NIETZSCHE HUMANIST

CLAUDE NICHOLAS PAVUR

MARQUETTE UNIVERSITY
PRESS

Marquette Studies in Philosophy
No. 15

Andrew Tallon, Series Editor

Library of Congress Cataloging-in-Publication Data

Pavur, Claude Nicholas, 1952-
Nietzsche humanist / Claude Nicholas Pavur.
p. cm. — (Marquette studies in philosophy ; no. 15)
ISBN 0-87462-614-5
1. Nietzsche, Friedrich Wilhelm, 1844-1900. 2. Humanism.
I. Title. II. Series: Marquette studies in philosophy ; #15.
B3317.P3 1998
193—dc21 97-45329

All rights reserved. No part of this publication may be reproduced, stored in a retrieval system, or transmitted in any form or by any means, electronic, mechanical, photocopying, recording or otherwise, without prior permission of the publisher.

Marquette University Press
Milwaukee

The Association of Jesuit University Presses

Contents

Preface

Supposing Nietzsche is a humanist—what then? Are there not grounds for the suspicion that we have not been well enough attuned to the ancient dimensions of our own identities to know what to do with this knowledge? Does our age's preference for the novel and the revolutionary mean that unmasking Nietzsche this way will amount to his inevitable diminishment—and might that not be for the best, after all?

We may have needed to see him—and in his later years he may have felt the need to present himself—as the radical overturner of all things, as the beginning of a new millenium. We do want to feel that things are moving forward, do we not? And if they leap forward, then so much the better! But self-presentation as dramatic as Nietzsche's makes us wonder. Might it have been a strategy for obtaining a readership, one worked out during years of increasing isolation? Or was it perhaps compensatory grandeur for his utter neglect, or therapeutic ventilation, or the beginning of his breakdown? It is not at all impossible that he was simply caught up in a creative whirlwind as he fashioned his own Galatea, and that his intellectual art began to operate independently, following its own dynamics and seducing the artist whithersoever it willed. Or maybe the author was simply collapsing, as any mortal would, under the rush of a breathtaking in-breaking vision that he indeed was the first of the race to behold.

Perhaps, too, his late visions were deeply implicated in a long-labored upward-and-downward spiralling climb through many and many a beloved text—ah, through many a beloved *meaning*—toward what he had hoped would be his own beatitude. In that case, this "unmasking" might result not in the diminishment but in the expansion of Nietzsche's own meaning.

At least we have had a convenient screen that would allow us to use him for certain ends. And that, of course, has a certain legitimacy. But Nietzsche the *classical scholar?* Nietzsche the *humanistic pietist?!* The true companion of those recidivists Schopenhauer and Wagner, not to mention Emerson and Montaigne, Petrarch and Erasmus, or Plutarch and Seneca?

Do we recognize this Nietzsche? *Should* we?

2

As we near the hundreth anniversary of Nietzsche's death, it may be time for a revaluation of the revaluator, time to shake some of the amnesia that haunts our submodernist culture with its penchant for parody. We need to take another look at one whose dark thunderings and frenzied lightning bolts have provided *son* et *lumière* for each succeeding generation in the twentieth century. No doubt he intended to pull us from the arms of some collective Morpheus—using to that end music that was itself usually entrancing, though not always melodious, not always harmonious. His influence has been staggering, but has it "worked"? Maybe the opera is not yet over. We should not, prematurely confident, assume that we have heard it all. Even if we have, we may need to replay it several times in order to come to appreciate it. Philology is the art of slow reading, as Nietzsche reminds us. It also is the art of reading *widely* and the art of reading *repeatedly.*

There may be more magic here than we had at first suspected, more than we were ready to confess that we actually like—or deplore. At any rate, the right praise, the right blame are impossible apart from an adequate hearing. But *can* we discover Nietzsche now? His manner has made us suspicious. Did he hide himself in order to be discovered? Certainly he has eluded us, this man of knowledge, to the extent that we have not come to know ourselves. Perhaps his life and work were designed as a parable that would trick us into self-discovery.

3

I hope that this essay has some value for students seeking to understand modernity, and also for all readers of Nietzsche, be they naïve, amateur, casual, or professional. In addition, I address those who want to sharpen and deepen their conception of *Western humanism* as it is generally but not always explicitly understood. At the end of this study, I will raise certain relevant issues of contemporary culture and education that affect us all. It is in light of these larger concerns that these pages may offer something to all those who profess the humanities, from philologists to philosophers.

St. Louis, Missouri
January 19, 1997

Acknowledgments

I am grateful to my many conversation partners at Emory University, especially Walter Adamson, R. Bracht Branham, Daniel Carrere, Herb Golder, Robert Paul, Louis Ruprecht, Jr., and James Winchester. I am also much indebted to Walter Ong and to Daniel Conway for helpful advice and encouragement. The Society of Jesus and the Woodruff family of Atlanta provided the necessary support for this project, and the National Endowment for the Humanities contributed to it by making possible my attendance at a summer Nietzsche-seminar directed by Richard Schacht at the University of Illinois in 1991. The resources of Saint Louis University, and the generous spirit of the Jesuit Hall Jesuit Community assured that this work would be brought to completion. My special thanks to A. James Blumeyer, Edward O'Brien, and Anthony Daly for their patient assistance. My colleagues in and around Saint Louis University's Department of Modern and Classical Languages and its Center for Medieval and Renaissance Studies deserve credit for keeping my inspiration alive. I also acknowledge and thank from my heart the several translators whose careful philological efforts have enabled me to undertake this work.

Any product of human labor is a paltry, pitiful thing in comparison with those lasting gifts that we receive through the sacrifices made in the context of family life. I acknowledge here that my greatest debt is and always will be to my whole family, and especially to my parents for their abundant kindnesses to me, early, middle, and late. To Edward John Pavur, Sr., and to Gertrude Gentilich Pavur, first and best of all my teachers, I dedicate this book.

...*learn* to read me well—!

Nietzsche, *The Dawn*

The Bridges of the Greeks. We have inherited them but we do not know how to use them.

Simone Weil, *Gravity and Grace*

1
Reading Nietzsche, Knowing Humanism

"What kind of a man are you?! Don't you even like *dolphins*?" Zorba asks his scholarly companion.

"Who is this that even the wind and the sea obey him?" the disciples wonder aloud about the prophetic stranger in their midst.

We scholars and disciples can hardly refrain from posing similar questions of identity and genre with regard to that *enfant terrible*, Friedrich Nietzsche, once we have gotten to know something of him. In the traditions of contemporary literature, philosophy, and social, cultural, and psychological reflection, he seems to lie under every cover. He has become part of the very self-image of modernity and post-modernity. Many thinkers do not doubt that our self-understanding would limp if we failed to engage with his ubiquitous spirit. But hard to lose, Nietzsche remains elusive. Questions of identity and type nag at us as this centaur and mercurial masquerader proclaims "At bottom I am every name in history" while demanding "Hear me! For I am such and such a person. Above all do not mistake me for someone else" and asking "Have I been understood?" (1954, 686; 1969, 217; 335). Such utterances echo all the more insistently as we swim about in the ink-dark sea of interpretations that have teemed forth left and right, most of them finding good support from the wealth of Nietzsche's styles, opinions, arguments, and moods. For example, is he radically nihilistic or radically anti-nihilistic? Perceptive readers can certainly argue either side, as Arthur Danto and Walter Kaufmann once proved (Berman, 1988). To what extent, then, can we say that Nietzsche's writings reveal a discernible set of positions and concerns on a related range of questions and problems? To identify him as a chameleon is not quite enough. Even under the assumption that the author has assumed strikingly different masks, we might ask about the one who has chosen to assume just these masks—the one who is inevitably defined in quite a meaningful way by these particular choices. Why might he have made them? If he is a Proteus who changes into an astounding range of terrible shapes, can we possibly, like Odysseus, hold on long enough to know the god himself?

Beyond the question of his importance for our times, we have good reasons for not abandoning the search for an integrated understanding. First and foremost among these is our constitutional investment in the search for coherence, postmodern enthusiasms notwithstanding. We naturally tend to perceive things as wholes. We try to understand any intelligible connections, setting them out on our own grids. At least thus argue gestaltists, structuralists, intentionality analysts, and common human experience. If we suspect that greater accuracy or closure is possible and do not abandon the subject matter under investigation, we will continue to be frustrated until we achieve what we deem to be within our grasp. In the case of Nietzsche, we desire to end the "cognitive dissonance" that results both from the author's contradictions and from the interpreters' disagreements: a coherent understanding of Nietzsche will entail a better evaluation of the secondary literature as well as of the corpus that is our main concern. Of course, some critics would be eager to suggest that the search that we are undertaking is a vain one. It has been proposed that

> Nietzsche was above all an experimentalist, who tried out ideas as he tried on styles, not so much later rejecting them as moving beyond them, occasionally reaching back and borrowing from them. There is no Nietzschean *überhaupt*, no single theme, and those that are most often promoted to fill this role—the *übermensch*, the will to power, and eternal recurrence—do not bear even slight scholarly scrutiny. There are, of course, grand and personal concerns that permeate Nietzsche's work—the nature of morality, the pathetic motives of much moral and Christian thinking, the historical role of Socrates, the Greeks, and Jesus—but there is hardly a single theme or set of themes that tie the entire corpus together.... While his work certainly adds up to a life-long masterpiece, his philosophy is not of a piece." (Solomon and Higgins, 1988, 7-8)

The point does not appear to be unreasonable, but it merits our suspicion until we can confirm it for ourselves. Too many have sensed and found some type of coherence for us to simply accept this statement without question. In fact its very words paradoxically point to the feasibility of the alternative view: *some* idea of wholeness is evoked by the idea of permeating concerns and by the image of a "life-long masterpiece." Even while he affirmed that this profuse variety of Nietzsche's intellectual eruptions was the leading interpretive difficulty, Karl Jaspers maintained that this material was not therefore diffuse and random. Rather, these thoughts were deeply connected in a way that a reader could not suspect from any collection of isolated fragments. Jaspers believed that philosophical Nietzsche-scholarship ought to concern itself precisely with the discovery of the connections that would enable us to understand the unity behind the manifold variety of Nietzsche's utterances (Jaspers, 1980: 51). At any rate, there is little doubt that Nietzsche himself found the ideas of "coherence," "the whole," "totality," and so on, extraordinarily important, and that he spoke frequently of the importance of a "unity of style." It is also certain that he thought of himself as a man with a great project or mission. We therefore ought to assume that a correct articulation of the nature and direction of his efforts, if this is as possible as his apparent self-understanding seems to imply, might allow for some kind of comprehensive, unified overview of great interpretive value.

I will argue that we can best attain the coherent understanding that we desire only after we find the most appropriate framework for reading Nietzsche. Here we can not avoid a recurring hermeneutical phenomenon that can most easily be perceived by reflecting on how we habitually use our knowledge of literary genres. Identifying, even in a subsidiary way, the *kind* of text that we are reading gives us a basic set of "foreunderstandings" in terms of which we can paddle our way through the whirlpool of possible interpretations. We do not take a fable by Aesop as a biographical narrative. As we read we also construct, at some level of consciousness, not only categories into which the *work* most appropriately fits, but also categories into which the *author* most appropriately fits. There is often an ellision of author and work: we "read Shakespeare." This union of the text, authorial character, and authorial intentionality is full of significance for the Western literary tradition. Common sense will ally itself with the established practices of literary understanding to caution us not to read Homer as if the author were primarily a psychologist or a cosmological allegorist or a lyrical poet—even though we can easily grant that his songs contain much acute psychological perception, a wide range of resonant larger meanings, and an artfully expressive sensibility. At least we instinctively tend to know that we can not undertake such readings with too strident a claim that we are faithfully hearing and appreciating Homer.

"Constructed authorial personae," then, as well as ideal-types, paradigms, and genrecategories, guide us in the process of interpretation, a process which must be situated in a whole traditional web of practices of interpreting signs. Thus Nietzsche rightly feels that he himself is somehow quite personally involved when someone is trying to understand what he has written. The audience has, in this case, a specially complicated task of coming to know an author who attempts to express many aspects of himself in many different modes of writing. We could not be content with a simple identification of Nietzsche as, say, an epic poet or fabulist, even while it remains true that through the reading of all of his literary material, the process of our construction of some larger authorial persona continues and constantly affects our interpretations. We want some kind of framework for interpretive guidance. Nietzsche is the unseen agent choosing to address us now with a parable, now a personal confession, now a polemic. What *kind* of author are we dealing with, then? We must try to find, or if necessary, to help create the category that will aid interpretation. This effort is especially significant because the words themselves do not always give enough clues. We need to know whether the personality that is writing those words happens to be communicating them with irony, hesitation, conviction, dogmatism, desperation, exasperation, evasiveness, prankishness, solemnity, or some such spiritual quality. We can only come to identify such tones through an attentiveness to many texts, styles, ideas, traditions of expressions, and so on, in conjunction with one another. Perhaps part of the secret of the fascination Nietzsche wields is that the complexity of his texts attains an unusually close approximation to the same kind of complex patterns of interpretation and understanding that go on as we come to know the living individuals around us. The more lifelike, the more personal and immediate the author is. The more powerful the authorial presence, the harder it is for readers to be satisfied with generic patterns that serve us so well with the formal and the unfamiliar.

But we can admit that individual authors are precisely that—individuals—and that they, like the persons we know, may require special interpretive strategies on our part, and yet there nevertheless are "types" of authors and "types" of authors as well. Since the authorial type that forms the basis for our understandings has to be constructed in interaction with the material and with what we know of its relevant cultural-historical context, it can be quite misleading to impose and then to maintain the illusion of some inappropriate authorial persona. Consider what happened to Homer in the hands of the allegorists. The type, "epic poet," was stretched to include the personae of different, though related, traditions, with the resonance of the original meanings transmuted into new signficances that set audiences at a new distance from the original voice. Such an imposition does not have to be explicit or rigid to distort the communication. On the other hand, to type Homer as "epic poet" does not erase all his distinctive authorial individuality, his utter unrepeatability, his unique achievement. Rather, it is only when an appropriate identification has been made that Homer's particularity can emerge. Naming the type does not end the hermeneutical quest; it really allows it to begin in a meaningful way. It enriches and guides our understanding.

I believe that Nietzsche-criticism has suffered from a distortion because of a false option with regard to the "authorial personae" repeatedly evoked in the history of Nietzsche-interpretation. Even when this false option is not *explicitly* present it can unduly influence critical interpretations to the detriment of a good understanding of the author. It therefore needs to be addressed directly. With this study, I propose a perspective on his writings and authorial character that will give us the coherence that we seek (and that some of us have apparently already despaired of finding). Our present focus is thus on Nietzsche-hermeneutics, that is, on *how we should go about reading Nietzsche*, rather than on the specific interpretation of Nietzsche's works. Of course the hermeneutic circle does not allow us to disregard entirely the latter entirely. The motivating question that I hope to answer through these reflections is "In broad terms, within what horizon, or according to what primary authorial persona, should we best (i.e., most faithfully and comprehensively) read and understand Nietzsche?" I do not claim that the "false option" is valueless or even that it blocks the best insights, but rather that we are well-served by altering the received hermeneutic framework. In the midst of the complexity, volume, and subtlety of learned scholarship, I hope to bring a certain clarity to something so fundamental that it is all too easily overlooked. It is also something so basic that it is implicated in issues of far greater moment and urgency than that of the professional advancement of Nietzsche-scholarship. These larger concerns will emerge in due course.

The essential immediate import of my efforts might be conveniently expressed as follows: *The Nietzsche-criticism often tends to place Nietzsche either in the stream of thinkers canonized by disciplinary philosophy (with its characteristic questions, orientations, etc.) or in the stream of literary artists and critics for whom technical philosophical issues are decidedly peripheral or subordinate to "effect." I contend that the context of the history and concerns of humanism adequately embraces the philosophical and literary dimensions of Nietzsche's work and gives us a most appropriate hermeneutical horizon for the interpretation of his works and general project.* We have now reached the point at which it is helpful to dissolve the pervasive and simplistic hermeneutical question of "philosopher or poet?"—without, however, ignoring the clearly relevant domains of philosophical thinking and literary creation. Nietzsche wore many masks, including those of philosopher and poet. But to privilege either of these, purely and simply, or the very option itself, even in a subliminal way, will sooner or later lead us quite astray.

Now I am not implying that Nietzsche does not belong to disciplinary philosophy. He does because it has adopted him. *The question is whether our inherited interpretive predispositions really promote a satisfactory framework for understanding.* And here I must make a further essential qualification: the general reading that I am constructing rests upon a distinction between our typical understanding of *philosophy* and Nietzsche's own. He does indeed evoke the philosophical persona for himself, but that is no proof that he thereby hoped to evoke its current disciplinary associations. Nietzsche was aware of older and richer concepts of philosophy, and we must think in such terms to understand him well.

I will not rehearse in detail the history and the currents of Nietzsche-interpretation. I will note, however, that those who do provide us with such overviews often hint at the simplistic dualism that has been affecting the reading of Nietzsche. Since it is important that we have some sense of how deep and widespread this hermeneutical issue has been, I will offer a few examples. Jörg Salaquarda (1980b) tells us that Nietzsche was largely regarded as a poet and mythologist till the 1930's, when professional philosophers began to exposit his work. At the time of his review-essay, the poetical, musical, and philological sides of Nietzsche were more appreciated than they had been, but they were still to be subordinated to Nietzsche's own "primary interest in cognition." The philosopher-persona has been dominant. Such a bias appears in recent English-language works by Arthur Danto (1980), Richard Schacht (1983), and Robert Solomon (1980). Danto perhaps gives the most direct expression to it, placing the disciplinary philosophical approach over against all others, when he writes that

> [Against the prevailing opinion] I wanted to show that whatever else he was or was not, he was certainly a philosopher, in just the way everyone who is one is one: that he thought systematically and deeply about each of the closed set of questions which define what philosophy is, that he gave serious, original, and coherent answers to them all. Whatever else he was, he was a philosopher. The title [*Nietzsche As Philosopher*]—and of course the text—was an effort to rescue this man for my own discipline from all those poets, politicians, pot-heads, and photographers from Princeton. (9)

Bernd Magnus (1983, 95-103) reviewed the traditions of Nietzsche-scholarship and discerned three noticeably different groups, the first two of which follow lines of the standing dualism: (1) the analyticals, who discover, investigate, and evaluate arguments that Nietzsche can be found to be making about issues like metaphysics, cognition, and morality; and (2) the deconstructionists, who stress the historical conditioning of the texts and of all interpretations. The third group Magnus calls "reconstructionists." They work out interpretations on the basis of careful consideration and evaluation of the texts to find out where Nietzsche himself seems to have stood, regardless of present-day ideologies. Despite the tripartite division, Magnus evokes an essential dualism when he refers to the "gap between Nietzsche as philosopher and as psychologist, critic of culture, literary figure" (95). Magnus seems to prefer to place Nietzsche in the philosophical camp, even to the point of claiming that Nietzsche is "our last hope of overcoming that artificial and counterproductive split between traditions termed loosely 'analytic' and 'continental'" (103). In a later essay, Magnus (1986) suggests how problematical even this apparently secure place in philosophy really is. Anyone familiar with Nietzsche-interpretation will have to be aware of vast differences in interpretations. Radical questions continue to be asked. What is his philosophy? Did he have one? Did he intend to have one? Or did he want to prove that the very goal of having a philosophy was itself a foolish and futile one (79)? This later essay raises the dualism in a new form. Magnus comments that those who wish to consider the notes and the published writings together (the "lumpers") seem to want to ally Nietzsche with their own conceptions of the traditions of philosophical practices. They tend to overstate the importance of categories like the *Übermensch* and the Will to Power. The "splitters" do the reverse, stressing style, but they have a hard time explaining why philosophers should attend to him in any serious and sustained way if he is not offering us something that might be recognized as epistemology, ontology, ethics, and the rest. In this essay, Magnus ultimately wishes to keep to the philosophical designation, but he would do so by changing the dominant concept of philosophy to mean the intellectual expression of a particular historical moment.

Again, the same interpretive dualism has been sharply portrayed in a condensed hermeneutical overview given by Michael Allen Gillespie and Tracy B. Strong (1988). They show how the philosophical model runs up against the problem of Nietzsche's own contradictions and difficult doctrines, which it tended either to ignore or to accept too easily as a necessary consequence of the Nietzschean doctrine of a purely chaotic and self-contradictory universe. The poetic or stylistic model, they say, tends to make of Nietzsche an aphorist or an inevitably self-referential writer. The first option tends to ignore the actual range of his works; the second to reduce them to their effects on the reader. Gillespie and Strong promote a view of Nietzsche that valorizes his own claim to have transcended the distinction between philosophy and poetry. Content can not be separated from its style and from its effect on us. Nietzsche's philosophy is music and poetry. It is not merely informational data but formative and transformative performance. Their words show that the hermeneutic dualism is so strong as to have provided the very terms in which they suggest their position on Nietzsche, even as they strive to overcome the gap that it implies.

An awareness of the heritage of this double stream of interpretation helps us to situate recent criticism and it may point us in the direction of what is still lacking, many fine insights notwithstanding. That the primary tendency is still to treat Nietzsche above all in the context of philosophical argumentation can be seen in Allan Megill's *Prophets of Extremity: Nietzsche, Heidegger, Foucault, and Derrida* (1985), where he posits an admittedly partial image of an "aestheticist" Nietzsche for whom the world is an artistically self-creating phenomenon. He rejects the idea of a "naturalist" Nietzsche who campaigns against current morality for the sake of a more "natural" human existence. Megill testifies to the fact of a general dominance of the philosophical persona by suggesting that his view "will strike many readers as perversely out of tune with their own prior knowledge" of Nietzsche, the usual view being that Nietzsche was a "naturalistic philosopher" (29). His own essay still seems to treat Nietzsche according to the philosophical paradigm by proposing Nietzsche's aestheticism as essentially a radically idealist and solipsistic philosophical position (101). Aesthetics supplants ethics, metaphysics, and so on, but Nietzsche still appears as primarily within the horizon of systematic philosophical stances.

Another most interesting, highly explicit attempt at hermeneutical gap-filling can be found in Alexander Nehamas's much-praised work, *Nietzsche: Life as Literature* (1985). Nehamas is clearly reacting to a hermeneutic dualism that either highlights content and thus caricatures Nietzsche's actual doctrines (of *Übermensch*, etc.) or focuses on form and thereby eviscerates Nietzsche's work of any positive content. In his own reading, he tries to do justice to both sides in a new, creative way. He shows how, in a sense, style is all for Nietzsche. It is the key content of his work when interpreted correctly as self-creation. Nehamas, however, also seems to lean heavily toward the side of the philosophical paradigm by claiming that Nietzsche adopts this literary self-creation as a means to support his "position" of perspectivism. Was the non-dogmatic assertion of a philosophical position really "Nietzsche's central problem as an author"? Did he really adopt the many styles "as all part of his single project to present an interpretation that demands to be believed even as it says it is only an interpretation"? I remain unconvinced that this is an adequate expression of Nietzsche's major project or that his epistemological stance was so overarchingly important in his own estimation. Indeed, Nehamas meditates well enough to communicate much that is important about Nietzsche, and he does suggest profound dimensions of meaning in Nietzsche's texts, but I suspect that the old dualism, and his attempt to transcend it, may be exerting an unfortunate influence in his interpretation. Consider some lines from his summation:

> None of this is to say that Nietzsche avoids or escapes from theoretical or philosophical thought, that he has no positive views of his own, that we should read him as an 'artist' rather than as a 'philosopher,' or that he has accomplished something that, as he himself may sometimes have thought, had never been accomplished before. But along with figures like Plato's Socrates and Kierkegaard, he both engaged in philosophical thought and, for his own reasons, mistrusted it. His texts yield not only philosophical views but also a view of what it is to be engaged in giving philosophical views. This one view among many possible others is deeply ambivalent and gives Nietzsche himself a deeply equivocal position in the history of this tradition. (233)

Two paragraphs later, Nehamas claims that the "final consequence" of his reading is that both Nietzsche's model and product are literary, soon adding, though, that "The content of his works...remains a set of philosophical views." Here we have an ingenious mixture of the traditional hermeneutical opposites in Nietzsche-interpretation.

Nehamas's work demands attention because he calls our attention to some fundamental literary dynamics and intelligently links them to Nietzsche's underlying motivations. But the question remains whether working out an interpretation in terms of the old dualism is the best option. Furthermore, Nehamas's study manifests the common tendency in some leading Nietzsche-criticism to overstress the later works, those written after 1883. I will suggest that such a procedure has been most misleading for anyone who seeks a comprehensive understanding of Nietzsche—or even of the late works themselves. Nietzsche's late texts in fact frequently send us back to his early ones.

The dualistic framework is therefore a demonstrably pervasive and still-current feature of Nietzsche-criticism. But we should also realize that it is not at all recent. We find its basic terminology, which is redolent of the classic discussions of philosophy versus poetry, in the remarks of the young T. S. Eliot (1916) when he writes that "Nietzsche is one of those writers whose philosophy evaporates when detached from its literary qualities, and whose literature owes its charm not alone to the personality and wisdom of the man, but to a claim to scientific truth." And we find it even in Nietzsche's own writings, as, for example, in these words:

> "Suitor of truth? they mocked me; "you?
> No! Only poet!"
>
> ...
>
> Thus I myself once sank
> Out of my truth-madness,
> Out of my day-longings,
> Weary of day, sick from the light—
> Sank downward, eveningward, shadoward,
> Burned by one truth,
> And thirsty:
> do you remember still, remember, hot heart,
> How you thirsted?
> *That I be banished*
> *From all truth*
> *Only fool!*
> *Only poet!*
> (1954: 410, 412)

If my proposed reading of Nietzsche as a humanist is to be an effective "cure" for the misleading dualism indicated by these words, which happen to be sung by the magician's "evil spirit of magic and deception" (414), then we must begin by trying to articulate the meaning of humanism. But it is important to recognize that a comprehensive and precise definition of the term is not feasible here for several reasons. First, the richness of the concept would make for an exposition too lengthy and distracting to help our immediate purposes; it is better to deny the false implication that we need a higher degree of accuracy than we do to use the term meaningfully. Second, the various meanings, levels, and manifestations of humanism need to be perceived in a continual process of cultural-historical interpretation.

To some extent humanism must be defined via concrete examples that *establish a field rather than delineate a single object.* No simple formula can accomplish that work. Thus we are dealing with a still-changing "open concept," that is, a meaningful designation that cannot be exhaustively or precisely defined (Weitz). Examples of open concepts include ideas that we commonly use, such as *Hellenism*, *American Dream*, *Romanticism*, *paganism*, the *East*, *the Judaeo-Christian tradition*, *liberalism*, *modernism*, *art*, and of course *philosophy* itself, which includes such a vast range of practices and contents. Positing Nietzsche as a humanist involves us in a reciprocal hermeneutical play within a special field of meaning: we come to know and to understand both Nietzsche and humanism in a somewhat different way because of the affinities and tensions between them. This study will significantly depend upon arguments for and concrete illustrations of the entwinement of Nietzsche and humanism, drawing on the reservoir of meanings that most educated readers can be expected to sense in the term, and it will allow for the possibility that Nietzsche could be a new and distinctive moment in the history of humanism. But still, a working definition is possible and it offers us some helpful orientation. I therefore suggest the following provisional glosses of three words that best evoke the relevant field of meaning: *humanism*, *humanists*, and *humanities.* The definitions are ideal: they prescind from historically concrete examples and present a composite, positive overview. They have been fashioned with the help of several summary sources (Trinkaus, 1963; Ong, 1967; Hadas, 1972; Levi, 1973; Grudin, 1987; Kristeller, 1988).

Humanism is a type of vision, a kind of orientation, a quality of consciousness, and a web of cultural attitudes and practices. It implies a reflective anthropocentrism that stresses human experience, powers, and values, especially ethical ideals, communication, freedom, critical reason, imagination, historical consciousness, and the cultivation of their harmonious development in the individual human personality. Perhaps its most basic motivating questions is "What are the best ways and means by which we can become most fully human, as we can best imagine such an ideal?" It tends to be holistic, personalistic, and sapiential in approach, not theoretical, technical, or systematic. It affects and promotes an ideal of superior education and personal integrity, but, though it might stand over against the dominant popular cultural values of its time, it is not elite in the sense that hermetic circles are or in the way that ruling class ethos may be. Rather its attitude is shaped by the belief that the heritage is a shared possession, open to all who want to profit from it in a great variety of ways, across generations, cultures, languages, and social strata. The kind of humanism to which I am referring here is historically rooted in but not limited to the appreciation of Western classical literature and its dominant ethos. Like any human achievement in consciousness, it bears the marks of its particular historical genesis, even while it maintains a universal relevance.

The *humanist* stays close to the human life-world, not getting disproportionately absorbed in theory, dogma, scholarship, spirituality, art, science, or politics, but rather taking interest in all of these areas and in their most timely, valuable combinations. The humanist aspires to be literate, creative, self-possessed, realistic, aware, engaged, well-balanced, discriminating, effective in communication, and informed by a broad cultural background. Increasingly aware of human capacities *and* limitations, the humanist is oriented toward both *appreciation* and *critique* of relevant cultural and historical phenomena. This attitudinal polarity within humanism means that it can support affirmative, dogmatic, universalist, generalist orientations as well as critical, skeptical, pluralist, particularist ones; but it favors neither to any disproportionate degree because at the limit of either tendency the life-world recedes and humanism dissolves.

The *humanities* traditionally include moral philosophy; history; literature, language, and art, when these are taught not so much for technical "professional" expertise, as for the present enjoyment, fruition, and integration of a range of human potentials, and for the sake of mature, self-conscious, self-critical cultural-historical awareness, understanding, and discernment. Maturity is understood to involve a generative self-appropriation and a responsible autonomy affiliated with traditions that are attentively received and creatively transformed.

We begin to flesh out these ideal definitions by noting that there have been four premiere moments in the cultural history of humanism: the times of Classical and Alexandrian Greece; of late Republican and early Imperial Rome; of Renaissance Italy and its European derivatives (ca. 1300-1600); and of German *Klassik* (ca. 1795-1830). The first gave us *paideia*, a system of education explicitly conceived according to a formational ideal; the second, the concept of *artes liberales* and *humanitas* (sometimes used to translate *paideia*); the third, the *studia humanitatis*, a curriculum opposed to the dominant theological curriculum (not to theological questions pure and simple), and the term *humanista*, designating a teacher in this new curriculum; the fourth, the term *humanism* itself as a designation for a particular type of classical education. These four moments represent the times at which humanism attained a particularly intense cultural expression. Ancient Greece, though it depended in many ways on the heritage and ongoing contributions of the great civilizations of northern Africa and the Near East, has come to stand as *the primordial, originative humanistic culture* from which the later moments drew much of their inspiration. There are aspects of Renaissance culture, however, that seem to make it the *paradigmatic cultural moment* of the humanist tradition, perhaps largely because of its more modern configurations of communication and social organization. By the time of the Italian Renaissance, the selection of the center of a particular "humanistic" canon had occurred, and this set of texts was even more precisely defined with the rediscovery and careful editing of many ancient works. The Greek culture at the root of this movement was of course a complex cultural-symbolic network, and it sent out many different kinds of humanistic impulses so that one might begin to distinguish the particular features of humanisms that might be designated Homeric, Hesiodic, Solonic, Socratic, Platonic, Aristotelian, and so on. Furthermore, the tradition as a whole contains dynamic tensions between these various strains. Thus, in the thirteenth century, Aquinas had absorbed a good bit of Aristotelian humanism, but it was evidently not cultivated in such a way that the later scholastics were immunized against the early Renaissance humanists' charges of formalistic and irrelevant abstractions. We must always realize, therefore, that we are dealing with large composite realities that are variously differentiated and interrelated.

As I work towards a general reading of Nietzsche in the context of the history of Western humanism, I will not be especially concerned about the question of precisely to what extent he is affiliated to each of these four major moments. My primary interest here does not lie in any kind of detailed delineation of a "history of ideas and their thinkers" but rather in basic hermeneutical considerations that will ground a new general reading of Nietzsche's works. The point that I most wish to establish is *not* about how closely Nietzsche resembled or differed from the humanists of this or that time: I am not polishing a nugget of intellectual history. My point is about how profoundly Nietzsche affiliated himself to this tradition, whatever his own particular terms of self-presentation, and it is also about how this humanistic identification might make a difference in our understanding of him and his entire project. How Nietzsche becomes a new moment in the history of humanism will emerge only after we understand the intelligibility and the appropriateness of interpreting him in light of that history. Understanding Nietzsche in the context of the field of meaning established by these terms and moments will open a way forward in Nietzsche-interpretation. A strong version of my thesis sets forth the humanist persona as *the* superior generic-hermeneutical key by which the best possible (most integral and most faithful) reading(s) of Nietzsche can be achieved. A weaker version asserts merely that this persona is heuristically helpful and allows for new, valuable, or interesting insights into Nietzsche. My reflections and my experience of this author firmly set me much closer to the former position than to the latter. I realize, however, that a solid confirmation of such a radically-framed and far-reaching proposal would require an extensive analysis of Nietzsche's texts and comparision of Nietzsche-interpretations. I would be obliged to probe a wide range of the scholarly literature to estimate relative deficiencies, and I would have to argue out, in the context of the primary material, all the apparent advantages of my approach. Once again, the danger of distraction into byways leads me to leave such efforts for the most part in abeyance. Let the reader decide how strong a version ought to be held. It is enough for now to make explicit how *there are excellent grounds for reading Nietzsche first and foremost as a humanist.*

Some of these grounds have already been generally indicated, even if they are of a negative nature: the confusion, failure, and growing self-criticism of the current major interpretive traditions, as expressed, for example, by Bernd Magnus above. Nietzsche-interpretation is still diffuse, controversial, and evidently insufficient. The split that has been so persistent a topos in the field encourages all the more, I believe, the hermeneutical use of the humanist persona, wherein both "philosophical" and "poetical" dimensions can be taken into account in a way that is more consistent with the sources and with Nietzsche's own apparent self-understanding. The sphere of possible evidence for this view will be relatively large. We need restrict ourselves neither to Nietzsche's published texts, nor to these as supplemented by the posthumously published notes, though both of these sources obviously have a certain centrality and value. Also important are Nietzsche's lectures, letters, and conversations with others as they later recounted them, since all such material can give us insight into Nietzsche's intentions, his character, and the primary meanings of his projects. They therefore bear upon the fundamental hermeneutical issues with which we are concerned. In fact, even though some of this material contains "unpolished" insights, I do not think that such evidence can be ignored for an adequate large-scale interpretation of Nietzsche. Imagine for a moment—if we were to discover that Nietzsche repeatedly spoke to others of how he felt a great need to somehow establish the validity of an aestheticist and perspectivist position in the face of the positivists and idealists, and if, furthermore, this was the almost the only way in which he presented his chief concerns, then we would tend to read the same texts in a particular way because of that knowledge. Our recourse to the larger field of evidence is necessary in virtue of the fact that, because the same object can often be given different meanings, we require contextualization and a more careful process of interpretation. This phenomenon is well-represented in Gilbert Ryle's example of two boys contracting their right eyelids. Is it a twitch? A signal to someone? A parody of someone else's wink? A practice for an intended deception or parody? "Thick description" carries with it a more exact idea of the import of an event than does the "thin description" of the brute physical fact (Geertz, 1973: 6-7). In a way, the main thrust of this essay amounts to a plea for a "thicker" description of Nietzsche than is generally available.

My strategy will be to suggest several arguments that provide important reasons for the validity of understanding Nietzsche primarily in the context of the history of humanism. These arguments are in no way intended to flesh out at length the many issues raised, nor are they, all taken together, meant to be an exhaustive coverage of possible arguments for this particular approach to Nietzsche. They merely provide sufficient evidence for the great value of using (not necessarily restricting oneself to) the humanist paradigm in Nietzsche-interpretation. There is no question of "painting the definitive portrait," as it were. But painters often seek what might be called an "optimal perspective" for their purposes. And some undoubtedly "get the shape" of their subject or in some ways suggest its character better than others, sometimes even with fewer lines. Just so, Nietzsche will, I hope, actually be better illuminated by what we consider. But the form of the argument will be shaped more by the intention to suggest a framework of vital ideas than by the desire for elaborate them completely. Using a bit of poetic licence, I have named the arguments as follows:

The *Genealogical* Argument: Out of what intellectual or cultural spheres did Nietzsche's work, intellectual habits, projects, and self-image primarily develop?

The *Analogical* Argument: To what kinds of authors and thinkers is Nietzsche most similar? By what authorial personalities is Nietzsche most influenced in his own self-presentation as an author?

The *Thematic* Argument: About what kinds of things does Nietzsche tend to write and think?

The *Horizonal* Argument: What are the primary cultural-historical objects that circumscribe the extent of Nietzsche's vision?

The *Teleological* Argument: What is Nietzsche's purpose?
The *Doctrinal* Argument: What is Nietzsche's message?
The *Rhetorical* Argument: In what forms and ways does Nietzsche communicate? What kind of attention does he give to the manner in which he communicates?

The underlying assumption is that all these questions are involved in fundamental hermeneutical questions in Nietzsche-criticism. Even though I am aiming only for adequacy rather than completeness, it should be apparent what a wide range of source material will be relevant. The *genealogical* argument will especially highlight the biographical, professional dimension of Nietzsche's involvement in the humanist tradition as a classical philologist. The *analogical* will suggest similarities on the basis of formal parallels probed by a number of scholarly studies that have not yet been gathered into a single place. The *thematic* will attend to the specific configuration of issues in Nietzsche's works. The *horizonal* will suggest the larger cultural-historical and material context into which Nietzsche fits (suggesting a transbiographical "genealogy"). The *teleological* will attempt to make clear the core complex of purposes and values that unifies all of Nietzsche's life and works. The *doctrinal* will attempt to isolate Nietzsche's key positive doctrine as a vital link with the humanist tradition. The *rhetorical* will attend to the form, genres, and styles in which Nietzsche expressed himself and to the type of significance that he gives them.

These arguments are in no way meant to be absolutely discrete, and before they have run their course, several of them will be melded together explicitly. Any one of them could serve as an instructive starting point leading through the considerations taken up in the others. What justifies this particular form of presentation is merely that the approaches and principles of the arguments differ even while the object is the same and the relevant matter inextricably interrelated. This arrangement is merely one way of bringing order into a very complex, multi-leveled field. It also will provide a wide-ranging setting for beginning to address larger concerns that motivate this undertaking. These concerns are not the contemporary currents in Nietzsche-interpretation, nor the interpretations of Nietzsche's particular works as such, but they are *the entire realm of values, attitudes, and practices that are signally at stake in and around Nietzsche's works.* It is within this context that Nietzsche becomes all the more momentous a figure. It is this horizon that he himself continually kept in mind. This study therefore also has a place in a larger scheme of purposes that is not merely my own, nor Nietzsche's, nor Nietzsche-scholars', nor Academe's. This attempt to understand Nietzsche in a better way will aim us, as he himself would have it, towards matters of greater moment. But to get there with the advantages that this way offers us, we must first accept the task of trying to establish a more adequate orientation to Nietzsche and his work. When we will have done that, we may be better able to testify that we do indeed have a good idea of what kind of man this is.

2
Nietzsche's Humanist Genealogy

An emphasis on the late writings, especially on that posthumous pastiche of notebook-material called *The Will to Power*, characterizes much Nietzsche-interpretation written since Heidegger. As a result, many college students are now getting to know Nietzsche through *On the Genealogy of Morals*, or even through *Twilight of the Idols*. Plausible reasons can be adduced for such choices, no doubt, but beginning with such texts exposes readers to the dangers of distortion and early negativity. Over against that basic fascination that we all seem to have with what appears defiant, transgressive, or revolutionary, we need to gauge the extent to which this predilection for the most provocative works has skewed our collective attention. A more comprehensive vision of Nietzsche's meaning will emerge if we can strategically counter the prevailing emphasis by attending to the earlier works. Then we might read the corpus dynamically, in its whole process of "coming to be." This approach seems especially right for the interpretation of one who so consistently stressed the development of cultural and psychological phenomena from originary structures. Some might nevertheless insist that it is better to look to the mature form of a phenomenon in order to appreciate it. But we must realize that in this case we are not sure what the most mature form would have been, and we must take care to distinguish maturity from "degeneration." Since he had no time for retrospective nuancing, we lack Nietzsche's own careful reconsiderations of his last material after a decent interval. Any interpretive refinements will therefore have to rely upon some consideration of the earlier writings. Of course, the author might warn us not to take any single moment of his career early or late as an entirely adequate carrier of his deepest purposes: he criticized his own productions along the way, and he seemed always to have something more to add as the delight of fresh thoughts and new voicings of old ones beguiled his Dionysian sensibility.

Nevertheless much can be said for the turn to the beginnings. It has a powerful *prima facie* interpretive appeal, since few would argue that knowing origins, developments, and endings is a hermeneutical option necessarily inferior to knowing only endings. A vast amount of collective wisdom also seems to confirm the value of such a turn. For both the ancient Greek world (van Gronigen, 1953) and modern psychoanalysis (Pomper, 1985), beginnings (*archai,* in Greek) can possess a privileged status in any attempt to understand a phenomenon's essential principles (also called *archai*). Other authorities have expressed the same wisdom in a number of ways: "The child is the father of the man," Wordsworth says. "In my beginning is my end," Eliot adds. Long before them Virgil had written, "Happy the one who is able to discern the causes of things." And yet earlier, a proverb had it that "the beginning is half of the whole." Such witnesses betray our intellectual impulse to understand things in terms of their origins. This is in fact one of our most habitual, one of our most pervasive ways of discerning, establishing, appreciating, and extending meaning. Even as both traditional and modern societies delight in telling stories of their own genesis, historically or cosmologically, so current scientific research carefully attends to the origins of things to determine their natures. The word *nature* itself refers to the process of birth: the origin of this word implies that you will know what a thing is if you can know its coming-to-be. This very type of etymological understanding that I am now using indicates what kind of illumination can be achieved by ascertaining early meanings. Many of us can personally confirm that we tend to want to know where our acquaintances have come from. Such information helps us to "place" them in some kind of framework of understanding. For a similar reason, cultures often satisfy this need by employing things like patronymics to identify individuals. There is simply something psychologically unsatisfying about *not* knowing—or not even being able to imagine—origins. No wonder both early philosophy and primeval myth have sought the Starting Point, the Source. We almost inevitably look for some kind of developmental account as well. We ask how did *homo sapiens,* how did novels, how did democracy arise? Even a bad answer stands in as a comforting placeholder until we can do better. And so it is important to attend to such a perspective as we shape our understanding of Nietzsche.

Taking this approach does not mean that we must fall into the "genetic fallacy," whereby one assumes that all relevant material is contained in something's first form. Nor does it imply that a knowledge of origins is sufficient or necessarily determinative of the understanding of a particular phenomenon. Rather, the use of such an approach and the explanatory weight given to it are conditioned by what we want to know and by our sense of appropriate parameters, based on what we perceive (in a hermeneutically circular manner) to be a coherent and largely continuous development. The meanings involved in the beginning *may*—not *must*—significantly inform our general understanding. They could quite possibly have profound implications for later developments. Otherwise, they might simply become an important part of a reading that aims at a certain kind of comprehensivity. No doubt major transformations—we might call them "new beginnings"—could limit the applicability of the genealogical approach. An author's greatest signature work, for example, might well be achieved only after a personal conversion and at the end of a career. An actor, peanut farmer, or playwright might become the president of a nation, with a variance in the degree of continuity between the two professions. However, in the case of Nietzsche—a relentlessly ruminative personality who achieved a very early maturity, and who gave himself so intensely to his first undertakings—I would prefer not to begin with the assumption that such a break occurred.

Though Nietzsche does indeed sometimes criticize his early work, especially in the 1886 preface to *The Birth of Tragedy*, his remarks in *Twilight of the Idols* and in *Ecce Homo* leave no doubt that he thought his first book a highly important text. This estimation coheres with a life-long respect for origins that affected Nietzsche's whole style of thinking—as well his deep-set orientation toward what he considered the wellsprings of Western culture. The famous "genealogical method" seeks to explain things by the ulterior motivations revealed in a consideration of the likely history of their coming to be. J. Daniel Breazeale (1975b) has called this method the one that above all deserves to be described as "characteristic of Nietzsche." It posits the importance of examining origins, and especially *purposes* (302). Purposes themselves concern ends, but they are usually operative at the very beginning, both initiating and conditioning the agent's activities.

It is completely consistent with such an orientation that Nietzsche should value his early efforts and think familiarity with them a prerequisite for a correct reading of his later ones. In the preface to the *Genealogy of Morals*, he states:

> If this book is incomprehensible to anyone and jars on his ears, the fault, it seems to me, is not necessarily mine. It is clear enough, assuming, as I do assume, that one has first read my earlier writings and has not spared some trouble in doing so; for they are, indeed, not easy to penetrate. (1969b, Section 8, 22)

Facing the issue of his own hermeneutical question—*How am I to be understood?*—Nietzsche structures *Ecce Homo* as a review of his life that includes a temporally ordered consideration of the entire series of his writings. Perhaps his own project of self-understanding made this type of retrospective review inevitable, given his methodological alliances. Nor can we rule out the intriguing possibility that the radical, aggressive, and self-conscious prose of his last writing was, at least in part, a grand rhetorical ploy to get the public finally to attend to a message that he had been trying to broadcast from the time of his earliest works. In that case, the later efforts might have been undertaken, to some extent, "in service" of the earlier ones, to redeem them from oblivion, or to provide a megaphone for what had not been noticed adequately. They may well contain the most straightforward expression of his aims and the best clues to his deepest purposes. Asserting that they do would not be equivalent to saying that Nietzsche did not develop in his understanding and goals, or that he did not value such changes highly, but it would imply that we need to attend to the earlier material and that we need to be on the alert for reformulations of older material. At any rate we can say that when we are dealing with Nietzsche's writings, there are considerable hermeneutical justifications for taking a "genealogical" approach seriously, even though its weight will depend on a retrospective evaluation made in the light of many other factors. The implicit claim is not for the *necessary* interpretive priority of the *temporally* prior—that could take us back to Nietzsche's grammar-school work or earlier—but rather for *the importance of giving earlier material the full weight it proves to merit.*

Turning to the early Nietzsche, we can not avoid one overwhelming fact. The young thinker is rooted, heart, mind, and soul, in the domain of humanistic classical philology. The biographical data are fairly well-known, even if not adequately used: Nietzsche's precocious excellence in classical studies at Schulpforta; his appointment at the age of 24 to a university teaching position in Basel; his associations with other classical scholars like his teacher Ritschl and his companion Erwin Rohde; and his ten-year tenure as a professor of classics (1869-1879), fully half of his "professional" life as a writer. We even possess a detailed record of Nietzsche's "abundant" teaching-activity (Janz, 1974). He had absorbed classical materials more deeply than most of us can begin to imagine today. From the very first, then, even before we address the question of his personal absorption of classical ethos, we can suspect that the connection with the humanist tradition is a relevant and foundational one: modern philology is an intellectual-cultural tradition most indebted to those paradigmatic humanists of the Italian Renaissance who are distinguished precisely by their scrupulous, enthusiastic involvements with classical texts. They sought "grammatical" accuracy, stylistic elegance, and a progressively penetrating understanding and appropriation of antique culture, especially in the context of educational purposes. The ancients served as models for both communicational style and, closely connected therewith, human character. But concern with the "*bonae litterae*" alone was enough to merit one the designation of "humanist" (Giustiani, 1985). There is no doubt that Nietzsche too had both technical competence and a highly charged personal investment in those letters. He produced some solid academic philology, but he attempted something special when he wrote his first book, *The Birth of Tragedy Out of the Spirit of Music.* In this rich text, his consideration of Greek dramatic and spiritual culture so far exceeded the classical profession's horizons and technical strictures as to be deemed to belong to another sphere altogether. The philological side of classical humanism had become less ethically than technically oriented: but Nietzsche was aiming for the comprehensive, integrated vision that could not leave out *ethos* because it was based on it. Very early on, Nietzsche realized that beyond the "letters" of ancient culture there was the living spirit. And the letters were worth nothing without the spirit. Over against any type of supposedly dispassionate "scientific" or aestheticist "antiquarian" practices, there stands the type of studious engagement that seeks to promote deeply personal purposes. Nietzsche can be placed all the closer to the Renaissance humanist ideals inasmuch as he took to heart the original literary-educational vision that constitutes the primary field of humanist meaning. Those who first carried the designation *humanist* were to a large extent educational reformers, theorists, and practitioners (Kristeller, 1988, 114; Ong, 1962, 149-63). Again and again, throughout Nietzsche's life, it is the paideutic impetus that seems to constitute the core of Nietzsche's motivations and projects. He says, in a revealing aside to Peter Gast, "for ultimately I am a *teacher*..." (letter of August 20, 1882, cited in Nietzsche, 1974, 20). An ever-expanding bibliography on Nietzsche and education confirms the importance of this dimension of Nietzsche's professional self-image (Cooper, 1983; Golomb, 1985; James W. Hillesheim, 1969b, 1985; Loew, 1984; Murphy, 1984; Rosenow, 1986).

What then, can we make of Nietzsche's acerbic rejection of philology and withdrawal from the academy? Does it not perhaps indicate the tentative nature of Nietzsche's commitment to the educational sphere? Actually, there is little doubt raised here. Nietzsche's critique is so shrill because he had already given so much of himself to the profession and was so deeply disappointed with the lack of any appropriate kind of reception by a field so obviously in need of his help. The beginnings of this disillusionment come through most poignantly in a letter that also reveals the depth and sincerity of his commitment:

> You will not take amiss my astonishment at not having heard a single word from you about my recent book [*The Birth of Tragedy*]—or, I hope, my candour in telling you of this astonishment. The book, after all, is something of a manifesto, and the last thing it invites is silence. Perhaps you will be surprised at the reaction I anticipated from you, my revered teacher. I thought that if you had ever met with anything hopeful in your life, it might be this book, full of hope for our classical studies, full of hope for the German spirit, even if a number of individuals should be ruined by it.... I seek nothing for myself, I hope to achieve something for others. Above all, I am concerned to win over the younger generation of philologists, and I would consider it a disgrace if I failed in this...I hope I may remain assured of your good will. (Letter of January 30, 1871 to Friedrich Ritschl, cited in Silk and Stern, 1981, 91-92.)

The increasing distance between Nietzsche and his profession had the air of the alienation that follows a love affair gone sour. But his later scathing attack on the academy and its teaching methods actually only helps to confirm a case for his humanist persona, since the Renaissance humanists were equally incisive critics of the method and content of the scholastic traditions of their day (Ong, 1962). Actually, Nietzsche was critical, even at an early date, of "mere" scholarship in the positivist or antiquarian sense. But he did not lose all respect for the field even as his alienation grew deeper (e.g., 1986, Section 270). His distance from the Academy after his intense engagement with it might even be taken as parallel to the relative independence enjoyed by some premiere humanists. Petrarch, Boccaccio, Erasmus operated *outside* of the university milieu, even though the beginnings of the humanist movement must be associated with it to some extent (Kristeller, 1961, 102).

We can define Nietzsche's place on the philological map yet more precisely. Within the confines of the professorial world, Nietzsche clearly belonged to what has been identified as the "magisterial tradition" of German classical philology, a notably humanistic stream of the tradition of classical studies (Whitman, 1986). In this he followed the pattern set by August Wolf, elaborated by August Boeckh, and promoted by his own early champion, Friedrich Ritschl. This tradition stressed the comprehensive and ordered totality of the sciences and subject matter of antiquity as well as its subjective achievement in the person of the experienced master. Such a *magister* would have attained a powerful vision and understanding on the basis of an interdisciplinary synthesis drawn from a life-long penetration of the various concrete manifestations of the classical *Geist.* By Nietzsche's day, this mode of classical scholarship had been terribly weakened by the enthusiasm of a rival positivists who aimed primarily at the accumulation of all the concrete details of classical life (*Realien*). They too could claim descent from Wolf, on the basis of his conception of *Altertumwissenschaft* as a totalizing scientific study, but they had lost an important humanistic goal contained, though not well developed, in that original program—*the understanding of humanity.* Wolf's new science had been predicated on three features: its professionalization, its scientific rigor, and its orientation towards the empirical knowledge of human nature (Bolter, 1980, 87). This last goal was always, of course, the hardest to realize. Nevertheless, the minority tradition of classical studies as an essentially humanistic wisdom that incorporated science, or actually rested upon it, was still alive in Nietzsche's day, and some of his early works manifest his close affiliation with it. It will therefore be worthwhile to investigate with some specificity the humanistic orientation of Nietzsche's academic vision. From the many possible sources we will select three especially significant ones.

The most direct piece of evidence for Nietzsche's concept and practice of classical philology is to be found in a rarely-printed work entitled *"Einleitung in das Studium der classischen Philologie"* (1910, Band XVII, 327-52) dating from the summer semester of 1871. It is Nietzsche's "*Encyclopaedie,*" a formal overview of the field for advanced students, largely comprised of philosophical and methodological considerations and a general orientation to some of the particulars of classical literature and philosophy. The prefatory outline contains a larger number of headings than are actually developed in Nietzsche's text: some of them refer to the history of philology, types of criticism, rhythmics and metrics, ancient religion and mythology, and so on. The notes that follow the outline of headings may well provide us with a good indication of Nietzsche's special interests, that is, those areas on which he thought it especially valuable to develop introductory commentary, even though we can not be completely sure that he did not also explore the other areas as well, whether spontaneously or in notes not known to us. The first line of the main text, for example, is a brief reference to the history of philology. Nietzsche seems simply to have selected a single salient item from the longer list of historical topics given in the outline. In this case, it is an item quite suggestive in the present context. It reads, "The discovery of antiquity with the Italians." When we turn to the paragraphs of explication for the sections that Nietzsche did expand upon, we are not limited to such meager hints, for there long-standing humanistic traits are evident even from a cursory reading. They are also so closely interconnected that we will do best to sketch out various major strands. Naming them will help us to sharpen our understanding of some generic humanistic features even while we investigate Nietzsche's particular presentation of these traditional ideals.

1. Belief in the normativity or "classicity" (Classicität) of the Hellenic tradition in ancient world and the importance of the idea of the "classical." The classicity of antiquity is the "philosophical presupposition" of classical studies (329), which wishes to comprehend a "classical" form of existence (*ein classisches Dasein*, 329). By the term *classical*, Nietzsche seems to mean paradigmatic, archetypal, setting an ultimate standard. Thus he stresses the use of the greatest works of the greatest authors of the greatest culture, the study of the highest phenomenon of all (*allerhöchste Erscheinung*, 329). And, in consonance with such a position, he recommends avoiding those writings that the moderns have surpassed (333). One should tend to associate only with the greatest of all reality (*den allergrössten Wesen*, 333). Greek art is a matter not of average but highest humanity (*höchste Menscheit*, 335). Lower criticism deals with antiquity as a set of remains (*das Überlieferte*); beyond that, all is left to hermeneutics, except for the "trans-temporal" and "trans-spatial" judgments that answer the highest questions of higher criticism. These last make of the Hellenic heritage a living tradition (*Überlieferung*) of eternally valid laws (*ewig giltige Gesezte*) that assume various local manifestations (338). Essentially, one can look with profit back to the ancients in "every modern science" (e.g, mathematics, medicine, agriculture, horsebreeding), but they achieve the peak of their classicity as philosophers. That unrepeatable series of thinkers comprise living manifestations of "all philosophical possibilities" (349).

2. Educational or formational aims. This exemplarity we have just discussed is closely related to Nietzsche's educational orientation, for as in the humanist tradition, it is precisely by means of the "greatest examples" that one is presumed to learn best and most deeply. Nietzsche himself directly says that dealing with authors and monuments is merely a "midpoint"— understanding the classical is the goal (342). One cannot miss in this text Nietzsche's concern for the vocation of the teacher (*Lehrerberuf,* 329). He stresses that along, with a joy in antiquity and a pure eagerness for knowledge, a pedagogical inclination is absolutely requisite "in the essential character of a 'higher teacher'" (330). Being a scholar cannot suffice. The vocation of teaching requires the very self-formation of the teacher (an insight Zarathustra was to receive in the course of his own career, which was also profoundly absorbed in conceptions of future and higher humanity):

> To be a pedagogue in the high sense, he must comprehend the classical. But since he cannot convince the young about classicity, he must seek a broader field for his vocation as an educator. He must be the ideal teacher, for the most capable stages of life: Teacher and bearer of educational material, the mediator between the great geniuses and the presently developing geniuses, between the great past and the future.
>
> Tremendous reproductivity, a brilliant virtuousity, over against creative genius.—This is his gradient (*Tendenz*) for life. His first task is to become a good gymnasium teacher. (332)

Nietzsche returns to the educational theme often, and his passion reveals itself most strikingly in the sole apostrophe to his audience, in the section on general methodological observations: "Keep a tight hold on the classical tendencies of the Gymnasium, my good men!" (341)

3. Sense of current cultural needs, with an eye to the future. The citation about being a pedagogue in the highest sense is also a good example of another underlying humanistic trait evident in this text: concern for the present. The production of future geniuses is a culturally vital undertaking. Though Nietzsche clearly believes in the classical, the normative, he is equally concerned about using it in a way that bears on his immediate cultural situation. In these notes he does not set forth a general critique of modern culture, though he does indicate his sympathy with that Romantic position decrying the fragmentation and one-sidedness of modern humanity (336). He speaks at greater length of the professional crisis of philology, which has tended to degenerate into a mighty battle between the methodically fastidious linguists and the positivist historians (343). Method has become a standard criterion but it has been blind to the *educative* dimensions. Thus, the gradient towards the classical has been "quite lost." Nietzsche would have the classical *Tendenz* dominate even the scholarly impulse (344). But the wider sense of the present is clearly a key factor for the very possibility of the emergence of a capable philologist. To learn antiquity truly (and thus to be nourished by its classicity), one must know the present: "The most important expedient (*Förderungsmittel*) for becoming receptive to antiquity, is to be *a modern person...*" (333). But such a life-project requires being truly linked with the *modern* greats, especially through an intimate familiarity with Winckelmann, Lessing, Schiller, Goethe, in order to attain a truly profound sympathetic understanding of what antiquity is for the moderns (333). Once again, in humanist fashion, an *open* canon of leading examples and sources provides the way to understand and appropriate a given cultural reality. The recent thinkers are not excluded because they were not Greeks; rather they are included on the basis of the usefulness of their achievement for the larger task.

4. Enthusiasm and delight in the study of ancient culture, with stress on literary study. Nietzsche explicitly stresses how radically important for classical philological study are the qualities of personal attachment and delight. The second fragment reproduced in Holzer's edition runs "Understanding of antiquity, loving immersion (*liebevolle Durchdringung*)" (329). Nietzsche's second major requirement for an authentic philologist is "joy in antiquity" (330), a theme he returns to a little later (333), saying

> The most important thing (and the most difficult) is to enter lovingly (*liebevoll*) into antiquity and to experience the difference. Only then can one be educated by antiquity (the child must love the father if the father is to educate it), but also only then will he become a productive scholar (only out of love do the deepest insights arise).

Philological training should include, besides exegetical preparatory reading (340) and seminar-exercises (341), the "reading of the correctly methodical philologists, that is, those who present with love and care (*mit Liebe und Sorgfalt*), not only give results" (341). The affective dimension can not be left out, or the educational project will be spoiled. Such a perspective on literary practices of academic research reflects the humanistic concern for "the whole person." It is especially interesting that the reading must remain rooted in feeling. "Only out of love do the deepest insights arise." The approach stands over against any one-sided search for "correct" and dispassionate judgements.

5. Aesthetic sensibility. In line with the sense for the affective life of the learners, Nietzsche has a particularly keen sense for the aesthetic dimensions of the philological enterprise. The point of departure for attaining a comprehension of classical existence is the ancient's artistic superiority (329). Scholars can not be classical philologists if they are "unaesthetic" (331). Knowing the distinctive character of antiquity requires a "practical art-activity" (333) and the contemplation of ancient art (333). At first, of course, it is not a matter of achieving particular aesthetic perceptions, but a gradual familiarization and "*Liebgewinnen*" (a "taking a fancy to," 333). Ultimately, important hermeneutical judgments depend upon a sound aesthetic judment (338).

6. Concern for a profound and authentic, active, personal appropriation of antiquity. Just as important as a general orientation is experiencing "what it means really to appropriate (*sich aneignen*) the ancients" (334). Classically humanistic in this regard also, Nietzsche's sense of the relevance of the individual's personal horizon of philological study is paramount. This feature is corollary to his educational-cultural conception of the work, and it coheres with his methodological sensitivity for differences of perspective. The whole issue of objective normativity versus subjective relativism is present here, both sides having a definite place in his general scheme. On the very first page of the text, Nietzsche stresses the possibility of plural interpretations of the same data: "One grasps after history and finds in it a collection of examples for one's own perceptions. The more one is an independent thinker (*Selbstdenker*), the more will one perceive in the past" (329). The sentence immediately following turns to the idea of classicity as the presupposition of classical philology. Our task is to grow to be one with it. Manifold talents are also presupposed: "Each will perceive something and seek a sphere appropriate to himself" (329). A similar juxtaposition of ideal and yet individual perspective occurs later when Nietzsche speaks about the need for attaining, with the help of Plato and Kant, an idealist transcendence of naive realist perspectives, with the result that paradoxes lose their fearsome force (336-37). The scholar "must have the courage to seek his way alone" (337). Avoid the distracting, non-classical effects of comparative linguistics, Nietzsche also urges "Greek or Latin is never just one language among others." It is precisely a matter of the nonfamiliar; "with this one must gradually become fully accustomed" (*sich hineinleben,* 342). Bulk of material is clearly secondary to the "How?" Scholarship only gives minimal bases for definite perceptions (344).

> The best thing is that each has a quite individual inclination to approach antiquity. Our task is only to give him indications how he might most easily and reliably arrive at the particular areas. The main thing always remains: that there is a need to learn and to experience something. The skillfully noted and collected items remain dead, i.e., it is not assimilated into the productive nucleus; it does not transfer into flesh and blood, yes—it oppresses and injures the person like a lead bullet in one's head. (344-45)

7. A balancing of subjective and objective interests. Because Nietzsche is interested in a personal appropriation of an objective classical existence that is really quite different from our own (333), he seems to present us with a typically humanist balancing of perspectives on the subjective self. The ego is important, but it is not everything. It destroys us when it is inflated. Only the Greater Self, the genius, has the right to devotion and discipleship. Very early on, Nietzsche states "I am against the activity of the egoistic desire for knowing (*Erkennen-Wollens*). Above all else, taking joy (*Freude*) in what is at hand and carrying it farther is the teacher's task" (329-30). Here, in a striking way, the humanist's values of joy and educational orientation are combined with Nietzsche's anti-egoism. The "donkey-work" (*Kaerner-arbeit*) of collecting huge amounts of data is always necessary, but the donkeys must be guided! "If [such scholars] try to build themselves, woe to them and to science!" (340). These words show that Nietzsche does indeed have a living interest in the positive achievement of "science" (*Wissenschaft*)—he includes a "pure eagerness for knowledge" among the three essential traits of a philologist (330)—but his understanding of it exceeds that of a simplistic positivism. Hence he recommends that one should read not many things but with much depth, quoting the old Latin maxim "*Non multa sed multum*" (340-41). He stresses the time-element, the gradual familiarization that derives from the repeated reading of the same material. Philology is indeed a matter of sound understanding and judgment (337). It has laboriously won the basis for important insights into antiquity (339). Even though Nietzsche has stressed delight in antiquity, he does not mean to foster an anti-scientific animus. Respect *Wissenschaft*, he urges, which "has nothing to do with enjoyment (*Genuss*) beyond pleasure (*Lust*) in the rigorous truth" (338). But Nietzsche clarifies: the aesthetic is "not a matter of mere enjoyment," i.e., dilettantism (338). What is really at stake is "the highest elevation towards an ideal"; in that "the truth is included again" (338). The objective and subjective dimensions are neatly encapsulated in Nietzsche's assertion that every classical *Tendenz* aims for two things: a scientific approach to antiquity and an accurate active possession of it. It is important, therefore, to limit quantity of material in order to obtain as much meaning as we can from each detail (344).

8. A philosophical horizon, especially as manifested through one's concern for (an ideal) fundamental anthropology. Nietzsche's valorization of the "highest elevation towards an ideal" in which the truth is included (338) is another key indication of Nietzsche's profoundly humanistic orientation, absorbing and transcending scientific truth for a higher philosophical and ethical one. He is clearly concerned with the idea of human existence at its fullest, as is so much of the humanistic tradition. The following passage is quite revealing:

> In all things, one must reflect, but not all too tenderly, and without the naive presupposition, that now everything might possibly be beautiful. Above all it is important that one does not misunderstand the concept of humanity: it has nothing to do with "essential rights." We must always maintain that the ideal person is something very rare: namely with a higher total endowment and a balancing of instincts: contemplative, gentle, artistic, political, beautiful, noble forms. How must we seem over against Sophoclean Athens? With our Roman veneer of education and our one-sided virtuousity and atrophy of the rest. (336)

The humanist anthropology of ideal and harmonious personal integration is evident, even while there is an appeal to remain realistic: not everything can be beautiful and don't be too tender. And one must work from the right concept of humanity. We also find here a suggestion of Nietzsche's critique of socialist ideology and modernity's fragmentation, further evidence for his presentist involvement in contemporary cultural criticism. Elsewhere, his openness to, even involvement in, the philosophical sphere stands out especially clearly. The often-recommended one year of philosophical studies for the philologist is not adequate, he finds, since the philologist "must continually hold fast to philosophy so that his claim of the classicity of antiquity over against the modern world does not sound like a laughable presumption" (334). The profound issue of Christian versus pagan perspectives is really not helpfully framed: "the fundamental question is pessimistic or optimistic towards existence (*Dasein*)" (334). The philologist's very task of perceiving the available, universally known facts as data worth explaining and using in a contemplative reflection on the contrast of ancient and modern modes of cultural existence is "the true distinctive trait of philosophers" (336). The positivist accumulators are not "predestined philologists" because they are not philosophers and are they are unaesthetic (340). The conclusion to the *"Einleitung"* stresses the exemplary naive genius of the Greeks, who combine simplicity and depth. Nietzsche hopes to have illuminated for his audience the essential philological task: "as a means of clarifying existence (*Dasein*) for oneself and for the youth that is coming of age. In the Greeks will we learn, with their examples in hand will we teach" (352). This last sentiment is quintessentially humanist. In fact, one might partially define the core of Western humanism as *a thinking of, through, and by means of the Greeks for the sake of a well-informed and promising present.* The greatest hope is that such a dynamic anamnesis will lead the age to the achievement of its own perpetually memorable personalities and events.

Classicism, educational interests, presentism, enthusiasm for ancient culture and literature, aesthetic sensibility, personalism, integration of subjective and objective dimensions, ethical-existential philosophical horizons—all of these traits taken together suggest how consistently humanistic Nietzsche's classical philology actually was and how consciously he committed himself to the direction of this tradition. Two other sources lend weight to this conclusion. One is Nietzsche's inaugural lecture at Basel, "Homer and Classical Philology," delivered in 1869 (1964d). Its title is not self-explanatory. Nietzsche ostensibly engages nothing less than the long-standing philological question about the existence of the poet Homer, but he uses his answer as an occasion for important reflections on the science of philology. His investigation is meant to show how such *Wissenschaft* is not at all merely a destructive discipline that necessarily results in the demythologization and therefore deflation of classical Greece as a generative matrix of the highest cultural ideals. In fact, Nietzsche suggests, it actually leads us in the direction of a new reverence: "I should like to make it clear by an example that the most significant steps of classical philology never lead away from the ideal antiquity, but to it; and that, just when people are speaking unwarrantably of the overthrow of sacred shrines, new and more worthy altars are being erected" (150-51). A great disruption had occurred when Friedrich August Wolf declared his "Homeric atheism," believing that there was no single person responsible for the Homeric poems. These were merely primitive bardic lays. "Homer" was not "individual" but "folk" poetry. Nietzsche casts this division aside as a false dualism. All poetry—even popular poetry—"requires an intermediary individuality" (160). No group as a whole could possess genius. From the time of Peisistratus on, however, critics turned the individual "Homer" into an essentially aesthetic judgment, denoting the beautiful passages as genuine and the others as deriving from the tradition (162). In fact, "Homer" was originally a material designation used to distinguish a particular type of poetry, that is, heroic poetry, over against that didactic poetry labeled with the name "Hesiod" (163). Nietzsche proposes, on the basis of his aesthetic and philosophical principle, that there was indeed an original inspired poet who composed pieces without any sense of a whole. There was also another person, a "designer," whose genius was to make from these earlier poems a uniquely effective synthesis, thus achieving "something relatively great in [his] conscious technical composing" (166). In this way, Nietzsche arrives at his thesis: "We believe in a great poet as the author of the Iliad and the Odyssey—*but not that Homer was that poet*" (167). This genius "sacrificed his name on the altar of the primeval father of the Heroic epic, Homeros" (167).

Nietzsche reconciles the results of the supposedly "destructive" critical philology with the idealizing tendencies of classicism, which elevates inspired, paradigmatic individual achievement. The older Homer was "only too great" before Wolf, i.e., held to be responsible for far more than he actually achieved. Science has given a more differentiated and adequate understanding, without giving up the idea of the original genius and the aesthetic unity of the poems. Also, it has even helped to "make" the greats: how known or accessible was Homer before Wolf's "brilliant investigations"? (169). At the end of his address, Nietzsche states his own confession of faith, reversing an old Senecan phrase: "What was philology has become philosophy" (170), that is to say, "all philological activities should be enclosed and surrounded by a philosophical view of things, in which everything individual and isolate is evaporated as something detestable, and in which great homogeneous views alone remain" (170). Interpretive, global holism should overcome analytical, scholastic, and positivist particularism: this is what seems to define an authentically philosophical approach. Nietzsche concludes with a reference to himself as a servant of the public trust, "fulfilling the confidence with which the highest authorities of this community have honoured me" (170). Here we have, then, the same themes that we have already noted in the *"Einleitung,"* especially those of incorporating but transcending science; affirming but relativizing the power of the individual; and maintaining a philosophical horizon. Nietzsche is clearly an idealist in the humanist sense of the word. For him, the classical world still towers over us as the peak of human culture. A correctly practiced science will ultimately tend to support this understanding.

If we turn back to the introductory paragraphs where Nietzsche expounds on the mystery of this "centaur," classical philology, we will also see that the question of unity is a disciplinary as well as a poetic question. And we will finally understand the reason why the title's paralleling of Homer with classical philology is so appropriate: "At the present day no clear and consistent opinion seems to be held regarding Classical Philology...The cause of this lies in its many-sided character, in the lack of an abstract unity, and in the inorganic aggregation of heterogenous scientific activities which are connected with one another only by the name 'Philology'" (145). Just as the Homeric poems required an anonymous, self-sacrificing "designer," Nietzsche implies, so does the discipline of classical philology. He proposes that there are various components that constitute this discipline. It even "conceals within itself an artistic element, one which, on aesthetic and ethical grounds, may be called imperatival—an element that acts in opposition to its purely scientific behavior" (145). In addition to the aesthetic and the natural scientific, Nietzsche mentions the historical (145), perhaps as an ally of science and standing over against fanciful imagination. But each of these three fields (aesthetics, history, science) were later to be objects of his own enduring interests and definite dimensions of his typically composite humanistic mentality.

Here Nietzsche stresses the duality of science and art, compares them as both ways of transfiguring everyday reality (148), and connects them by proposing as their common purpose a single trans-individual, modern cultural attempt at merger with antiquity:

> The entire scientific and artistic movement of this peculiar centaur is bent, though with cyclopic slowness, upon bridging over the gulf between the ideal antiquity—which is perhaps only the magnificent blossoming of the Teutonic longing for the south—and the real antiquity; and thus classical philology pursues only the final end of its own being, which is the fusing together of primarily hostile impulses that have only forcibly been brought together. (150)

Nietzsche seems to aspire to a "realistic idealism" with regard to Greece. The issue of homogeneity of vision can only be solved, he finally suggests, by that horizon that is "a philosophical view of things" (170). But with these contents, his philosophy is clearly more than an abstract account of epistemology, metaphysics, etc. Ultimately Nietzsche does not want to lose that "wonderful creative force, the real fragrance, of the atmosphere of antiquity...that passionate emotion which instinctively drove our meditation and enjoyment back to the Greeks"

(148). This concrete and enthusiastic sensibility is what helps to us to identify him as a humanist. Though a professional, he is no bloodless technician of *Altertumwissenschaft*, just as he is no dilettante, despite his wide-ranging exuberance.

In 1875, six years after his inaugural address, and three after the disappointing non-reception of *The Birth of Tragedy*, Nietzsche attained a new peak of self-conscious disciplinary reflection, expressed in his notes for the aborted fifth Untimely Meditation, "We Philologists" (1973). This is the third and last example we will examine for the purposes of the present argument. Although we have only this collection of experimental and sketchy fragments, they show, even as they exhibit the major humanist features of the earlier works, the special turn that Nietzsche's classical humanism was taking. More extensively than before, the idea of classical philology is understood in a large cultural and historical context, and it is discussed with an intense disillusionment about its failure, but still with an equally intense desire for its radical reform. A fundamental question seems to be How can the classical philologist presume to be "teacher and moulder of the human race"? (7[7]). The philologist stands on trial for contributing to the "bad state of modern culture" through either unfortunate lack of judgment or a miserable weakness of will. Presumably, Nietzsche was going to introduce the body of his essay with the summary statement and charge (7[7]): *"If the philologist wants to prove his innocence, he must understand three things: antiquity, the present, and himself. His offense lies in the fact that he understands neither antiquity, nor the present, nor himself."* Thus Nietzsche essentially adopts a self-critical and revisionary stance *within* the classical humanist tradition: Humanism, especially in its paradigmatic Renaissance instantiation, was a movement concerned precisely with a knowledge of antiquity, the present, and the self.

In these notes, Nietzsche maintains his profound educational allegiance and continues to support the idea of some kind of exemplarity in the classical Greeks, although this latter is now darker and more "realistic." A thorough analysis of the entirety of these reflections is not required here. A sampling of key texts and a summary overview will adequately indicate Nietzsche's passionate humanist commitment, as well as his own strenuous efforts to rethink the significance of Greece and the cultural and educational mechanisms, dynamisms, and needs of his own time. Especially noteworthy is Nietzsche's continuing educational obsession, with which his new vision of Greece is sometimes entwined. The following citations reveal some of his typical sentiments on the Greeks and education:

> It is only the relation between a people and the education of the individual that interests me. In this respect there are certainly among the Greeks some things very favorable to the development of the individual, deriving, however, not from the nation's *good quality*, but from the conflict of evil instincts...My hopes lie here: in the training of significant men. (5[11])

> Until now the history of Greece has always been written optimistically. (5[12])

> To bring to light the irrational in human affairs without any shame—that is the purpose of our brothers and colleagues. As a result a distinction will have to be drawn between what in this is fundamental and cannot be improved, and what can still be improved. But "Providence" should be kept out of it; for this is a concept by which things are oversimplified. I want to breathe the breath of this purpose into scholarship. To advance the knowledge of man! The good and the rational in man is something fortuitous, fictitious or the opposite of something very irrational. Someday the only thought will be of education. (5[20])

> My religion, if I can still use the word, lies in the task of producing the genius. Education is everything we can hope for; all consolation is called art. Education is love for the procreated, an excess of love beyond love of self. Religion is "Love beyond ourselves." The work of art is the image of such self-transcending love, and a perfect image. (5[22])

> Educators, educate? But first educators must educate themselves. It is for these I write. (5[25])

Nietzsche's revalued classicism posits a distinction between humanity and "the humane": the Greeks are superlative revelations of the former, *not* of the latter (3[12]; 5[72, 100, 145]). And yet, Hellenic existence is still somehow ideal: The Greeks are "not to be imitated directly, but they teach how art achieved its highest perfection to date" (3[74]); they "shine in the splendor of a higher *humanity*" (3[76]). They provide us with "a classical archive of examples for the enlightenment of our entire culture and its development," being a means for "*understanding ourselves*, for judging our own age and thereby surpassing it" (6[2]). They are also praised for having a higher moral nature, for being "whole" and "simple," thus giving us "pleasure, as the sight of animals pleases us" (6[36]). Clearly Nietzsche still valorizes some kind of imitation of the exemplary, according to the subjective state and position of the learner. In fact, "The criterion of the curriculum is this: we should study *only what incites us to imitation,* what we understand with love and which demands to be passed on" (5[171]). If classicists had truly appropriated classical antiquity they would not be the disappointing examples that they are (3[18]). Repeatedly, Nietzsche makes the point that we have not understood antiquity; nor, therefore, have we adequately evaluated it (5[148]; 6[11,51]). Thus the entire humanist tradition must be seen skeptically: it is an incomplete or even failed project, even though it can be given credit for some solid achievement.

We can find in this text some essential insights into Nietzsche's complex attitude to the history of humanism and begin to sense something of what he himself thought of humanism and the Renaissance, as he uses these very terms in a few of the notes. It seems that he regrets the Carolingian, Saxon, and Christian humanism in general: they seem to represent the victory of Christianity over Hellenism (5[33,107]). In another place, Nietzsche suggests that humanism "badly understood and wholly falsified" antiquity, which "when clearly understood" is "evidence *against* humanism" (5[60]). This statement seems to be a striking challenge to the present thesis, but it is neither surprising nor irreconcilable in context. Nietzsche immediately clarifies his understanding of humanism here with an explanatory phrase "the notion of human nature as basically good, etc." Thus, he seems to want to hold a distinction between Hellenism and humanism, with the latter word perhaps connoting for him, at least in this particular context, a Christianized, "optimistic" understanding of life. He wants his idealism to be more "realistic" and more "pagan," founding it upon a clearer understanding of how very different the Greek vision is from our own. Nietzsche evidently has some trouble here, insofar as he also finds a definite continuity between Christianity and ancient Greece—a connection that he will later tend to keep out of sight—and he is embarrassed by the "victory" of the former over the latter (3[13]; 5[148]). Therefore he attempts to make a distinction between the Hellenic achievement and the religious bases of Greek culture, which were pre-Greek and revived by Christianity (5[155,156]). But the more relevant issue has less to do with religion as such and more to do with humanism and the university milieu in which Nietzsche found himself. He in fact often juxtaposes the modern classical scholar, who might, with some justification, be thought of as a derivative of the culture of Renaissance humanism, with the vital humanity exemplified by the Greeks themselves. One of the most incisive and vitriolic examples of this is the note immediately preceding the one that speaks of evidence "against humanism" (5[59]). It is important to remember that from the time when it was introduced in the early nineteenth century, the word *Humanismus* had an especially strong *academic* connotation, as did the Renaissance *humanista.* Our use of the word may carry formational implications without the same institutional implications. It can therefore be problematical to use the word *educator*, with its suggestions of our academic context, as a simple synonym for *humanist.* Nietzsche's problems with the Academy may be emerging here in a critical reflection on the history of humanism.

But even in these notes, Nietzsche does not unequivocally distance himself from humanism. In fact, he sometimes praises the Renaissance movement, which stood over against the German Reformation's use of antiquity to defend Christianity intellectually. The Italian Renaissance, however

> in a *purer* but quite anti-Christian way, begins classical studies...a serious inclination to the classics makes one unchristian...*Friedrich August Wolf* is remarkable...because he freed his profession from theology. But his achievement was not wholly understood since an aggressive, active element—of the sort we associate with the poet-scholars of the Renaissance—was not developed. Scholarship profited from the liberation, not men. (5[107])

Hence the new Renaissance culture was actually "*unpopular*," Nietzsche exclaims (5[108]). Modern classicists are terribly misdirected: since they do not achieve a truly emulative appropriation, theirs is a "*curriculum* of *desperation*" not a "*curriculum* of *competition* (Renaissance, Goethe)" (5[167]). Given a choice, then, Nietzsche certainly prefers the older Renaissance humanist tradition to the current "scientific" and "historical" one (5[178]): "Out of the very imperfect philology and classical scholarship [of the Renaissance], there issued a stream of freedom. Our own highly developed classical scholarship enslaves men and serves the idols of the state." Thus, Nietzsche's final judgment on contemporary philology seems to be that it should pass away, out of the self-consciousness of its own terrible educational failure and bad faith. One sketch for his essay shows that he considered having the concluding section deal with "The philologist of the future as sceptic of our whole culture, and thereby destroyer of professional philology" (5[55]). But these words also indicate the survival of philology in a new "transvalued" form, for there *will* be "a philologist of the future."

We have dwelt at length on evidence that pointedly reveals how deep and broad Nietzsche's humanistic foundation was. What especially encouraged this textually-specific approach was the general lack of attention to Nietzsche's early period despite the hermeneutical importance of genetic considerations. Dealing with these more obscure texts has allowed us to examine more explicitly what precisely is involve in the humanist tradition in which Nietzsche stands and to specify more concretely the particular type of humanism that Nietzsche seems to have been developing (as it cannot be named simply "Renaissance" or "Goethean," humanism, for example). Of course the points made here could be illustrated in many of Nietzsche's other works, like, for example, *The Birth of Tragedy*, which stands as an important early statement of so much of Nietzsche's later thinking, and which was undoubtedly the summit of Nietzsche's attempt to interpret Greek culture and simultaneously reform both classical studies and modern Germany (Heftrich, 1989). One who acknowledges the depth of Nietzsche's early humanism might yet reasonably wonder what relevance it has to the works by which he is chiefly known. A genealogical interest naturally leads beyond the identification of origins to the tracing of specific "lines of descent." Here we can at least notice some examples of the later reverberations of this early period in Nietzsche's later writing. For those who want substantial evidence of how Nietzsche continued to think about the Greeks, the selection of Nietzsche's thoughts made by William Arrowsmith (Nietzsche, 1963a, 1963b, 1963c) will be helpful. For those interested in the perduring methodological significance of philology in Nietzsche's later theory and practice, Alan Schrift (1987) has provided a good overview. And for those who want to investigate how thoroughly the appropriation of the content of Greek literature and thought informed Nietzsche's later positions, there is no better analysis than the book-length work by Patrick Moroney (1986) on precisely that theme. What I will add here are only a few suggestions that can be made on the basis of *Wir Philologen*, focusing on early forms of the famous, perhaps "hypermythologized" motifs associated with the "mature Nietzsche."

The foreshadowings of Zarathustra's coming *Übermensch*, along with a hint of the philosophers of the future prophesied by *Beyond Good and Evil*, could be said to appear as an anonymous counter-image to common, dull, and feckless existence:

> Men obviously do not regard themselves as *really* being *individuals*.... Only in three forms of existence does man remain an individual: as philosopher, as saint, and as artist. Simply observe how the scholar murders his own life...Here too we see, then, how innumerable men

> really live only as a forerunner of a real man: the scholar, for instance, as a forerunner of the philosopher, who knows how to use the scholar's ant-like labor to express an opinion on the *value of life.* (3[63])
>
> *The scholar must be a scholar from self-knowledge, that is, out of contempt for himself. In short, he must know himself as the servant of a higher man who will come after him. Otherwise he is a sheep.* (3[69])

A similar relationship of forerunner to a coming messianic figure is clearly basic to the opening of *Zarathustra.* We may find a hint of "eternal return" in this same context. Seeing that we are a "multiplication of many pasts," we must give up the idea of a "final end," Nietzsche observes; in any case, we generally would prefer to contribute, even modestly, to a lasting tradition.

> But this is actually the Danaids' jar. It is no use. We must do everything over for ourselves and only for ourselves. (3[69])

Of course, this is not the same as the idea of living one's life again and again for all eternity, but it does arguably have a significant amount of the same existential, "anti-teleological" import, which I would express in something like this exhortation: "Come to grips with your own life as it is, for that is all that is or ever will be for you! Do not falsely and unrealistically console yourself with the idea of being part of an ascending Hegelian stream of progress!" Nietzsche certainly shows some discomfort with the "hothouse of historical optimism" that Germany has become, perhaps at Hegel's hands (5[58]). The Eternal Return would be the "doing everything over for ourselves" and only for ourselves, appropriating the past not in a blind accumulative positivistic spirit, but with a sense of ourselves as somehow unique individualities who can not be denied a certain completeness or finality simply because historical "progress" will roll on beyond our biographical boundaries. We do not exist for the sake of another time. At best, in Nietzsche's understanding, we might in a way exist for the Great Individual whose coming will transform culture and whose qualities will lift humanity to a higher plane of being.

This line of thought is closely connected with an intensification of the presentism we have already pointed out as a standard humanistic feature. Nietzsche connects the prospect of a full living in the present with the idea of eternity in fragment 5[85], revealing there a Greek source for the connection: "The *heightening* of the *present* into the *vast and eternal,* e.g., in Pindar." This intensification can easily be tied to the whole lively realm of the Dionysian and the closely connected theme of Will, which are constants in Nietzsche's intellectual career. The concern for a present liveliness shows up repeatedly, for example:

> Happiness lies in swiftness of feeling and thoughts; everything else is slow, gradual, and stupid. The man who could experience the movement of light would be a very happy man, since light is very swift. (3[75])

> The Greeks lacked sobriety. Excessive sensibility; abnormal excitement of nerves and brain; vehemence and ardor of the Will. (5[81])

> Supreme judgment on life only to be passed by the supreme energy of life. The mind must be utterly removed from *apathy.* (5[180])

Though he here seems to be challenging any impassive version of the ancient Stoic ideal of *apatheia*, that freedom from the trouble generated by the passions, Nietzsche does seem to aim for his own parallel to Stoics' traditional ideal of the *sapiens* (sage). He opposes his own figure of wisdom to Christianity's quite bluntly and thus even raises the prospect of his long and labored attack on Christianity through the disturbing concept of the Anti-Christ. This theme, which he was to elaborate so vehemently in the last months of his career, clearly appears in a section entitled "*Aims*":

> The *wise man* must oppose the designs of the unintelligent good, since his goal is the reproduction of his type. Least of all can he *promote* the ideal state.—Christ promoted the stupidity of men; he arrested the production of great intellect. Quite consistently! His opposite would perhaps be an obstacle to the production of more Christs.—*Fatum tristissimum generis humani!* (5[188])

We can not attribute Nietzsche's extreme ideas, therefore, to any "incipient madness" of the late period, for he had begun long before to entertain them, albeit with the suggestion of regret suggested by the last line here, a sorrow that was only going to deepen for him. Nietzsche holds to a tragic conception of the individual, heroic, human vocation: he does not want the Kingdom of God and the joy of the Resurrection, but god-like kings and the pained glory of a Great Battle.

The weight of this genealogical argument will be determined partly by one's sense of the colors, tones, proportions, and interrelationships of the various themes that appear in Nietzsche's early writings. It would not be hard to point out that matters of concern to "rigorous" philosophy also occupied Nietzsche deeply during his early years. In fact, such seems to be the import of the fascinating collection of material published as *Philosophy and Truth* by J. Daniel Breazeale (1979). These notes make clear the intense epistemological speculations of the young Nietzsche. In fact, of the many projects Nietzsche was planning in those years, the one "overshadowing" all the others was a book that was going to deal with the nature of philosophy, truth, and knowledge. Not only does Breazeale agree with Arthur Danto's sentiment that Nietzsche never altered the theory of truth contained in these early unpublished writings, but he goes on to assert that they "contain by far his most explicit, detailed, and sustained treatments of basic epistemological issues" (1). While they support the idea of an early "maturity" in Nietzsche, such observations would appear to be another challenge to the present thesis, since they could suggest that we should find Nietzsche's center of gravity in a systematic philosophical rather than humanistic milieu. I would argue, however, that the center is and remains "humanistic." It is not clear that Breazeale himself would disagree, for he sees that the framework for the "Philosopher's Book" was to be "an historical exposition of the ancient Greek philosophers"; it was to be a companion piece to the *Birth of Tragedy*; and its trans-philosophical, humanistic character seems to be indicated by one of the proposed titles, *The Philosopher as a Cultural Physician* (xxi, xxiii).

Nietzsche's ultimate concerns have to do not so much with the exposition of a systematic epistemology as with life and culture. It is better to contextualize his radical epistemological reflections within a humanistic horizon without necessarily denying their importance or systematic nature. For Breazeale himself, "culture" is the great leitmotif of Nietzsche's entire life. He also indicates that Nietzsche's reflections on knowledge are profoundly dependent upon his philological background (xxxiii ff.). In fact other research has made clear how the history of humanistic philology itself provided an ample horizon for many probing, epistemologically significant reflections on how language is a constitutive cultural practice and not a neutrally instrumental reality (Leventhal, 1986). Nietzsche does not pursue rigorous argument as much as he seeks *appropriate evaluation and enhanced experience.* This is what most clearly seems to speak for the value of our hermeneutic use of the humanist paradigm over against a straight, disciplinary philosophical one. As Breazeale wisely points out, the selections he has translated do indeed contain significant epistemological reflection, "but one misses the point of these passages unless one remembers that Nietzsche wished to find out what knowledge *is* primarily in order to be able to find out what it is *worth*" (xxxviii).

Such an insight corroborates our main thesis. The importance of this issue of the *value* of knowledge is also underscored by an interesting correlation of two summary accounts, one of Nietzsche and the other of humanism, that intersect just at this point. An expert on humanism has suggested that in the most comprehensive sense it is simply "*the quest for value.*" It is to be distinguished from a concern with either distant transcendental realms or neutral unspirited "nature" (Levi, 1969, 15). An equally prominent Nietzsche-scholar has posited that this very idea is just the one by which Nietzsche's entire philosophy might be most coherently organized:

> The question arises as to where we are to find the thread of Ariadne to guide us through the labyrinth of Nietzsche's thought: where is Nietzsche's most fundamental problem on which all his philosophic labors are focused? This crucial question is easily overlooked; but asking it almost means answering it—so little doubt does Nietzsche leave concerning his primary concern: values...Modern man finds that his values are worthless, that his ends do not give his life any purpose, and that his pleasures do not give him happiness. Nietzsche's basic problem is whether a new sanction can be found in this world for our values; whether a new goal can be found that will give an aim to human life; and what is happiness? (Kaufmann, 1974, 121-22)

General and abstract as this correlation is, it remains interesting that these summary formulations of humanism and of Nietzsche should coincide so neatly. And in fact, expressing the meaning of humanism in terms of "values" is not a completely vague description when interpreted in context. It does indicate a particular direction. It implies, for instance, that the mere satisfaction of the knowledge-drive, is woefully inadequate for the spiritual health of humanity. Nietzsche moves eagerly towards an idea of philosophy that is "art as well as knowledge" (Breazeale, 1979, xliii). With a humanist paradigm framing our interpretation, we can more readily sense why Nietzsche even when reflecting upon philosophical themes treated them as a part of a whole network of issues (science, culture, knowledge, language, art) that he was going to organize around the "common hub" of "the general problem of early Greek antiquity" (xliv). Clearly Nietzsche, like a true humanist, was employing the Greeks as a model by which to understand the present and to achieve insight into the primary principles of culture in the West. By using as a framework the idea of Greek existence, to which he had privileged access as a philologist,

Nietzsche's cultural reflections could attain a certain radicality as well as a definite *concreteness.* This latter quality is again a pre-eminently humanistic predilection, standing over against the abstractness and theoreticality of "rigorous" philosophy.

There are many complex, reciprocal interconnections here. The humanistically-developed profession of philology consisted in scientific practices that involved Nietzsche in issues of language, poetry, rhetoric, and in a highly artistic, paradigmatic cultural complex whose peak of classicity was reached in philosophy; philosophy in turn explicitly raised questions of knowledge, truth, and culture. From another vantage point, the educational or "formational" aspect of humanist practices gave Nietzsche from the start a bias towards the therapeutic use of "knowledge" for the sake of the individual's own personal wholeness and maturation. Such a tendency already makes the teacher one who is striving not so much to pass on some ultimate "objectively valid" concrete fragments as to tap the life-enhancing potential of cultural materials. For Nietzsche, the priority of human value over "scientific validity" was no doubt ultimately supported by the whole dynamic of the scientific quest itself, since the "fundamental secret" of science has to do not with a pure and simple "truth" but rather with our *search* for truth, as Lessing discovered. Thus science itself is carried along by a metaphysical illusion that takes it repeatedly to that point at which it becomes art (Nietzsche 1967b: Section 15, 95-96). Logic turn and bites its own tail (98). The earlier Greeks, in Nietzsche's view, give us, in the creative philosophers of the Tragic Age, effective conquerors of this tyrannical compulsion (1979, 11). To imitate the greatest of the Greeks therefore necessarily means not letting ourselves be dominated by an eternally insatiable hunger for knowledge. Thus Nietzsche's particular type of Hellenism, which venerated the spirit of the pre-Socratic Tragic Age and saw Socrates as an agent of decline, could also have driven him more deeply into epistemological questions. Through his interpretation of the unfolding of Greek cultural history, he came to believe that the Western agenda should be that of curing ourselves of the now powerfully instinctive scientific illusion that some "one Truth" is attainable. To be a true follower of the early Greeks, Nietzsche simply had to engage and attempt to overcome the presuppositions of the contemporary scientific intellectual regime.

No doubt Nietzsche's epistemological interests are overdetermined by a whole composite of cultural and intellectual phenomena that would have to include that modernizing philosophical turn taken in the radical reflections of Descartes, Hume, and Kant. But if we wish to identify more clearly the personal generative origins of this web of reciprocally intensifying dynamics, there may be a most important point yet to make. Nietzsche's humanist origins largely comprised two interrelated areas that served as the original soil for all of his later intellectual productions: (1) The (proximate) *object* of classical humanism, i.e., ancient Mediterranean culture, especially Hellenic, and its own range of discoveries, insights, values, achievements; and (2) the modern *practice* of humanism in its form as modern scientific philology—the royal road to an adequate knowledge of the ancients. We might in fact ask if Nietzsche's early obsession with knowledge itself did not have a deep, biographical, professional basis, insofar as his *"Einleitung"* treats the desire for knowledge as a trait of the ideal philologist even while it constitutes a serious threat to the Gymnasium's *classisches Tendenz.* Did Nietzsche perhaps become obsessed with the nihilistic character of knowledge precisely on the basis of the example of a philology that he knew at first hand and that he felt it was his mission to reform? Certainly *The Birth of Tragedy* analyzed the sources of sterile "Alexandrianism" in the decadence of Socrates, so that we can say that Nietzsche found a material basis for this principle at work in the decline of Greek antiquity. Breazeale raises the important thesis of Schlecta and Anders that "Nietzsche's insight into the nihilistic character of knowledge dates from the early 1870's and is the main theme of the notebooks of this period" (xxxviii-xxxix, note 32). It is proposed that Nietzsche's interest in Greek science and philosophy derived from the ancients' ability to offer "neat historical illustrations of his independently developed theoretical arguments and conclusions concerning the meaning of the knowledge drive and the fate of theoretical optimism" (xxxviii-xxxix, note 32). However we have already seen that even in Nietzsche's *1869* inaugural address, he was dealing with the "destructive" character of critical philological and historical knowledge. Here is perhaps a crucial part of the early germ of Nietzsche's whole later obsession with nihilism. The "independently developed theoretical arguments" of the 1870's need not be given a complete independence. The meaning and value of the practices of classical philology had already involved Nietzsche in questions of scientific knowledge and the effects that the scientific quest must have on the souls of scholarly seekers.

In conclusion, then, our genealogical argument posits that Nietzsche must be understood as a thinker rooted first and foremost in a humanist context. Professionally, intellectually, affectively, his absorbing concerns and themes were established during that time when he gave himself wholeheartedly to the Hellenic spirit and tradition for the sake of a full, this-worldly life and for the renewal of contemporary civilization.

3

In the Region of Likeness: Family Resemblances

"The Absolute never sleeps." Nor does that vast dimension of our psyches that Augustine might call *memoria* and depth psychologists "the Unconscious." Whatever we might imagine what goes on beneath, behind, or beyond our focal awareness, and whatever ontological status we might give that dimension of our mental lives, we can be sure that, when we involve ourselves in the complex act of reading, our operations depend upon others that remain relatively obscure. Yet we do know enough to be able to assume that we are constructing our understandings on the basis of habits that we have developed, contents with which we have made ourselves familiar, and categories according to which we have learned to interpret the data that we register. The adequacy of our readings, and our very ability to judge adequacy, depend upon practices worked out and passed on through our culture's larger literary histories.

But even more is involved. There are inescapable modes of understanding, "a priori" structures of consciousness that we can never suppress completely and that are not limited to our particular historical situations. For example, we like to put things into context and to interpret them holistically. We like to gather things that are similar and enumerate them. Such operations help us to fill out some of the dimensions of a hidden, ideal, heuristically helpful "totality." No matter how ghostly that construct may be, it remains with us in some form. It is not only Lévi-Strauss's "savage mind" that totalizes, but every mind. Given such mental dynamics, we can easily understand how something like Homer's catalogue of ships might be considered aesthetically satisfying, and why some persons have invested their energies in achieving things as disparate in scope as Linnaeus's great categorization of plants and a teenager's private baseball card collections. We press on toward a vision of "completeness," real or imagined. We enjoy the process, the progress, and the prospect of the final achievement. It does not matter that we never encounter that framework itself as an independent object among other objects that are publicly accessible in our daily lives. It does not matter that the vision is never truly complete.

In this second argument, I would like to summon a gallery of specific cultural-historical *personae* in order to examine some of these hidden yet foundational aspects of our interpretations of Nietzsche. First, a simple thought-experiment will highlight one major element in contemporary readings of Nietzsche. Let us ask ourselves: Do we tend to place Nietzsche with figures like Aristotle, Descartes, Kant, Hegel, Marx, Dilthey, Russell, Heidegger, and Wittgenstein, or is it rather with the likes of Socrates, Quintilian, Petrarch, Vives, Montaigne, La Rochefoucauld, Voltaire, Goethe, Emerson, Matthew Arnold, and Gerard Manley Hopkins? It appears to me first, that *de facto* the disciplinary practice of philosophy has promoted the former option, despite the fact that Nietzsche himself might well have preferred the latter, and second, that this choice— or prejudice—is not hermeneutically trivial. At the minimum, my larger argument suggests that it is quite valuable to try to think of Nietzsche in the context of the latter group while attending to the possible different resonances in interpretation that may result. I do not at all deny the justifiability of using the first group as a context within which to read Nietzsche, of course. Many things encourage it. But the understandings derived on such a basis would be decidedly limited and in some ways misleading.

Now I do not want to suggest that there are two mutually exclusive categorical boxes that we must posit, "the Humanists" and "the Philosophers." It would not seem much of an advance to replace one specious dualism with another. There are, however, cultural practices, just as there are conceptual distinctions, that lead us to sense immediately that there is some validity in the construction of a formal and practical distinction between the two groups of thinkers that I have just named. Notice that the distinction that I am making here is not at all about the humanistic *implications* or *foundations* or *possible uses* of one's thought; it is not about the humanistic qualities of one's *pasttimes*; rather it is about the *relevant features of one's authorial persona.* Immanuel Kant and Thomas Aquinas both elaborated systematic philosophies of powerfully humanistic tenor. Someone writing a "complete history of Western humanism" (if we for a moment allow ourselves to imagine such a project being attempted) could not easily omit either as a major contributor. But whether they themselves are best understood *primarily* as humanists is quite another question. Likewise, many humanists had much to do with something they would call "philosophy." But lumping them with different kinds of philosophers only serves to occlude those features that I would like to highlight here.

In contrast with the genealogical argument, our reflections will now operate at a much less specific level. We need not dwell explicitly upon the many parallels between Nietzsche and his humanist analogues, because in most of the cases raised, this has already been achieved in an excellent scholarly fashion. My intention is not so much to duplicate the results as to indicate their direction. This overview will suggest that there are indeed already signs of a long-standing and even growing critical appreciation of Nietzsche's humanistic character and that, taken together, the insights emerging from these lines of interpretation cohere with Nietzsche's self-understanding. They constitute yet another reason for considering him as first and foremost a humanist.

I have called this argument "analogical" because it depends upon our ever-active ability to perceive similarities. This power is holistic, pre-analytical, intuitive. I am therefore attempting to evoke a recognition rather than to fashion a thoroughgoing bio-literary analysis. I am not studying "influence" as such, although there are complicated material interrelationships involved in the examples that I will raise. People tend to become like the people whom they have had occasion to get to know well and have grown to like; or they tend to like and engage people that impress them as being like themselves. But on the other hand, similarity does not exclude harsh criticism, especially in Nietzsche's case. What I wish to stress is synchronic affinities rather than larger diachronic cultural-historical relationships. Questions of influence are not as relevant as similarities in the overall literary-intellectual gestalt.

In whose company, then, does Nietzsche best seem to belong? Where does he seem to want to put himself? What kinds of thinkers is he most like, whether or not he happens to know them? What influences, which structures of thought did he absorb and cultivate in his writing? Answering these questions is no arid intellectual exercise. It will draw us a little closer toward a more direct encounter with Nietzsche, and, as we survey the relevant figures, we shall also attain what amounts to a concrete, historical definition of Western humanism. To know what humanism is, look to its leading practitioners. Contemplate the ones who "set the standards."

Goethe. At the height of the German neohumanistic *Klassik* stands Johann Wolfgang Goethe. Louis Leibrich, convinced of Nietzsche's humanist character as it is revealed in his likeness to this pre-eminent humanist figure, fully admits the self-contradictory side of Nietzsche, especially noticeable in his last period, that stands over and against the humanist dimensions. Yet he asserts that Nietzsche's "existential experience and his spiritual quest, regarded as a whole, stem from an authentic humanism" that continues to the end of his career (1983, 287). Vis-à-vis the thought of Goethe, Nietzsche's writing manifests his kinship: "Their common orientation aims at exploring human nature in depth and at working out an optimal line of conduct for life" (287). At issue is the meaning of human existence: how should it be best understood and how should it be qualitatively transformed (288)? Clearly this is a core obsession in Nietzsche's life. Leibrich presents an impressionistic parallel sketch of the two men, having to do with five areas in particular: psychology, anthropology, epistemology, ethics, and metaphysics. He critiques Nietzsche for having an immature idealism, an erroneous anthropology, a dichotomous epistemology, and a contradictory morality (311). Goethe, by contrast, is praised for avoiding Nietzsche's failures. He rejected any Nietzschean pretention to the super-human; attained a more positive integration of his corporeal sensibility as a basis for thinking and acting than did the ascetic and eremitic Nietzsche; arrived at a socially attuned ethical vision that contrasts strongly with Nietzsche's more solipsistic emphasis on the will to power; and conceived of an open and optimistic metaphysics rather than the dead-end of eternal return (332). But both writers developed their positions from the "same fundamental aspiration: the profound need to promote the quality of the human species" (332). Between them there exists no "basic incompatibility." They "belong to the same spiritual family, to the great humanist tradition" (332). Leibrich does not expand upon his idea of the constitutive features of this tradition, but he has elegantly opened the way toward a fuller understanding of Nietzsche. If we seek a confirmation of this view in Nietzsche's own work, there is probably none better than those sections on Goethe in the the very late *Twilight of the Idols*, where Nietzsche's words even seem to suggest that Goethe might be an ideal alter-ego for him:

> *Goethe*—not a German event, but a European one: a magnificent attempt to overcome the eighteenth century by a return to nature, by an *ascent* to the naturalness of the Renaissance—a kind of self-overcoming on the part of that century.... What he wanted was *totality*; he fought the mutual extraneousness of reason, senses, feeling, and will (preached with the most abhorrent scholasticism by *Kant*, the antipode of Goethe); he disciplined himself to wholeness, he *created* himself. (1954, 553-54)

Here Nietzsche sets himself apart from Kant and scholasticism, and he positions himself on the side of Goethe, the Renaissance and the humanistic ideals of self-creation and wholeness. He goes on to say that Goethe represents for him the liberated spirit who has a faith that is "the highest of all possible faiths," the one that Nietzsche has "baptized" as Dionysian (554).

Montaigne. Among the many notables of Western humanism, Michel de Montaigne has a leading place. And so it is significant that Nietzsche's acquaintance with the *Essais* was as long and deep as his opinion of their author was exalted. Brendan Donnellan (1986) has masterfully traced the relationships between the two, summarizing Montaigne's most attractive features for Nietzsche as residing in his character "as one of the greatest figures of the Renaissance; as a model of the contemplative life; as a radical sceptic; as a writer with an unprecedented capacity for revealing himself with confessional frankness; and not least as an outstanding model of the aristocratic French moralistic culture" (1). Particularly noteworthy is their sharing of the crucial humanistic themes of the cultivation of one's own individuality or personality (13) and the sense of the wide plurality of cultural practices. The struggling, posturing, laboriously self-mastering Nietzsche was probably most inspired by Montaigne's "candid self-presentation of a harmonious personality which is the lasting literary achievement of the *Essais*" (14). Nietzsche was, of course, a more self-consciously heroic, tragic, tense, conflicted and contentious figure, but it is possible that he admired and even envied Montaigne's serene harmony of body and mind, and his "apparently effortless combination of detachment and self-control with a higher acceptance of sensuality,"—traits also present in the example of Goethe (16). Despite the obvious difference of temperament, Nietzsche's bolder, more self-assertive stance does not entirely cover over a kind of "nostalgia for this Renaissance miracle of detached personal culture and completeness," which had a naturalness that Nietzsche's age did not know (17). In his famous meditation on Schopenhauer, Nietzsche attested directly to his high estimation of this Renaissance virtuoso, saying that he could not even glance into his work without "growing a leg or a wing" (Nietzsche, 1983, 135). David Molnar (1993) has specified Montaigne's influence on Nietzsche, focusing especially on issues of the connection of philosophy and physiology, style, and "Montaigne's authentic self-representation in the *Essais* as a model of honest, creative valuing, which is the ideal of Nietzschean aspiration, pre-requisite to any *Übermenschlichkeit*" (81-82). One senses that we would miss much of Nietzsche's heart if we did not attend to the special relationship he had with this writer of the high Renaissance.

Emerson. A third long-time hero of Nietzsche's was a contemporary, the American essayist Ralph Waldo Emerson, who exerted a profound influence on him from 1862 on, even to the very end of Nietzsche's career. Emerson is a decidely humanist thinker in the style and content of his works, as Michael Moran makes clear when he concludes that Emerson must best be read not "as one would a philosopher like Kant, Schelling, Hegel, or even Coleridge," but as a writer with great powers of imagination and literary style. He was "neither a critical philosopher nor an idealist metaphysician but an intuitive sage-poet" (1972, 477, 478). He followed the tradition of the *pensée* (Montaigne, Pascal, Goethe) and preferred the essay-form. His abundant, unsystematic discourses would make a concise summary of the Nietzchean parallels very difficult, but we can point to a common stress on the individual; the heroic; the process and importance of self-development; educational and ethical concerns. They both manifest a self-asserting freedom from external, rigid, non-critical views and authorities. Knowing something of the complexity of experience, they favor intellectual flexibility and variability. They romantically exult in feelings of life and vitality and in the power of nature. They cultivate in expression their own aesthetic sensibilities. They both make an effort at cultural criticism and renewal. There are echoes of Emerson's Oversoul in Nietzsche's *Übermensch* and of his idea of a universal *nisus* in Nietzsche's Will to Power (Nietzsche, 1974; Stack, 1989). George J. Stack (1992) has now given us a comprehensive study of Nietzsche's debts to Emerson. His work brings to a culmination the direction of earlier suggestions. Rudolf Schottländer (1940) had expressed the essential relatedness of the two men in terms of the Dionysian spirit, interpreted as the youthful, spontaneous antique Greek way of life, with which both would have had extensive contact by way of their classical education. Hermann Hummel (1946) gathered many Emersonian citations that seem to anticipate Nietzsche, going so far as to say that "Everything considered, Nietzsche seems to have been influenced in a higher degree by Emerson than by anyone else" (84). Whatever our judgement may be on this issue, Nietzsche clearly expressed his affinity for Emerson on several occasions, at one point calling him "a brother soul," (see Hummel, 66) and at another point, writing: "Emerson. I have never felt so much at home in a book, so much in my own house as,—I ought not to praise it; it is too close to me" (cited by Hummel, 65).

T… … we have discussed thus far suffices to make the essential point: informed scholars agree with Nietzsche himself that he shows many affinities to, and has powerful affections for, exemplary humanist figures. His long, direct involvement with their works raises questions about influences in conceptions, attitudes, and so forth, which tie Nietzsche materially and dispositionally to the humanist traditions. But these *personalities* also exert an abiding power over Nietzsche. They live with him, as it were. He, as a humanist, can reject their ideas yet remain impressed with their behavior as well as with their literary style. He can see them as important players bringing special spiritual forces to a larger cultural drama. In fact, such admiration is a humanist trait that leads Nietzsche to attend carefully to all "culture heroes," even if they are not known primarily as humanists. Let us now amplify our "short list" of humanist analogues with several others, especially in the light of recent research.

Matthew Arnold. Donald Stone (1988) has written of the striking parallels between Nietzsche and Matthew Arnold, with special attention to their work as educationists, Hellenists, critics of religion, and promoters of a Goethean type of creative individualism. Though apparently unaware of each other's works, they strenuously fought against the complacency of "cultural Philistinism." They exhibited a many-sided, broad-minded openness that detested any diminishment of individual vitality and creativity. In this characteristic we might find some explanation for the elusiveness or complexity of their own "doctrine." The tensions accompanying such intellectual and spiritual versatility might also be a constitutive factor in the concern each had with the modern fragmentation of culture and personality, and in their similar quest for a coherence and wholeness in life. Nietzsche worked in a more exclusively intellectual sphere but chose to exalt the Dionysian dimension; Arnold, more of an activist, favored the Apollonian. Unlike Nietzsche, Arnold held a more democratic vision of education and culture and affirmed Christianity, at least in it symbolic meanings. His elitist counterpart chose to create a virulent counter-Christian persona. Both men were strongly anti-systematic and anti-dogmatic without being able to avoid tendencies towards those very qualities. The Englishman seems largely positive and cheerful, with a critical overtone; the German more critical, even if it is for the sake of affirmation. We can perceive this complementary contrast in the epigraphs Stone has chosen, from *Culture and Anarchy* and from *The Gay Science*, respectively (289):

> What we want is a fuller harmonious development of our humanity, a free play of thought upon our routine notions, spontaneity of consciousness, sweetness and light; and these are just what culture generates and fosters.

> We negate and must negate because something in us wants to live and affirm—something that we perhaps do not know or see as yet.—This is said in favor of criticism.

People today may sneer at he Arnold's "sweetness and light"—it has become a catch-phrase for prettifying idealizing—while Nietzsche is spared because of his grittier storm-and-stress. But there are moments when he too revels in the prospect of serenity and joviality. Ultimately, both Nietzsche and this Victorian arch-humanist wish to be joyful yea-sayers to human existence.

Diderot (with reference to Pico della Mirandola). Joseph Molitorisz (1983), under the direction of Ernest Behler, has given us a study devoted entirely to laying out stylistic, methodological, and substantive parallels between the thinking of Nietzsche and Denis Diderot, specifically as "fathers of modern humanism" (1). Both figures, he says, transcend the standard philosophical "*ésprit de systèm*e" with a dynamic, open-ended, dialectical "*ésprit systématique*" that is anti-system and anti-ideology (13-16). Though there is no record of any intense involvement of Nietzsche with Diderot's thinking, many similarities can be discovered in the areas of scientific, cosmological, ethical, and aesthetic reflection. Both make use of an essentially developmental dialectic, and both work toward their imagistically-presented understandings of human fulfilliment (Diderot's creative genius, Nietzsche's *Übermensch*). The culmination of their dialectics in fact is "the assertion of the philosopher who is complete in his repertoire of techniques, bold in their application, and steadfast in his determination to unveil each new insight for man's self-perfection within nature's self-development" (229). Humanity shapes itself through its native abilities. Part of what emerges in this study is Nietzsche's critical posture towards static, pre-set idealizations of "perfect humanity," especially if tainted with a pietistic "humanitarianism" that stifles or even reverses the transcendental self-developmental dynamic towards substantial and independent individual creativity (cf. 47-48).

Such a position recalls the radical freedom attributed to humanity in Pico della Mirandola's "Oration on the Dignity of Man," a premiere and programmatic humanist document:

> [The creator] took man as a creature of indeterminate nature and, assigning him a place in the middle of the world, addressed him thus: "Neither a fixed abode nor a form that is thine alone nor any function peculiar to thyself have we given thee, Adam, to the end that according to thy longing and according to thy judgment thou mayest have and possess what abode, what form, and what functions thou thyself shalt desire. The nature of all other beings is limited and constrained within the bounds of laws prescribed by Us. Thou, constrained by no limits, in accordance with thine own free will, in whose hand We have placed thee, shalt ordain for thyself the limits of thy nature...(Cassirer, 1948, 224-25)

A full appreciation of this transcendence of single fixed standards for humanity can help to explain how Nietzsche can be profoundly humanistic and simultaneously "anti-humanistic." His critique of a crude or dangerous humanism, that is, one that is based on a too particular or inflexible hypostatization of certain ideals, does not dissolve his own strong bonds to the humanist tradition. Here we have a way to help us to characterize Nietzsche's own special type of humanism: it is one that is highly self-conscious about its own tradition and about its shadow-side.

Voltaire. Another leading humanist of the Enlightenment and also a strong, demonstrably direct influence on Nietzsche, was Voltaire. Peter Heller (1976) has made very clear to what extent we can find evidence of "Nietzsche's worship of Voltaire, a sense of affinity, and an ambition to be Voltaire's heir, to succeed Voltaire, and to replace him" (110). He quotes a telling section from *Ecce Homo*: "Voltaire was above all, a *grandseigneur* of the spirit—precisely what I am. The name of Voltaire on one of my writings—that was truly progress on the way toward myself." (110, from Nietzsche, 1969a, 283)

Nietzsche had begun a reflective acquaintance with Voltaire as early as 1861 and he evokes him as late as the penultimate sentence of *Ecce Homo*, with its "*Ecrasez l'infâme*!" He finds him attractive essentially because he is a free spirit whose individualistic liberty nevertheless opposes the regressive revolutionism of Rousseau with aristocratic elegance and personal culture. Above all, Nietzsche admires Voltaire as one who can "dance in his chains," facing difficulty and limitation with lighthearted, brilliant wit. Not infrequently, the *philosophe*'s humor was turned in typical humanist fashion against scholastic philosophers and their ludicrously over-valued principles and methods. Nietzsche would go far beyond Voltaire's "pietistic" humanitarian faith and his naive Enlightenment trust in the cognitive powers of humanity (132), but the relationships of character, style, and aspirations remain evident. And even towards the end, Nietzsche would find an ally in the Frenchman who "still conceives of the comprehensive "*umanità* in the Renaissance sense and retains an appreciation for Renaissance virtues, that is: for *virtù* free of *Moralin*, free of the moral poison" (Heller, 127).

Petrarch. Nietzsche himself places Voltaire in the company of humanists *par excellence* when he looks forward to our being able to "bear the banner of the Enlightenment—the banner bearing the three names Petrarch, Erasmus, Voltaire—further onward" (1986, 26). Erasmus, the "prince of humanists," spent much very productive time in the city of Basel, where Nietzsche later worked. He may well have meant a great deal to Nietzsche as the closest that a dedicated philologist had ever come to being a cultural hero of major proportions. His wit, satirical criticism, and independence were also quite in line with Nietzsche's values. But now I would prefer to turn to the first figure in this list of banner-carriers, the representative and founder of Renaissance humanism, because he offers an even greater abundance of material for our purposes. Certainly if we consider the whole of Petrarch's career, it would be non-controversial to assert that each of the eight defining humanist traits delineated in our treatment of Nietzsche's "*Einleitung*" applies to him as well. Of course they wear a different color since Petrarch hails from such a different cultural, historical, and linguistic context. For example, we could not expect to find in him any really close parallel to Nietzsche's post-Schillerian aesthetic theory or to his post-Winckelmannian Hellenism—Petrarch never learned much Greek despite his enthusiasm for it. Nevertheless, the general gestalt is similar. One salient feature is his abiding, notably self-aware concern for the claims of the creative drive (Baron, 1975, 35) and of poetry, which he discusses in his *Africa*, Book IX, and in his "Coronation Oration." Nicholas Mann has even maintained that "[t]he *Canzoniere* is as much about poetry, and the process of writing poetry, as it is about a love-affair, a spiritual crisis, and the ironies of the human condition" (1984, 66).

Turning to philosophy, we see that Petrarch gives evidence of a strong affinity for that very Greek thinker to whom Nietzsche felt closest, Heraclitus (Françon, 1936). In fact, "his awareness of Greek philosophy and literature did affect his outlook and orientation" (Kristeller, 1972). Petrarch also shared with Nietzsche an abiding distaste for his age and a profound yet conflicted need for solitude that increased as he grew older. Like Nietzsche, he moved from philology to moral, not to systematic or metaphysical philosophy, adopting a strong anti-scholastic stance (Rico, 1986). He too wrote texts of keen psychological penetration and self-analysis like the *Secretum.* That work brings to the fore the whole problem of melancholy, which is part of a complex set of phenomena so important to Nietzsche: acedia, world-weariness, a negative judment on life, sickness of soul, and nihilism. Like Nietzsche, Petrarch had a more nationalistic artistically-framed political vision in his youth; he set out to compose a grand epic glorifying the great Roman Scipio Africanus (Baron, 1971, 29). Just as Nietzsche, against prevailing interpretations, "leapt over" the classical Greeks to exalt the archaic age, so did Petrarch downplay the empire to celebrate the earlier times of the Roman republic. It was not political structure that caught his imagination, but the virtue of the Roman citizen; Nietzsche discussed the greatness of Greek individuals much more than the types of their government. Nietzsche's turn from devotion to distaste for Schopenhauer can be paralleled by Petrarch's move from admiration of the "philosophical" Cicero to a certain distance when he discovered from the Roman's letters that Cicero had not followed his own philosophical admonitions to inward serenity. Petrarch, like Nietzsche, looked for a genuine existential coherence of the philosophical position with the personality and life of the author. But Petrarch did not abandon Cicero; nor could Nietzsche entirely cast aside Schopenhauer or other great heroes of his youth like Wagner.

Petrarch had, as well, a vision of a new culture and worked to the end on a synthesis of opposing forces (in his case, classical and Christian). Like Nietzsche, he practiced invective, not only against "fraudulent" professionals like some of the schoolmen and doctors, but also against cultural-religious institutions like the decadent papal court at Avignon. There is an asymmetry of intensity and poetic expression between Petrarch's public celebration of Laura and Nietzsche's own "Ariadne" (Cosima Wagner), but there is a similar romantic strain in both that gets expressed in various ways. Romanticizing often figures as a humanist trait, as does a certain nostalgia. Both features recur in the humanist complex. They seem to be connected with humanism's in-built disposition to give special attention to models that are presented as great and worthy of admiration or even love, howsoever distant they may be. Hence we hear of the "glory that was Greece and the grandeur that was Rome."

Both Petrarch and Nietzsche also desired their own glory. They looked for fame and for discipleship from "posterity," yet both were pointedly aware of earthly mutability, transiency, the all-too-human aspect of things. Thus they scorned the objects of their own passions in order to cultivate yet greater passions. Over the courses of their careers, Petrarch and Nietzsche had occasion to elevate and to depreciate poetry: the laureate Petrarch attributed great difficulty to great poetry, and Nietzsche boasted of the precocious brilliance of *Zarathustra*, yet eventually the former dismissed his love poetry as trifles, and Nietzsche wrote frivolous rhymes like those that frame *The Gay Science*. In both we can find anti-feminist and anti-popular sentiments that do not tell the whole story about them. They both exude an enthusiastic love for the world, manifesting itself in a remarkable sensitivity for landscapes and moods. Both were given to mountain-top inspirations and scenic retreats.

Like Nietzsche and so much of the humanist tradition, Petrarch believed in the primacy of the will over the intellect, and he sensed the importance of rhetoric and pragmatics: "Truth is not scientific; truth is psychological and fruitional, the vision that reconciles man to his divinely created universe and redeems him from his worst impulses" (Trinkaus, 1979, 25). Both writers humanistically combine poetry and philosophy in a process of seeking "a wholeness and integrity of the self" (Trinkaus, 1979, 48). Petrarch rejected the idea of *Fortuna*, Nietzsche that of Providence, but both, stressing personal autonomy, actively looked for at least a kind of salvation from beyond, whether from a leap of grace and the after-life or from a movement of Dionysian inspiration and the coming *Übermenschen* (or philologists or philosophers of the future).

Both of these many-sided moralistic pioneers of new ages were life-long travellers figuratively and literally, restless and passionate letter-writers and bibliophiles. Both of them absorbed, engaged, synthesized various elements of, and strove to transcend their literary heritage, constantly starting projects destined to remain unfinished, constantly revising what they had written. Highly sensitive to the variety and complexity of the world, both expressed their understanding in subtle texts that give their authors a kind of elusiveness as well as a special kind of presence. Perhaps most interestingly of all, both men were partly constituted and re-fashioned by their very own obsessive writing; hyperconscious of their own self-image, they were eventually engaged in the process of making their very lives "a work of art." Nehamas (1985) has written extensively on this aspect of Nietzsche. Nicholas Mann has said that "the whole corpus of Petrarch's writings constitute a vast, diffuse and constantly evolving portrait of the self, not exactly idealized, but seen through so many different prisms as to become almost kaleidoscopic" (1984, 102). And the grand spiritual-intellectual dramas of Petrarch's and Nietzsche's lives began with humble, painstaking philological labors, Petrarch on the text of Livy, and Nietzsche on that of Diogenes Laertius. Given such parallels on so many levels, It is not hard for us to perceive a formal resemblance as well as an inner kinship between the two men.

Socrates. All of the figures that we have so far discussed found it important at some time or other to state their opinions about that ancient Greek whose primordial hegemony in both philosophical and humanistic arenas is undisputed (see Spiegelberg, 1964). Likewise Nietzsche. "Socrates I simply admit it is so close to me that I almost always find myself in conflict with him." (1973, 352)

Careful studies have clarified the complex relationship between these two thinkers. (Schmidt, 1969; Kaufmann, 1974, 391-411; Dannhauser, 1974). Without negotiating that terrain again, we can certainly affirm that, even on a superficial reading, Nietzsche's attitudes are amply evidenced in his writings. With its meditation on Socrates and Socratism as the counter-instinctual, counter-tragic expression of the Greek development of the theoretical realm, *The Birth of Tragedy* claims that "we cannot fail to see in Socrates the one turning point and vortex of so-called world-history" (Nietzsche, 1967, 96). At the other end of Nietzsche's career, *Twilight of the Idols* begins its argument, after the introductory maxims, with a section entitled "The Problem of Socrates" (1954, 473-479). We should not be misled by the criticism we find here: Nietzsche's great devotion to self-overcoming could sometimes necessarily entail the "destruction" of his dearest exemplars.

No doubt Nietzsche sensed a kinship with this open-minded, ironic critic, always more clever than his opponent, a *provocateur* who elusively played with even the deepest-held values of his society to the point of "criminality." Though Nietzsche opposed the rationalism of the post-Socratic philosophical tradition (but perhaps primarily because he thought that his own age had intoxicated itself with it), the personality of this Greek sage must have suggested to him that naturally cheerful freedom of spirit that he often praises. Nietzsche seems the most anti-Socratic in his pompously dogmatic assertions, such a far cry from the Greek's self-deprecating demurral. But the two appear to stand closer to each other when we realize that their respective rhetorical strategies were drawn up against two very different cultural moments: both prankishly prodded at the substructures of their societies' traditional values. The following citation speaks elo-

both of Nietzsche's admiration for Socrates and of his under-
g of his humanistic character:

> *rates.*—If all goes well, the time will come when one will take up the memorabilia of Socrates rather than the Bible as a guide to morals and reason, and when Montaigne and Horace will be employed as forerunners and signposts to an understanding of this simplest and most imperishable of intercessors. The pathways of the most various philosophical modes of life lead back to him; at bottom they are the modes of life of the various temperaments confirmed and established by reason and habit and all of them directed towards joy in living and in one's own self; from which one might conclude that Socrates' most personal characteristic was a participation in every temperament.—Socrates excels the founder of Christianity in being able to be serious cheerfully and in possessing that *wisdom full of roguishness* that constitutes the finest state of the human soul. And he also possessed the finer intellect. (1986, 332)

Thus Nietzsche continues the absorption with this figure who had at one time constituted the center of a Renaissance cult. Socrates had been, in fact, a "focus" in the sixteenth century "for those who passionately believed in man, with or without the benefit of the clergy" (Krailsheimer, 1978, 25; see also Marcel, 1951). There was abundant reason for the choice of such a hero, as we quickly discern from the radically humanistic characteristics of Socratic thinking that Laszlo Versenyi (1963) has highlighted so well. Versenyi sees Socrates as intimately linked with the Sophists' rhetorical and educational project, transcending it in method and orientation, but like the Sophists deeply desiring "to improve and educate man, to cultivate human excellence, to promote the art of living" (73).

> [Humanism is] the type of thought that is centered upon man himself, that raises questions concerning his ultimate nature, and that tries to answer them without transcending the limits of what is human. In this sense humanistic thinking is the cultivation of man, his self-cultivation and self-unfolding into full humanity. Socratic philosophy is the highest embodiment of this type of thought in the history of man…it still challenges us and shows us the way to authentic human existence. (1)

historical Socrates, like Nietzsche, was never tempted away from
fe-world and the significant ethical issues that inform so
ly life. No wonder, then, that Nietzsche, himself also

sophistic in so many ways, should find this constantly engaging humanist figure a momentous and inspiring event.

Burckhardt. To test our conclusions, it will serve us to consider a few individuals who might conceivably be proposed as counter-examples to this argument, starting with Nietzsche's long-time acquaintance Jacob Burckhardt—a Renaissance-scholar, art historian, Hellenist, and premiere academic humanist at the University of Basel. In the Nazi madness of the 1930's, a conscientious scholar undertook to contrast these two figures, finding the elder Burckhardt too "Alexandrian," refined, traditional, historically informed, and intellectually nuanced to be classified as part of the same world as the radical, wide-ranging, "anti-humanist" Nietzsche (von Martin, 1947). Without denying the basic truth of many of von Martin's assessments within his own framework, I would suggest that his own picture is not really nuanced enough, particularly because of his avowed method of placing the stress on the "final" rather than on what he sees as merely "preliminary, intermediate, and peripheral" (8). In this way he justifies using the extreme currents especially of the later Nietzsche as a basis for a whole reading. Such an approach parallels the common tendency to overemphasize late elements in Nietzsche, and frustrates the intention of a really balanced and comprehensive understanding. I simply call attention here to the profound affinity Nietzsche feels with the professor and even with his essential project. Nietzsche's letter of September 22, 1886 is remarkable:

> Please read this book [*Beyond Good and Evil*] (even though it says the same things as my *Zarathustra*—only in a way that is different—very different). I know nobody who shares with me as many prepossessions as you yourself; it seems to me that you have had the same problems in view—that you are working on the same problems in a similar way, perhaps even more forcefully and deeply than I, because you are less loquacious. But then I am younger.... The mysterious conditions of any growth in culture, that extremely dubious relation between what is called the "improvement" of man (or even "humanization") and the enlargement of the human type, above all, the contradiction between every moral concept and every scientific concept of *life*—enough, enough—here is a problem which we fortunately share with not very many persons, living or dead. To express it is perhaps the most dangerous venture of all, not for the person who ventures it but for those to whom he speaks of it. My comfort is that, for the time, there are no ears for my new discoveries—excepting yours, dear and deeply respected man; and for you again the discoveries will be nothing new (1969c, 255).

Thus, even in his late period, Nietzsche clearly saw an extraordinary and exceedingly intimate parallel between his work and that of the humanist Basel professor. These words give us a valuable insight into Nietzsche's own understanding of what his own task was—not simplistically humanistic in the sense of promoting an optimistic progressivism, but nevertheless concerned with the "enlargement of the human type." Such an orientation can not be dissociated from the humanist tradition.

In fact this "enlargement" (*Vergrösserung*) amounts to what I will identify as Nietzsche's *Grundthema*, human greatness, the very subject upon which the young Nietzsche heard Burckhardt lecture in the fall of 1870. It was clearly a significant moment early in Nietzsche's professional career, so much so that he wrote about his experience to his friend Carl von Gersdorff, claiming that this was the first lecture he ever enjoyed, that he was probably the only one in the hall who fully understood the lecturer, and that it was a lecture of the type that he could give if he were older (1975-1984, II.1, 155). Von Martin would have us draw a heavy line between these two thinkers' concepts of greatness, with Burckhardt retaining a stronger link with civilization and the "humane," and with Nietzsche radiating a fierce, destructive, skeptical spirit (von Martin, 1947, 118-21). We shall see that these differences of accent are to some extent justifiable. Nietzsche did indeed make ever more forceful, more radical pronouncements. He stressed, more than Burckhardt ever apparently did, the destructive power of real greatness, especially in *Twilight of the Idols.* However Nietzsche believed that Burckhardt was not misleading, though he was largely quiet, about the most problematical issues; he may have considered Burckhardt's hesitancy something of a mask, even as his own "savage" persona no doubt was. For we must admit that Nietzsche, however feral he may on occasion appear, has many more moments of—indeed makes an art of—subtlety, restraint, indirectness, elegance, and pregnant silence. The humanistic lines of affiliation between these two men are terribly obscured if we do not contextualize Nietzsche's occasional fierceness and place it within his larger concerns and within his entire opus. Nietzsche's heroes remained predominantly *cultural* figures like Goethe, Emerson, and Burckhardt himself. And, whatever the rhetorical strategies used for the sake of insight and communicative effect, Zarathustra is far from being a wild and raving beast—if anything he suffers a danger from too much sensitivity and pity. We also will remain muddled about the relationship between Nietzsche and Burckhardt if we do not actually turn to some of Burckhardt's words and judge their relevance for ourselves.

When we examine the lecture on greatness that was later published as part of Burckhardt's *Weltgeschichte Betrachtungen* (1979), we find an unmistakeably "Nietzschean" array of themes. Burckhardt's Great Individual is "not set up as an example but as an exception" (296), a "strange exception from the moral code" (307-08). His life is more forceful, so therefore he is not condemned for yielding to his stronger passions (308-309). His crimes can also be justified as a way of ending or blocking the crimes of others (309-10). Yet there is an important relationship with the larger community. The Great Individual embodies it in a way, being the coincidence of the particular and the general (307; 292). We might think of Nietzsche's unique combination of personal and universal in his *Zarathustra*, a mixture which justifies calling it either a tragedy or a parody, a "Book for All and None" as the subtitle has it. Nietzsche (the "Good European," in his words) operates from the basis of an identification with modern civilization as surely as he stands defiantly several leaps beyond it. Burckhardt mentions the Anti-Christ in his lecture as an example of an image of greatness (291); Columbus as the only truly great explorer (275-76); Montaigne and La Bruyère as figures who provide the link between the philosophers and the poets (278); Euripides as the "most important evidence for a turning point in Athenian thought," towards the "ephemeral" and away from the "eternal" of Aeschylus and Sophocles (284-85). He comments on the Great Individual's plenitude (281), single-mindedness and intelligence (282); authority (292, 298); the consoling power of tragedy (279); the optimistic nature of visual art (286); music as situated at "the extreme frontier of art" and possessing superior revelatory qualities (288, 289). And even as to the destructive power of true greatness, Burckhardt is not at all completely silent:

> The great man's faculties unfold naturally and completely, keeping pace with the growth of his self-confidence and the tasks before him. It is not only that he appears complete in every situation, but every situation at once seems to cramp him. He does not merely fill it. He may shatter it.
>
> It is doubtful how long he will be able to keep himself in hand and be pardoned for the greatness of his nature. (296)

There is even a "Nietzschean" sense of the suffering of the Great Individual, with attention to cultural illusions:

> When the man of culture sits down to the banquet of the art and poetry of past times, he will not be able, or wish to resist the lovely illu-

> sion that these men were *happy* when they created their great works. Yet all they did was to rescue the ideals of their time at the cost of great sacrifice, and wage in their daily life the battle we all fight. It is only to us that their creations look like youth rescued and perpetuated. (289-90)

But the most important line of affiliation is the main theme, which never left Nietzsche's mind, heart, or soul. Even in his last year, Nietzsche was planning to use as a title or subtitle for *The Songs of Zarathustra* the phrase "The Way to Greatness" (1967a, 20). Perhaps, the "deconstruction" of all truth notwithstanding, Nietzsche shared at least this "absolute" with Burckhardt:

> [F]or the thinking man, reviewing the whole course of history hitherto, one of the few certain premises of a higher spiritual happiness is an open mind for all greatness. (Burckhardt, 1979, 315)

Admittedly, Burckhardt did not sense the affinity with Nietzsche that the latter felt with him, beyond their common reverence for Schopenhauer. But then again, Nietzsche was the better psychologist, and, more significantly, he knew Burckhardt better than Burckhardt knew him. Nietzsche was the one who attended the other's courses. It was Burckhardt who constantly claimed not to be able to understand the thinking in the books that his junior colleague faithfully sent him. We are fully justified, then, in taking Nietzsche's word for his profound sense of affinity with the most outstanding and famous humanist that he knew personally. Though critical of so many, he respected him unfailingly. Once he wrote to von Gersdorff that this singular individual spoke "completely from of our way of thinking and feeling" ("*zwar völlig aus unserm Denk- und Gefühlskreise heraus,*" Nietzsche, 1975-1984, 155).

Spinoza. I do not claim that Nietzsche cannot be placed beside the grand systematic thinkers, or that he does not consciously implicate himself in the line of thinkers that the discipline of philosophy has canonized. Very interesting and valuable work has dealt with Nietzsche's relationship to figures like Kant, Hegel, and Marx (Ansell-Pearson, 1987; Houlgate, 1986; Love, 1986). In fact, such figures are already implicated in the humanist tradition, without necessarily meriting the designation *humanist* as a primary hermeneutic key to their authorial personae. But Nietzsche himself never mentions Marx and tends to be quite negative about Hegel and Kant, demoting the latter from philosopher to critic at one point. He treats such figures from an existential, ethical, and cultural standpoint: What was their net effect on the ideals of Europe? Did they finally support or transform the prevailing ethos? What kind of cultural events were they, and how should they be assessed? What kinds of examples do their personalities hold out for us? Nietzsche's standpoint is that of "life." This type of treatment is not so much philosophical in the disciplinary sense as it is humanistic. Philosophy may engage "ultimate questions," but humanism, which in a quite relevant way stands back from the technical analyses of disciplinary philosophy, also evaluates, from the perspective of human life, philosophy's treatment of such questions. Its own stance is determined by common-sense, ultimately pragmatic, though still spiritually sensitive, educational and cultural concerns. Nietzsche expresses a strong antipathy to professional philosophy most emphatically in *Twilight of the Idols* (1954, 479-86). He rejects not the employment of, but any naive biases towards system, argument, concept, "reason," or determinate conclusions. This stance puts him closer to the humanistic figures that we have surveyed. And on this very point alone, it becomes clear that to understand him mostly in terms of his own arguments and reasons—his "position" on morality, for instance—will inevitably give us an understanding that would be at odds with his own.

The ultra-systematic Spinoza, however, presents an interesting counter-example to the figures assembled in this argument, for we do have an ecstatic postcard that Nietzsche wrote to Franz Overbeck on July 30, 1881, claiming him as a precursor and a close companion in his solitude (1969c, 177). Nietzsche is delighted to have discovered a similar general tendency "to make knowledge the most powerful passion" and to have found five major doctrinal similarities with his own thinking: the denial of "free will, purposes, the moral world order, the non-egoistical, evil." There is no doubt that Nietzsche's thought was in fact influenced by Spinoza in some of his key formulations, especially *amor fati* and the Will to Power (Wurzer, 1975). His enthusiasm is surprising and shocking, precisely because Spinoza's hyper-rationalistic "geometrical" thinking seems so utterly different from Nietzsche's.

Yet one could appeal to this very postcard to point out that Nietzsche was aware of the tremendous cultural, historical, *and disciplinary* differences between the two: "of course, the differences are enormous, but they are differences more of period, culture, field of knowledge (*Wissenschaft*)." Nietzsche later scorned the defensiveness and weakness he suspected behind "that hocus-pocus of mathematical form" in Spinoza (Nietzsche, 1966, 13). According to William Wurzer, who made an extensive study of the relationship between Nietzsche and Spinoza (1975), it seems that the former absorbed the latter's work indirectly, especially through a secondary account by Kuno Fischer (68-71; 141-48). The later Nietzsche was especially influenced by Spinoza, but he evidently never really attained a sufficient knowledge of Spinoza's psychology, cognitional theory, or metaphysics (146). Hence, Nietzsche could not fully critique the thought of a person that he had not yet really discovered. Wurzer claims that in a way, he might even be said to have refused to engage "categorical Western thinking" adequately enough for a true liberation from traditional metaphysics (148).

Nevertheless, it is possible to give the grounds of a *humanistic affinity* as the basis for an explanation of Nietzsche's curious enthusiasm, for Spinoza's philosophy was anticipated by an Aristotelian current of naturalistic humanism in the Renaissance, represented by Pomponazzi and Zabarella (see Cassirer et al., 1948). In Moses Hadas's view, Spinoza marks a signal return to an ancient humanistic vision: he "resumes the main lines of what is peculiar to the Greek outlook just where Philo had diverted it" (Hadas, 1972, 131).

Schopenhauer. The major philosopher that Nietzsche read deeply and enthusiastically at an early age was Schopenhauer, who has tended to be neglected by the profession from his own day until recently. But even here, we find Nietzsche attracted above all to the man's personality and alienated by the Romantic and metaphysical elements of the fourth book of *World as Will and Idea* (Heller, 1976, 112, citing Nietzsche, 1967a, 381f.). Peter Heller refers us to two notes of 1878 in which we find the following sentiments:

> The living Schopenhauer has nothing to do with metaphysics. He is Voltairean in essence; Book 4 is alien to him. (Nietzsche, 1967a, 353)

> My suspicion against the system from the very start. The *person* stands out, he [being] typical as a philosopher and promoter of culture. (Nietzsche, 1967a, 382)

These sentiments give us a direct insight into Nietzsche's humanistic approach. Perhaps, in fact, Nietzsche was especially attracted to Schopenhauer through the latter's books of aphorisms, in which humanistic concerns often appear. For example, listen to how he praises Petrarch for his music *and his thought*:

> For me my beloved Petrarch comes before all the other Italian poets. In depth and intensity of feeling and in the direct expression thereof, which goes straight to the heart, no poet on earth has ever surpassed him.... That our super-excellent '*Jetztzeit*' ventures to speak disparagingly of him merely confirms me in my opinion. As a superfluous proof of this, we may also compare Dante and Petrarch in domestic attire, so to speak, that is to say in their prose, by placing Petrarch's beautiful books, *De vita solitaria, De contemtu mundi, Consolatio utriusque fortunae*, and so on, so rich in ideas and truth, and also his letters next to Dante's barren and tedious scholasticism. (Schopenhauer, 1974, 443-44)

Thus I side with Charles Andler, whose lengthy study of Nietzsche (1958) devoted fourteen chapters to "Nietzsche's precursors," naming therein very few individuals who have been understood as philosophers: Goethe, Schiller, Hölderlin, Kleist, Fichte, Schopenhauer, Montaigne, Pascal, La Rochefoucauld, Fontenelle, Chamfort, Stendahl, Burckhardt, and Emerson. Nietzsche's closest, life-long "mates" can likely be found among figures such as those that we have discussed above and in the others that Andler names. Perhaps he himself would see many of the ones that we have named not only as peers, but as ancestors, members of his own *spiritual genealogy*. In that sense, our first argument about Nietzsche's origins is carried forward by this one. By attending to Nietzsche's relationship to the ensemble of his cultural champions, we will get a better understanding not only of his own character, but necessarily of his "philosophy" as well. As Nietzsche points out, ultimately a philosophy can not be separated from its thinker—nor can thinkers from their models.

4
A Single Web of Meaning

Nietzsche's positions on knowing, on truth, on being, on ethics, on ultimate reality, and so forth, possess a kind of logical priority that makes them hermeneutically significant, but attending to them apart from the whole web of Nietzsche's concerns leaves us with something like a portrait made from a rear view. Fundamental, yes—and ever-relevant too—but not enough. And if Nietzsche's often aphoristic, essayistic style, if his polytropic spirit and fancy pen-work trick us into believing that he is a "nomad thinker" having no particular haunts and no real destination, we would again miss too much. The experience would be like watching a movie with a selection of its scenes presented in random order. Readers of Nietzsche at some point have to raise these simple questions: *With what kinds of things does the author continually tend to concern himself? To what does he draw our attention? How are these things related to one another? How do they look all together? Do they change over the course of his career? Can he be said to have one particular focus?* When we can attend to his entire thematic range as a wellspring for his thought, we can then discover some of the coherence that he himself felt in it. When we can affirm that his range of themes has a certain unity and in fact comprises a landscape with many features quite similar to those that we find in the Western humanist tradition, then we will have valuable clues to his identity and mission.

Within this thematic argument there is also a "proportional" one. It is valid, it is helpful, but it is certainly insufficient to say "Whatever else he was or was not, he certainly was a philosopher" insofar as he "thought systematically and deeply about each of the closed set of questions which define what philosophy is" (Danto, 1980, 9). Leaving aside for now the question of what philosophy is, we must still go on from such a statement, if we really want a full reading and understanding of Nietzsche, to ask *how much* of his writing is accounted for by this approach. Proportionately how much *time* does Nietzsche spend on, how much *space* does he give to, how much *weight* does he place upon thinking about that "closed set of questions" as opposed to the wider complex of humanistic themes? If we do not raise these questions, we expose ourselves to the charge of not having learned to read Nietzsche well. The relative dimensions of the various facets of this versatile thinker should be of no little interest to would-be interpreters. As Nietzsche has taught us well, reasonings occur in a context highly relevant for understanding and evaluating them. The stronger version of my basic thesis, namely that the humanist identification is the best hermeneutical key by which to interpret Nietzsche, will be justified to the extent to which we come to see how we get so much "more" of Nietzsche with this approach.

The evidence for the coherent complex of themes is easily available to reader who attends to the contents of Nietzsche's works in their relative proportions. Of course, I can not perform such a "total reading" for the reader. I do however offer a beginning. Some of what I present here will amount to an inventory of certain works, gathering concrete particularities, as the last chapter did in its own way with regard to humanist analogues. I do this not because I think that a scan from a great height is sufficient for interpretation—though the best ideas can be born of the meagerest of data, and compact expression is often the key to insight—but because without such a survey both our general and particular readings of Nietzsche would suffer. The scan is orientational. It is the beginning of a patient process of attaining a better feel for Nietzsche's spiritual-intellectual cosmos. By getting to know the general dimensions of that cosmos and how Nietzsche moves about in it, we will grasp something basic about his literary habits, his quality of mind, and his intellectual style. We will get some sense of what he habitually connects with what. And we may even come to realize why he does so.

Nietzsche's themes are notoriously hard to summarize, especially for his aphoristic works. At first glance, it seems that practically anything and everything could be included somewhere in the labyrinthine wanderings of his expansive meditations. But there is one especially instructive way of finding Nietzsche's own approach to classifying his main subject areas. We can compare the headings that he writes for two works bridging his middle and late phases, *Human, All Too Human: A Book for Free Spirits*, of 1878, and *Beyond Good and Evil: Prelude to a Philosophy of the Future*, of 1886.

Human, All Too Human (Vol. I)	*Beyond Good and Evil*
Preface	
1. Of First and Last Things	1.On the Prejudices of Philosophers
2. On the History of Moral Sensations	2. The Free Spirit
3. The Religious Life	3. What is Religious
4. From the Souls of Artists and Writers	4. Epigrams and Interludes
5. Tokens of Higher and Lower Culture	5. Natural History of Morals
6. Man in Society	6. We Scholars
7. Woman and Child	7. Our Virtues
8. A Glance at the State	8. Peoples and Fatherlands
9. Man Alone With Himself	9. What is Noble
Among Friends: An Epilogue [poem]	From High Mountains: Aftersong [poem]
(1986, 3)	(1966, vii)

There are interesting similarities here. Both books have nine chapters with a closing poem. They each begin with a chapter about philosophy or philosophers (the ones who deal with first causes and ultimate ends). Both have a chapter on the history of morality, which is a key theme that becomes the focus of *On the Genealogy of Morals.* The third chapters focus on aspects of religious life. Chapters Two and Five seem to have subject matters that structurally "reverse themselves" as we move from the earlier to the later work: The central chapter of *Human All Too Human*, "Tokens of Higher and Lower Culture" can be correlated with "The Free Spirit" of *Beyond Good and Evil*, if we know something of the contents. The second and penultimate sections of the former chapter explicitly mention the "free spirit" in their titles. Culture and morality are in fact intimately related for Nietzsche, especially since he sees current morality as a roadblock to true freedom of the spirit, which is "higher culture." Even apart from Nietzsche's association of the two, *Sittlichkeit* (customary morality) is generally conceived of as something essential to culture, for without common, inherited patterns of action and valuation (Greek *nomoi*, Latin *mores*), cultural coherence is nil. The eighth sections of both books have to do with the state and politics, and the ninth with the typical Nietzschean move to a transpolitical individual sphere as something that was more elevated in his eyes—the "noble" ethos of the particular great personality. Other parallels may suggest themselves, but Nietzsche's themes are so interwoven that attempting to define all their interconnections precisely would be relatively useless. The titles suggest that special areas of concern for him are metaphysics, philosophers, and philosophy; morality and its history, and virtue; culture, cultivated existence, and cultures and national character; states of life, especially in the literary, artistic, religious, scholarly, and philosophical modes; social and political arrangements; family life; solitude and friendship; human interrelationships.

Jacob Burckhardt revealed how he understood the book when he wrote to Nietzsche on September 26, 1886, to commend his "astonishing survey of the whole area of current cultural movements" as well as his "power and art" in his "subtle delineation of details" (cited in Hayman, 1982, 300). But we are not completely without direction in this vast overview. Even the bare structures and variegated contents of these tables point to what the author considers particularly important. Especially with as musical a writer as Nietzsche, we expect a certain care in composition. Since climactic moments classically occur at the middle and the end of a work, it is interesting that here these sections treat of culture / morality (central sections) and individuality / nobility (concluding ones). First sections are also usually important and they often link with the last. Here the concluding visions of the solitary noble individual return us to the theme of philosophy, albeit in a new mode, for a topos of the tradition is that the *sapiens* is truly self-sufficient and nobly independent. More extensive reading bears out that these themes are in fact focal points for Nietzsche's entire effort. A brief exercise such as this can suggest the general dimensions of Nietzsche's thought-world better than many focused analyses. It also tells us something about the perdurance of certain themes over at least a considerable part of his literarily productive life.

We will find a similar coherence of themes if we expand the limits of our comparison and make a closer analysis of the textual contents for two works, one from the start and one from the conclusion of his writing career. Given the importance of beginnings, let us first turn to Nietzsche's seminal *The Birth of Tragedy Out of the Spirit of Music* (written in 1871 though dated 1872), asking the thematic question: What is it really about? It deals seriously with art and its place in culture; the origin and real nature of Greek tragedy and its chorus; Greek culture in its entire historical development and in its "authentic" character; lyric poetry; the metaphysical meaning of music; the underlying aesthetic principles of all culture and consciousness; the phenomenon of decadence in Western culture through Socratic rationalism and "Alexandrian" scholarship (*Wissenschaft*); "operatic culture"; tragedy in general and its possible revival in Germany through the art of Wagner; contemporary cultural renewal; pessimism and the ultimate meaninglessness of human existence over against tragic affirmation of reality; the aesthetic justification of human existence. Later Nietzsche claimed that it was also about morality as inimical to life, although this theme is not clearly stated in the work itself (1967b, 24). An early letter to his mentor Ritschl (January 30, 1872) indicates that the essay was an attempt to revive and to transfigure *classical philology* (Silk and Stern, 1981, 91-92, cited from Nietzsche 1975-1984, 281-82). He also later interpreted *The Birth of Tragedy* in a strongly autobiographical way, making it a self-presentation, a "parable and parallel in history for my own inmost experience" (1967b, 271). What we have is certainly a complex intentionality and an equally complex interweaving of themes that the author understood as organically related.

We can discover the coherence of the work if we can elucidate the essential principles on which it is based. Nietzsche seems to be looking for certain "keys" to the fundamental mysteries of life. His passionate reflection ultimately rests on certain long-held convictions, recent discoveries, in-breaking inspirations, and blossoming hopes. In shortest compass, these might be presented as follows:

> Greek culture is the key to understanding all culture. Greek tragedy is the key to understanding Greek culture. The Dionysian-Apollonian duality is the key to understanding art, and especially to understanding Greek tragedy, which is the greatest art. Schopenhauer's understanding of the relationship of music to the other arts parallels the Greek insight into the relationship of Dionysus and Apollo and illuminates the essential dynamics of reality (Will and Appearances). Art illuminates or is the means to authentic life. The Greeks cast a "philosophical" light on the ultimate dynamics of reality through their tragic drama. We moderns can today reach such a peak of authentic personal and cultural vitality by attaining a similar level of artistic tragic achievement. Wagner is at work on this project. Philosophical philology provides access to the core meanings of the most characteristic art of the normative culture and hence to the understanding of and appreciation for the most important cultural phenomenon needed for vital cultural life and authentic human existence today. And Nietzsche is on the scene performing this service.

Though Nietzsche called this work a "centaur," it is certainly a *tour de force* of integration of his leading interests as a young scholar. Its echoes continued through his career to the very end, and in a way they only grew stronger, as we see when we turn to what I will propose here as the late (1888) counterpart to *The Birth of Tragedy*: Nietzsche's *Twilight of the Idols or How One Philosophizes with a Hammer* (1954). For the author, this book represents his "philosophy *in nuce*." (Brandes, n.d., 92) First, after a brief and feisty preface, we find a section of forty-four maxims on a familiar range of topics: psychology; morality and virtue (e.g., truth, courage, honesty); philosophy and philosophers; human nature; the idea of God; the need for meaning; artists; the desire for disciples; women; the German spirit; historians; music; knowing and thinking; and Nietzsche himself. Moral issues again stand out as paramount. There is a significant autobiographical turn at the end of the series, even though in the thirty-fifth maxim he claims that "we psychologists," like horses afraid of their own shadows, need to turn our attention away from ourselves to see anything at all (35).

Over the span of his authorial life, we easily notice how Nietzsche's textual self-presence gradually intensified in his writings as he moved toward the grand climax of *Ecce Homo* and *Nietzsche Contra Wagner*. Here, in *Twilight of the Idols*, this theme of Nietzsche's self is presented in connection with his favorite motifs. Even the first maxim is self-referential, though it might not seem so because it sounds like such a detached sapiential pronouncement followed by a moralistic musing: "Idleness is the beginning of all psychology. What? Should psychology be a vice?" But because the original title for the work was *A Psychologist's Idleness*, we can surmise that Nietzsche himself is in some way at issue. Secondly, he evokes his favorite theme of morality: in the mention of vice. The number of maxims, forty-four, may carry a reference to Nietzsche, who is just about to turn forty-four years old at the time of the writing. The last maxims give us four important questions of conscience and an intriguing suggestion about Nietzsche's lifelong obsession with morality. The thirty-sixth one reads: "Whether we immoralists are *harming* virtue? Just as little as anarachists harm princes. Only since the latter are shot at do they again sit securely on their thrones. Moral: *morality must be shot at.*" (471-72) The book as a whole makes an autobiographical turn, the last two prose chapters being entitled "Skirmishes of an Untimely Man," a reference to his early *Untimely Meditations* of 1873-1876, and the plainly autobiographical "What I Owe to the Ancients."

This beginning and this ending might not lead us to expect that Nietzsche would survey the entire history of philosophy in the early chapters and go on to attempt to present the essential character of the human condition. Nietzsche begins with one of his old themes, a highlight of *The Birth of Tragedy*, the problem of Socrates as a decadent who casts a shadow over Western cultural history. He proceeds to other favorite targets, the problems of idealism and the notion of reason in philosophy. But for Nietzsche, philosophy is indeed an integral part of life—in *personal, moral, cultural, and religious modes*—and it is to be evaluated as such. This belief imparts a profound unity to the book and to all of Nietzsche's writings. Hence, in the middle of the work he attacks moral ideals as anti-nature and explicates how erroneous thinking about causality lies at the core of "the whole realm of morality and religion" (498). Nietzsche climactically declares his own doctrine in no uncertain terms: no God, no general human *telos*, no human ideal to measure up to, no responsibility, no unity of all things, only the whole and one's immersion in it. Accepting this doctrine is the only freedom and salvation (500-01). From this standpoint, one "*beyond* good and evil" (501) what is interesting to Nietzsche is the phenomenon of morality and the "psychology of the 'improvers' of mankind," whose undertakings Nietzsche ironically declares to be immoral (501-505). He turns now (unexpectedly only for those who do not know him) to a chapter on German culture ("What the Germans Lack") just as in *The Birth of Tragedy* he had leapt from Greece to Germany in the last third of that work. He speaks of the nation's lack of culture, the danger of its coming to (military) power as the end of its philosophy: "Power *makes stupid*" (506). With this idea we can parallel the opening of his very first *Untimely Meditation* (1873) on David Strauss, where there is a very similar point: Germany's military victory over France has nothing to do with the former's cultural superiority and may lead to the loss of German spirit altogether! Strauss is in fact soon directly mentioned in *Twilight of the Idols* as a praiser of beer, which Nietzsche sees as a dimension of degeneracy among the younger scholars (507). Nietzsche is still concerned with scholars. Here he polemicizes about Germany's spirit and lack thereof; its university institutions, *Bildung*, the requirements of good education, politics, cultural decline, and the loss of German philosophy. These topics cover ground that he had traversed in his 1872 lecture-series, "On the Future of Our Educational Institutions" (1964b) and in other writings of that time (see 1967d, Volumes 1 and 7).

So intensely personal is Nietzsche's passion about German culture, that it seems a natural transition to the more directly autobiographical chapters already mentioned. In the first section, which is long enough to make up about half of the entire work ("Skirmishes of an Untimely Man," 513-56), Nietzsche gives us a series of observations about a whole, again interrelated, range of topics. He makes brief evaluations of many different cultural figures from literature, music, philosophy, theology and spirituality, science (Darwin), and art. He now and then returns to aesthetical questions, to the Apollonian and Dionysian categories (we are back with *The Birth of Tragedy* again), and to the "psychology of the artist" (518). Raised in the early section on Socrates (whose ugly "criminal" physiognomy as the representation of moral degeneration already links aesthetics, philosophy and morality), the questions of beauty and ugliness return: hatred for the ugly is declared to be hatred for the "decline of [the human] type" (527). Schopenhauer is then discussed and worked into the discussion of the beautiful: unlike Plato, he found it a way to escape the demands of the will. Nietzsche sides with the Greek: art is, in fact, "the great stimulus to life" (529). In effect, Nietzsche had already in *The Birth of Tragedy* opposed Schopenhauer by praising the life-affirmation of the tragic Greeks. Here, Nietzsche continues with a series of variegated aphorisms, all relating to the key themes already pointed out, especially to those of morality, freedom, politics, religion, and health (an important motif of the preface and in the discussions of the Dionysian).

The last theme seems to bridge personal, physical, social, political, cultural, philosophical, and artistic spheres. Nietzsche is ever alert to issues of health and decadence at many levels. He once wrote to Malwida von Meysenbug, "I am, in questions of *décadence*, the supreme court of appeal on earth..." (1969, 314, letter of October 18, 1888). In a section entitled "Critique of Modernity," he refers to the first part of *Human, All Too Human*, commenting that there he had "already characterized modern democracy, together with its hybrids, such as the German Reich," as the form of decline of the state" (1954, 543). That same section ends with a paragraph on the loss of the rationality of the social institution of marriage as something connected with the modern loss of self-affirmation of the society as a whole. The health of individual, social, and political value-instincts are evidently interrelated:

> The whole of the West no longer possesses the instincts out of which institutions grow, out of which a future grows: perhaps nothing antagonizes its "modern spirit" so much. One lives for the day, one lives very fast, one lives very irresponsibly: precisely this is called "freedom." (543)

In Section 44 (with ironic self-reference again, perhaps?), Nietzsche speaks of his "conception of genius" (547). From there, he goes back to the idea of the criminal (again an issue in the portrait of Socrates), but this time as a *positive* feature: the criminal is really the strong human being made sick (549). Catiline is "the form of pre-existence of every Caesar" (551). Then we are back to beauty as something that must be worked for patiently in the health of the body. Here the Greeks are honored as "the first cultural event in history" (552). Nietzsche is still the Hellenist, despite any developments occurring since *The Birth of Tragedy*. He finishes off this penultimate prose chapter with an important laudatory section on Goethe, a figure who indeed combines many Nietzschean themes and ideals, some explicitly mentioned here, others not: German culture and transnational cultivation; health and naturalness; Hellenism; political activity and public engagement; self-creation; anti-Kantianism; freedom; affirmation beyond all negation; self-acceptance; the desire for totality; wholeness as the integration of reason, senses, feeling, and will; realism; the culmination of education; science; and—note especially—a *transmoral existence* for which "there is no longer anything that is forbidden" (554). This meditation on the last German he reveres (555), leads him to reflect on himself—how he is the first German master of the aphorism and how he has "given mankind the most profound book it possesses," *Zarathustra*, which is soon to be followed by "the most independent one" (555-56).

The concluding prose chapter in *Twilight of the Idols* reviews Nietzsche's debts and relationship to the ancients. Here we are definitely back at the home-port, in that world of classical philology from which Nietzsche set out as an aspiring youth. He even recalls his gymnasium days and the awakening of his sense of style there (556). He seems proud of the fact that he sought approaches to that ancient world and that he "perhaps found a new approach" (556). The discussion turns finally to the constant of his life and work, the Dionysian, which is, after all, present whenever he speaks of or is concerned with health, fullness, abundance, excess, vitality, life, wholeness, exuberance, joy, frenzy, dancing, affirmation, quickness, playfulness, prankishness, strength, creativity, realism, courage, art, tragedy, "strong" pessimism," and tragic heroism—that is, almost always. The last paragraph is full of the sense of return, with an explicit reference to *The Birth of Tragedy* and to its foundational status in his career:

> And herewith I again touch that point from which I once went forth: *The Birth of Tragedy* was my first revaluation of all values. Herewith I again stand on the soil out of which my intention, my *ability* grows—I the last disciple of the philosopher Dionysus—I, the teacher of the eternal recurrence. (563)

The Odyssean wanderer has come home, but in a way he never left this "soil" out of which his life-work sprang. Following this significant confession, Nietzsche appends a concluding quotation from *Zarathustra*: the address of "the Hammer," as diamond, to his brothers, as coal, exhorting them to hardness for the sake of the nobility and exhilaration of triumphant, creative, eternal, world-historical greatness. In one way this dream of greatness is the ultimate issue in Nietzsche and it pulses through all his psychology—in both his thinking and in his life. We will return to it later. For now, enough has been said to indicate the complex thematic range of *Twilight of the Idols* and its material connections with *The Birth of Tragedy* and other early compositions. The later work does show us an author far more self-conscious about his enterprise, an author who begins to thematize his very self in his writing. But the arena is the same.

The themes we have highlighted from these four works (*The Birth of Tragedy, Human, All Too Human-I, Beyond Good and Evil*, and *Twilight of the Idols*), which span Nietzsche's career from beginning to end, could easily be found in his other ones as well. It is clear that Nietzsche tends to keep in his mind and in his writing the following fields of meaning: culture and education; philosophy and philosophers; scholars and scholarship; history and historians; popular morality and ethical ideals; literature, poetry, art, music, opera, science, and religion; national and international culture, society, and politics; and psychology, interiority, and spirituality. Though he does not treat all themes in all works, he treats many in most—and certainly perceives the vital interconnection of all these spheres. A reader should expect any of these themes to appear at any time. Why, we might ask for example, is Wagner so important, the subject of two books of Nietzsche's final year of writing? The history of their relationship, of course, was a great personal motive. Nietzsche was still attempting to come to terms with his feelings about this early significant friendship gone bad. But Wagner (who had developed a distinctive and popular style and theory of art) was also a tremendous, increasingly exalted German cultural phenomenon that Nietzsche understood as significant for the issues of the health and sickness of modern society. Because Nietzsche considered art to be deeply intertwined with moral and religious realities, he abhorred Wagner's return to Christian themes and thus sensed Wagnerism to be an insidious cultural danger relevant to his great polemical project. *The Anti-Christ(ian)* was written in the same year as his final works on Wagner. Of course, by his own early promotion of the composer in works like *The Birth of Tragedy* and *Richard Wagner in Bayreuth*, Nietzsche himself was already a cultural event, and hence his autobiography was all the more relevant itself as a culturally relevant topic for publication at this time. So, we can surmise, Wagner is not the pure and simple issue here. An entire position on a tremendous range of elements—"Nietzsche" included—is involved. This attempt to deal with single items in light of the whole and vice-versa deserves to be considered a type of "systematic thinking": each issue is so closely connected with so many other ones that a single revision necessarily involves a shift in the others.

Because of the range of Nietzsche's major themes and because of his energetic, judicious involvement in all of them, he could rightly suggest that his intellectual vitality increased the farther he got from dull professional academic labor, "As *summa summarium* [over-all] I was healthy; as an angle, as a specialty, I was a decadent" (1969a, 224). His ability to take a general view, to look for the panorama, to deal with the "weightiest" matters lightly, to be swift and less than pedantically rigorous, even at the risk of being charged with superficiality—all this is an important part of what makes Nietzsche the scintillating intellectual personality that he is. Thus we can find Ida Overbeck's characterization an extremely apt one. After calling him "poet, musician, philosopher, pedagogue, philanthropist" she says: "Predominantly, Nietzsche was an eclectic of spirit and mind [*Eklektiker des Geistes*] with artistic powers of organization and verbal talent." (Gilman, 1987a, 107). But this must be supplemented by the comment that she makes a little later when she addresses the issue of Nietzsche's basic purpose:

> What was Nietzsche's cause? He wanted to conceive morality historically and to reform the philosophical conscience on the basis of the free individual who supplies the strength of the will with his capacities and passions. (109)

We are not entitled to call Nietzsche's "eclecticism" a species of dilettantism. His work was strongly united by a purpose, a great intention, a "mission." The forty-fourth maxim of *Twilight of the Idols* reads: "The formula of my happiness: a Yes, a No, a straight line, a *goal*" (1954, 473). The greatest Nietzschean testimony to his purpose and to the prolific but solid unity in his aspirations and works we discover in his preface to *On the Genealogy of Morals*. After claiming that his ideas on the origins of morality were first expressed in *Human, All Too Human* but were actually even older than that, he expresses delight that their continuance and their growing solidity and interrelationships might signify that they arose in him

> not as isolated, capricious, or sporadic things but from a common root, from a *fundamental will* of knowledge, pointing imperiously into the depths, speaking more and more precisely, demanding greater and greater precision. For this alone is fitting for a philosopher. We have no right to *isolated* acts of any kind: we may not make isolated errors or hit upon isolated truths. Rather do our ideas, our values, our yeas and nays, our ifs and buts, grow out of us with the necessity with which a tree bears fruit—related and each with an affinity to each, and evidence of *one* will, *one* health, *one* soil, *one* sun.—Whether *you* like them, these fruits of ours?—But what is that to the trees! What is that to *us*, to us philosophers! (1969b, 16)

At this point, one assumes that Nietzsche would cast a rather cold glance on interpreters who would like to fragment his works—or else that he would give them a bracing slap to bring them back to reality. One is easily reminded of another echo from *Ecce Homo*: "...I was many things and in many places in order to be able to become one thing—to be able to attain one thing" (1969a, 282).

His efforts were a grand unity, perhaps most especially because he was in fact ever rooted in his early humanistic period and was obviously never completely finished with his trinity, Schopenhauer, Wagner, and the Greeks, however many qualifications he added or reversals he experienced. It is interesting how even the philologist persona perdures in his writing, notably in the substantial philological exercises in *On the Genealogy of Morals*. He also lectures his readers on the necessity of "exegesis" in the preface to that work (1969b, 23) and he praises philology and "the great, the incomparable art of reading well" in *The Anti-Christ(ian)* (627 and 650). A couple of letters to Carl Fuchs in late 1888 show him giving extensive discussions of classical prosody (1969c, 308-310) and suggesting the application of classical rhetorical terms to musical articulation (1969c, 305-308). In *Ecce Homo* (1969a, 242-243), he claims that the last book he has read was one on Greek skepticism, a study "in which my *Laertiana* are also put to good use." This is indeed a noteworthy return, since his work on Diogenes Laertius are of the purest "philological" nature and take us back to 1868!

In his last years of writing Nietzsche was turning back to the early period with special fascination. In June of 1888, he claimed that the *Untimely Meditations* "deserve the closest attention for my development" (1969c, 299), and he took a profound delight in his discovery of the autobiographical natures of *Schopenhauer as Educator* and *Richard Wagner in Bayreuth* (1969a, 280-83). After reviewing all his books, he wrote to Gast on December 9, 1888, that "*Human, All Too Human* impressed me very strongly indeed; it has something of the tranquillity of a *Grand Seigneur*" (1969c, 333). Nietzsche's last "Untimely One" is significantly interwoven with *The Birth of Tragedy* of five years earlier as well as with his last year of writing, since it discusses the "modern Aeschylus," Richard Wagner and his dithyrambic art. The year 1888 found Nietzsche not only writing about Wagner again, but engaging in his own practice of that art in his *Dithyrambs of Dionysus. Ecce Homo* makes the point of the earlier connection well, since the discussion of *The Birth of Tragedy* in that work modulates so seamlessly into an enthusiastic reflection on *Richard Wagner in Bayreuth* that it can confuse even careful readers (see Kaufmann's note at Nietzsche, 1969a, 275). At this point in *Ecce Homo,* the profoundly (even mystically) self-revelatory quality of *Richard Wagner in Bayreuth* is made quite explicit and the work is very closely linked with what Nietzsche considers his masterpiece, *Thus Spake Zarathustra*:

> [In *Wagner in Bayreuth,*] in all psychologically decisive places I alone am discussed—and one need not hesitate to put down my name or the word "Zarathustra" where the text has the word "Wagner." The entire picture of the dithyrambic artist is a picture of the pre-existent poet of *Zarathustra*...the absolute certainty about what I am was projected on some accidental reality—the truth about me spoke from some gruesome depth. At the beginning of section 9 the *style* of *Zarathustra* is described with incisive certainty and anticipated; and no more magnificent expression could be found for the *event* of *Zarathustra,* the act of a tremendous purification and consecration of humanity, than was found in section 6. (1969a, 274-75)

Hence we have evidence that in Nietzsche's own understanding there exist very close connections between *Richard Wagner in Bayreuth, The Birth of Tragedy, Zarathustra,* and Nietzsche himself.

The Birth of Tragedy had a special significance for Nietzsche's late self-understanding. He had returned to it with a self-critical preface written for it in 1886, two years before his laudatory account of it in *Ecce Homo.* It indeed covered his core complex of themes, though morality and religion were to receive more explicit and focal consideration later. Most remarkable testimony to the essentiality of *The Birth of Tragedy* for Nietzsche comes from a letter to his friend Overbeck on July 13, 1885:

> Thinking out the principal problems...always brings me back...to the same conclusions: they are already there, as veiled and obscure as possible in *Geburt der Tragödie*, and everything I have since learned has become an ingrown part of them. (Cited in Hayman, 1982, 286)

This early work is, then, indeed the "soil" out of which his intention and ability grew (1954, 563). Here the genealogist says something of great genealogical importance about his thought.

The lines I have drawn to and from *The Birth of Tragedy* suggest its vital importance and that of Nietzsche's whole early period. Of course one could go on to point out many other connections between various writings, but here it will be especially helpful to indicate that the entire series of Nietzsche's works were indeed *in his own view significantly interconnected* (no matter where we might want to consider placing the emphasis, early or late). The case can be made concisely enough by reference to the author's own comments and clues. One of the most important for the entire early period is a rarely-noticed passage that appeared on the back of the original edition of *The Gay Science* (1882). There Nietzsche lets his readers know that he thinks of the book as the culmination of the several immediately preceding works. *Human, All Too Human (I and II), The Dawn, The Gay Science* were called a "series" having a "common goal" (1974, 28, 30). But this early period is then directly hinged to the middle one, since the fourth book of *The Gay Science* introduced Zarathustra in such a way that the two works actually share important textual material. It bonds the climax of one work and the beginning of the next, Section 342 of *The Gay Science* being "almost identical" with the first section of "Zarathustra's Prologue" (1974, 274, note 72). Nietzsche himself says that the penultimate section of *The Gay Science* gives the "basic idea of *Zarathustra*" (1969a, 296). It is hardly a leap at all from here to the late works, because Nietzsche himself indicates to Burckhardt that *Beyond Good and Evil* "says the same things as my *Zarathustra*," only differently (Nietzsche, 1969c, 255). Such a statement does not indicate that the relationship between the works is merely superficial; it points entirely to a substantial coherence. So does what we find regarding the relationship between *Zarathustra* and *On the Genealogy of Morals*, since the latter is "intended as a supplement and clarification of *Beyond Good and Evil*" (Nietzsche, 1969b, 11; cf. 17, 54-55). The *Genealogy*'s preface and body also explicitly refer many times to specifically designated sections of earlier works, pointedly unifying the various formulations of the author's lines of thought in a "historical" way (e.g., 1969b, 18, 66).

Important links between *Untimely Meditations, The Birth of Tragedy, Zarathustra, Twilight of the Idols*, and the late works on Wagner, *The Case of Wagner* and *Nietzsche Contra Wagner*, have already been suggested and they could easily be spun out at great length. One has only to think of the themes of Schopenhauer, Wagner, tragedy, music, and *Twilight of the Idols*'s reminiscences of *The Birth of Tragedy.* When we turn to the latest works, we find again that they are also entwined with each other as well as with the earlier ones. The fact that Nietzsche conceives of *Twilight of the Idols* as his whole philosophy in essence (see Nietzsche, 1969c, 312, 317) means that he in effect thinks of it as radically related to all his major works. Also the content of *Ecce Homo*, reviewing his life especially in terms of his writings, likewise necessarily connects it with all of them in an integral way. He describes *Ecce Homo* in terms that would seem to equate it with *The Anti-Christ(ian)*, telling Brandes that it, *Ecce Homo*, is "a ruthless attack on the crucified Christ" (1969c, 326). *Nietzsche Contra Wagner* is more than any other single work virtually fused with many earlier writings, since it is essentially a verbatim gathering of selections from *The Gay Science, Human, All Too Human, Beyond Good and Evil*, and *On the Genealogy of Morals.* What we are witnessing in Nietzsche's last period of writing is a grand summation and intensification of all his lifelong concerns.

To allow Nietzsche himself to set his seal of approval on this argument, we can attend to his highly significant words to Georg Brandes in a letter of May 4, 1888:

> These last weeks at Turin, where I shall stay till June 5, have turned out better than any I have known for years, above all more philosophic. Almost every day for one or two hours I have reached such a pitch of energy as to be able to view my whole conception from top to bottom; so that the immense multiplicity of problems lies spread out beneath me, as though in relief and clear in its outlines. This requires a maximum of strength, for which I had almost given up hope. It all hangs together; years ago it was already on the right course; one builds one's philosophy like a beaver, one is forced to and does not know it: but one has to *see* all this, as I have now seen it, in order to believe it. (Brandes, n.d., 84)

Ipse dixit! "It all hangs together." Even this very compact presentation of evidence allows us to conclude that Nietzsche's works possess a complex, yet coherent and comprehensive thematic core. Nietzsche knew them to be such a unity. Nietzsche wants his readers to appreciate them as such a unity. Recalling our first argument at this point, we can reason that if Nietzsche's corpus is indeed a unified whole, and if Nietzsche was intensely humanistic in his early formative years, and if the concerns and positions of those early years form the generative basis of those of later ones (as Nietzsche himself attests generally and in the cases of *The Birth of Tragedy* and *Untimely Meditations*), then we are justified in our suspicion of the essentially humanistic cast of Nietzsche's thought as a whole.

Our second argument, of course, also implies a similar conclusion on the basis of major analogies between Nietzsche and leading humanist figures with regard to major areas of concern. But, prescinding from this logic, let us ask directly, Can we meaningfully and appropriately designate the Nietzschean complex of themes (as it is, in early, middle, and late periods) as "*humanistic*"? A positive answer to this question follows immediately from our sense of common English usage, which makes *humanist* or *humanistic* a synonym of *cultural* (e.g., see Webster's *Third New World Dictionary*). A wide range of that with which Nietzsche is focally concerned—art, morality, philosophy, music, language, literature, history, education, scholarship—is obviously humanistic in this sense. Other areas, like religion, science, and politics (over against which the *studia humanitatis* are sometimes misleadingly said to have defined themselves, though they too are significant cultural phenomena) are treated in an obviously humanistic way: Nietzsche critiques these areas for their antihumanistic, culturally corruptive tendencies, while he adopts elements from them that seem to support increased human vitality, creativity, and freedom. For example, Nietzsche values the benefits of the science of critical philology; he admires the world-historical character of Napoleon; he adopts religious symbolism ("Dionysus") and biblical rhetoric (*Zarathustra*). But Nietzsche's themes are humanist in an even more radical way because they strongly parallel those found in the works of the Renaissance humanists. A popular unabridged dictionary's first definition of *humanist* (as an adjective) is "of or relating to Renaissance humanism or humanists." Not only does Nietzsche carry with him all through his career the idea of *classical antiquity as a reference point*, but he also, very much like his Renaissance forbears, gives himself especially to reflections on *morality, psychology, and spirituality.* These closely connected areas were of major importance for the Renaissance humanists and they as a complex whole represent the critical juncture of humanism and disciplinary philosophy. We know that it was moral philosophy and allied subjects like political thinking that were of leading interest to the humanists. The technical areas like epistemology, metaphysics, logic, and so on, were not anywhere nearly as prominent in the humanists' labors. They strove to write moral treatises and dialogues (Kristeller, 1988, 134).

The subjects favored in the *studia humanitatis* thus had a distinctly ethical tenor. According to Kristeller, the curriculum included *grammatica, rhetorica, poetica, historia,* and *philosophia moralis* (1988, 113) but rhetoric traditionally involved an understanding of the human psyche (and therefore of human character or *ethos*), and poetry and history would have been radically ethical in import, since they would have been appreciated especially for their presentations of exemplary figures. As we have seen, the theme of morality was a special obsession of Nietzsche's across most of his career, with even religion tending to be reduced to its moral manifestations. His early "On Truth and Falsehood in an Extra-Moral Sense," (1979, 79-97) can be seen as a use of basic reflection on language (cf. *grammatica*) to gain a perspective from which ethics can itself be judged. The position that cognition is primordially deceptive for the the sake of survival bears ethical as well as epistemological implications, and Nietzsche aimed to expose this hidden groundwork of morality as he strove to transform the prevailing ethos of his day. The relationship of truth and goodness appears as an important theme to the end, in *Ecce Homo* (1969a, 326-35). There it is clear that Nietzsche believes his radical achievement to have been a revaluation of morality: "Have I been understood?—What defines me, what sets me apart from the whole rest of humanity is that I *uncovered* Christian morality" (332). Though, at least in our eyes, his stance differs greatly from that of most Renaissance writers, Nietzsche's obsession with the ethical sphere places him squarely in their thematic milieu. As we have noted, ethical issues are thoroughly implicated in cultural ones. In the union of these two topics we have a fair description of what seems to be Nietzsche's "core theme" from which and toward which all else flows.

We can go yet further to link him with other interests of the Renaissance humanists, who instantiated a profounder *historical* sense, a keener *philological* science and *rhetorical* practice, a more self-conscious and theoretically-based practice of *art,* and a more incisive *psychological self-understanding.* Their concern with heroic individuals led to the practice of panegyrical *biographical essays* like Petrarch's *De Viris Illustribus,* and their intense sense of their own achievements to the writing of *panegyrical autobiographies* (see Ijesewijn, 1973, 209-18). All of these areas are ones to which Nietzsche contributed substantially, down to his own exalted evaluations of important cultural heroes like Schopenhauer and Goethe, and of course himself. He gloried in his stylistic achievements (e.g., *Ecce Homo,* "Books," 4,

265-66), echoing that Renaissance concern with excellence of style and its sense of style's ethical and cultural implications. In *Twilight of the Idols*, "What I Owe to the Ancients"), he even finally revealed a fundamental Latin bias despite his profound Hellenism and in this way too he parallels the largely Latinist culture of the Renaissance (cf. Boulby, 1976, 214-33). In addition to being a musician, Nietzsche was a composer of light verse, lyrics, and even his own epic poem, *Thus Spake Zarathustra.* Like the Renaissance humanists, Nietzsche was deeply concerned about national and political practices and ethos, albeit more as a critic than as a glorifier. I have already stressed in the first argument Nietzsche's profoundly humanistic concern with education, *Bildung.* It is a theme that can be found from *The Future of Our Educational Institutions* in 1872 to *Twilight of the Idols* (1954, 508-13) and *Ecce Homo* (1969a, 237), both written in 1888. He shared with Renaissance humanists the desire to educate or to prepare for exemplary figures (like the philosophers of the future), who could provide cultural and spiritual leadership. Did Nietzsche ever really renounce his fundamental educational aspirations? He once confessed "I know of no better objective I can have than somehow or other to become an "educator" in a wide sense (letter of 1874, cited in Hayman, 1982, 171).

Put this range of themes and interests together and it is hard to see how the designation "humanist" is not a most appropriate one for Nietzsche. Like many of the authors that he found worthy of careful attention, Nietzsche, from the start of his professional career to its end, concerned himself with that whole complex of themes that can be designated as "humanist" in either of its two major senses. Though so much more can be said about these and other themes in Nietzsche's works, enough has been said to secure the argument. We have inventoried his major topics, we have seen that his works are materially interconnected, that the author perceived this unity and explicitly invoked it, and we have gotten some sense of the humanistic quality of his leading concerns. Now we can now move to yet a sharper definition of Nietzsche's horizon and his message.

5
All in One: Horizon, Goal, and Doctrine

It is not surprising that Nietzsche—not as nomad but as range-boss—should roam the spacious terrain of themes that we have just surveyed. After all, he does belong to a long tradition of studied cultural return and advance. The pattern consists in society's absorbing, forgetting and re-discovering, then re-playing itself in a new key, perhaps with one or two new instruments added to the symphony. Ingesting new materials, sometimes from very different cultures, this tradition has grown ever more complex, but it has managed to maintain a recognizable identity. A generative core of contents and practices, attitudes and dynamics, directions and aspirations support a certain continuity. The repeated effort to stay in some kind of touch with its own sources constitutes what we might call a "renaissance dynamic" in Western cultural history. It has a universal aspect since it can be read as one form of the age-old attempt to tell one's myth of cultural origins for the sake of orientation in the world of meaning. The living communication of such a myth establishes in each generation's initiates a new relationship to that world. Transformative educational praxis involves a receptive and creative spiritual return to ancestors, to homeland, and to one's ultimate sources in order to connect more consciously with some "Center That Assures Life."

This process takes on a distinctive form in Western European societies because of the particular implications of their "technologies of the word," to borrow a phrase from Walter Ong. Textuality and literacy have played an especially important part in modernity's leap onto an entirely new level of interrelated dynamics of culture and consciousness, even as televisual and telecybernetic technologies presently carry us yet further. Repeated intellectual expansion, forgetting, return, selection, and differentiation have led to to the formation of an "open canon," a vast, composite cultural archive that embraces many authors, times, genres, styles, disciplines. In order to come of age in this tradition, one must be put to the task of learning to appreciate many of its representative realities. One can not be an informed participant without having gotten to know something of

Andromache *and* Achilles; Penelope *and* Odysseus; Homer *and* Plato; Aeschylus *and* Euripides; Parmenides *and* Heraclitus; Thucydides *and* Pheidias; Hesiod *and* Sappho; Euclid *and* Lucian, and so on, ultimately on to the inclusion of the Greeks *and* the Romans; pagans *and* Christians; gentiles *and* Jews; rhetoric *and* philosophy; arts *and* sciences; moderns *and* ancients. A trans-temporal and trans-cultural breadth constitutes an important part of the goal toward which humanist paideusis has ever aimed, group-bias and practical limitations notwithstanding. This vision has had important historical consequences. Some of the greatest interest in non-European cultures arose among European students of the classical languages: the close bond between language and culture meant that classical philology helped give rise not only to modern linguistics but also to modern anthropology.

Given such a horizon and such a gradient towards maturity, then, why should a humanist not ultimately attain both a critical *and* an affirmative stance, a tolerant yet a judicious sensitivity for various perspectives, a dogmatic anti-dogmatism, a power of evaluation that allows positive and negative attitudes to exist and develop side by side? This is what happened in the case of Nietzsche—and in those of countless others. One might of course protest that Nietzsche is too inhospitable to too many elements of his heritage for us to see him as such a humanist. Does he not side with the either/or rather than with the both/and? Does he not want to *separate* Aeschylus and Socrates, Christian and pagan, master and slave, Wagner and Nietzsche, male and female? He crashes his great cymbals with that ultra-dramatic ending to *Ecce Homo*: "Dionysus *versus* the Crucified!" How, then, can he be placed within a domain of a set of cultural practices that try to include and broaden rather than to exclude and sharpen? Yes, if one selects the right passages, Nietzsche appears to have fallen into the black hole of polemical oversimplification.

But even in cases of less obvious humanistic partisanship, the point is not that one judges each element equally good, nor that one comes to a definitive judgment in order to judge no more, nor that one can not make any definite affiliations because so many voices have been heard. On the contrary, humanists tend to engage any worthy moment and to weigh its value in the light of a particular ethos and existential stance. They also go on reading and understanding, expressing and reshaping the articulation of their stances. We might even say that humanists often act as if they believe that it is precisely through the effort of repeated, even passionate and hyperbolic articulation that they can achieve the deliberation necessary for holding a position that can finally be called their own. Humanistic intellectual examination thus tends to be "essayistic" rather than "analytical," interested less in *proof* than in *probing, approval,* and *provocation.* But facing the looming swell of the world's cultural-historical heritage does not necessarily lead to a confused relativism. Rather, such far-flung exploration often heightens our evaluative and deliberative powers, partly through the many inventive re-contextualizations of issues, and partly through the polemics and the panegyrics that characterize this highly rhetorical tradition.

Nietzsche is an exemplary modern re-incarnation of this old rhetorical humanist culture of praise and blame, from his denunciation of David Strauss (*David Strauss the Confessor and and the Writer,* 1873) to his most brutal, frontal attack on Christianity (*The Anti-Christ[ian],* 1888); from his glorification of Schopenhauer (*Schopenhauer as Educator,* 1874) to his exaltation of himself in *Ecce Homo* (1888). He is clearly undertaking the work of "appreciation," evaluating issues and personalities and cultures and entire eras, as he thinks within that expansive cultural-historical horizon that we can identify as a humanistic one. The polemics and the panegyrics are means to such an end. Humanists let rhetoric play its serious game without completely excommunicating the adversaries.

Ancient schoolboys, preparing for their days in court, might write epideictic compositions praising, then blaming Helen of Troy. Nietzsche eloquently castigates Socrates as an agent of decline in culture, and later he confesses that he truly admires the greatness of this man. He has both good *and* bad things to say of Epicurus, Goethe, and Jesus. Even as the Anti-Christian, he could confess, letting his own type of *pietas* show, that he *loved* Pascal. Did the Christian humanist scholars of the Renaissance not do something similiar, with their devotion to the likes of Seneca and Socrates and their eschewal of "their own" Christian scholastic philosophers? Humanism cultivates that curious art of saying both yes *and* no in its deliberative patience and continual reconsideration—no matter that it can now and again lead to a disjunctive assertion. The art of reading well allows the author some place in the development of the reader's thinking; it therefore formally demands some modicum of genuine tolerance and openness. Montaigne is most straightforward when he admits that even his own positions are constantly shifting. He claims that fifteen minutes are enough for him to assume a very different stance on a matter. Though Nietzsche strives for the dramatic simplicity of the either/or and uses radical dichotomy effectively as a rhetorical tool, he was too knowledgeable and too acute to rest with an oversimplification. We do not know how he might have recast his late blusterings had he recovered his health and looked back upon them from some years' distance. We will have to do without his retrospective reflections. He certainly differs from Montaigne in the cast of his thinking, once he has decided which parties he might best represent as the enemy. His deliberation seems to have become a kind of mental tragic production, a living intellectual fiction enacted to achieve a personal transformation in the soul of the thinker and then in the spirit of his age. But even in these moments, one who has come to know Nietzsche's tactics has ample ground to suspect that his polemics are rhetorical creations fashioned to further particular purposes—and that Nietzsche is not at all unaware of that fact.

At the origins of the Western humanism, that "Hellenic hubris" that separates the world into the two groups of Greeks and Barbarians is in fact belied by those specific moments in which the Greeks show a keen sense of what is superior in another culture and of what is shared in our common humanity. Homer's Priam and Euripides's Medea are are as compellingly personal as any Greek literary character. Egypt and the great Eastern civilizations could be admired and imitated by the Greeks, not only during the famous "Orientalizing period" antecedent to classical Greek art. Just so, within the bounds of the homeland, Sparta could be praised by Athens. The Greeks both envy the Persians *and* they define themselves over and against the Persians. This too is the art of saying yes and no simultaneously for the sake of the discovering how to muster the deepest and broadest *genuine* affirmation from one's soul.

We both are and are not "the Others." We try to do some justice to both sides of this hardly controvertible truth. But the larger drift of humanistic practices is finally not toward isolationism and exclusion. It is precisely in dialogue, in encounter, that they come to life. In the tradition of the international wisdom literature of the ancient Mediterranean world, Greek philosophy moves not only towards that other kind of universality that philosophy is famous for, but more concretely towards the practices of Stoicism, that most cosmopolitan world-view, and towards those of Epicureanism, which tends to distance the thinker from the world of relatively parochial political associations. Greek learning as a whole advances toward the vastly syncretic Alexandrian world. Of course, even long before Alexandrian scholars, Herodotus's title spoke volumes:

> Herodotus of Halicarnassus publishes this research so that what has happened among human beings might not fade in time, and so that great and wonderful works, some Greek and some barbarian, might

> not go unheralded, both why they fought with one another and other things as well. (Herodotus, *Histories*, Book I, translation mine)

Barbarian achievements are to be memorialized just as Greek ones are: they both belong to the history of humanity. If the Greeks do not have a strong reputation for what is today called "multiculturalism," they still can not be said to have failed to contribute substantially to its principles. Long after the ancient Greeks, as the humanist philological tradition found itself moving far along the road to modern anthropology, Nietzsche appears, with his own cosmopolitan considerations. He presents his famous "Blond Beast" as a phenomenon that appears in many cultures, including, for example, that of Japan. And he chooses the "eastern" Zarathustra rather than the good old Greek Heraclitus as his prime prophetic mouthpiece. Nietzsche's humanist sensibility makes him realize that, in the words of the old Terentian tag that is sometimes taken as the best motto of humanism itself, "I am a human being; I think that nothing human is alien to me." In this way there seems to be much sense in his late, "raving" claim that at bottom he is "every name in history."

But Nietzsche does not merely think out his thoughts in the context of this historical heritage. He intentionally practices, like a classical humanist, an *eternal return to the Greeks* and to their cultural progeny. There he finds the Center, the generative principle that unifies Western humanism's various manifestations through the centuries. He thus enacts, at an individual level, a special instance of that basic human desire to discover and define a *particular* center—that specific sacred mountain from which one can best mark out the farthest limits of one's own horizon. Even as he forges ahead into uncharted waters of a new era, he calls to mind the core cultural heritage that gave him his spiritual-intellectual birth. Though it may be a scandal to those who would like to highlight the most "progressive" elements in Nietzsche's vision, the classical and paradigmatic humanist cultures of antiquity and the Renaissance seem to be his constant reference points. He invokes them repeatedly and vigorously down through his latest writings. It is especially telling that these moments tend to occur precisely when Nietzsche is bringing a work to a climax. Right where he wishes to make his greatest challenge, to sound the most solemn notes of his exhortations, he seems to feel that it is essential to turn to his old, his ancient Muse. The ideas and the feelings expressed in these passages are important to recall because they show how, for all his flux, his own open canon has an easily discernible still point.

I am thinking, for example, of the conclusion to first essay of *On the Genealogy of Morals* (1969b), where Nietzsche scans the history of morality in the West. After commenting on Judaea's defeat of Rome he lets us see, without any embarrassment, something of his humanistic sympathies when he speaks of how "[t]here was, to be sure, in the Renaissance an uncanny and glittering reawakening of the classical ideal, of the noble mode of evaluating all things..." (1969b, 53). The second major essay of the *Genealogy* repeats this turn when Nietzsche tries to prove by means of Greece how having gods in one's culture does not necessarily entail an degradation of positive, primitive vitality: "...that is fortunately revealed even by a mere glance at the *Greek gods*, those reflections of noble and autocratic men, in whom *the animal* in man felt deified and did not lacerate itself, did *not* rage against itself!" (93-94). We easily sense the greater passion here. But among all examples of such classical turns of thought, *Twilight of the Idols* provides the clearest and *The Anti-Christ(ian)* the most intense examples. *Twilight's* entire final prose-section is entitled "What I Owe to the Ancients" (1954, 556-63) and in its penultimate chapter, immediately before the climactic evocation of the classical Goethe (48-51, the last sections of the chapter), Nietzsche makes his allegiances obivous, mentioning all of the elements in the humanistic trinity of Renaissance, Greece, and Rome, and positing them against the apparent object of his campaign:

> The danger that lies in great men and ages is extraordinary; exhaustion of every kind, sterility, follow in their wake. The great human being is a finale; the great age—the Renaissance, for example—is a finale. (548)

> Almost every genius knows, as one stage of his development, the "Catilinarian existence"...Catiline—the form of pre-existence of *every* Caesar. (550-51)

> It is decisive for the lot of a people and of humanity that culture should begin in the right place—not in the "soul" (as was the fateful superstition of the priests and half-priests): the right place is the body, the gesture, the diet, physiology; the rest follows from that. Therefore the Greeks remain the first cultural event in history: they knew, they *did*, what was needed; and Christianity, which despised the body, has been the greatest misfortune of humanity so far. (552)

This stark, exaggerated contrast of the classical cultures with Christianity is part of Nietzsche's effort to force his contemporaries beyond their own time's horizon. Ignoring Christianity's affirmation of creation in its idea of the Incarnation ("God so loved the and intentionally overlooking the many ascetic movements cal antiquity as well, Nietzsche strives here for one thing He does not intend to present a fair and nuanced account denying spiritualities, wherever they may occur. Rather he tries to make his fellow-travellers dissatisfied with themselves and with their most familiar assumptions. And he wants them to become enamored of a distant ideal, which they must not too quickly assume that they have already assimilated and surpassed. In such moments as these, it is not the mere fact of a classical reference that catches our attention, but the *quality of affect* that attaches to these evocations of Antiquity.

The notes of keen lament struck towards the end of *The Anti-Christ(ian)* are especially sharp. Towards the end of the work, the author exclaims:

> The whole labor of the ancient world *in vain*: I have no word to express my feelings about something so tremendous. And considering that its labor was a preliminary labor, that only the foundation for the labors of thousands of years had just then been laid with granite self-confidence—the whole *meaning* of the ancient world in vain! Wherefore Greeks? Wherefore Romans?...
>
> Greeks! Romans! The nobility of instinct, the taste, the methodical research, the genius of organizaion and administration, the faith in, the *will* to, man's future, the great Yes to all things, become visible in the *imperium Romanum*, visible for all the senses, the grand style no longer mere art but become reality, truth, *life*. (1954, 650; 651)
>
> The Germans have cheated Europe out of the last great cultural harvest which Europe could still have brought home—that of the Renaissance. Does one understand at last, does one want to understand, what the *Renaissance* was? The *revaluation* of *Christian values*, the attempt, undertaken with every means, with every instinct, with all genius, to bring the *counter*-values, the *noble* values to victory.
>
> The Renaissance—an event without meaning, a great *in vain*. Oh, these Germans, what they have cost us already! (1954, 653; 654)

This grieved passage can be balanced by a more temperate one taken from the finale of *Nietzsche Contra Wagner*, where he cites verbatim from the very last paragraph of the 1886 preface to *The Gay Science*:

> Oh, those Greeks! They knew how to live. What is required for that is to stop courageously at the surface, the fold, the skin, to adore appearance, to believe in forms, tones, words, in the whole Olympus of ap-

> pearance. Those Greeks were superficial—*out of profundity*. And is not this precisely what we are again coming back to, we daredevils of the spirit who have climbed the highest and most dangerous peak of present thought and looked around from up there—we who have looked *down* from up there? Are we not, precisely in this respect, Greeks? Adorers of form, of tones, of words? And therefore—*artists*? (1954, 683)

The strategically placed expression of sentiments such as these leaves no doubt that Nietzsche continues to think by means of the classical humanistic cultures of Greece, Rome, and Renaissance and that he explicitly and unmistakeably affiliates himself to them over against his own age, even through the last years of his literary life. The Greeks are so much a part of Nietzsche's intellectual life that his works pulse with the Hellenic heartbeat of the Western humanist tradition. A reader can not miss his love for the forms (of Apollo), the tones (of Dionysus), the words (of Socrates). They are so much a part of his soul that, in the last citation given above, he even declares *himself to be a Greek.*

But at the same time, we must admit that Nietzsche's *pietas* is as distinctive as it is profound. His eternal return to the Greeks and to other humanistic creatures has, in addition to the spiritual qualities of a reverent pilgrimage to the Center, a decidely antagonistic flavor. His is enacting the motive of self-overcoming on a grand, trans-personal scale. His own maturity is the outcome of an often repeated inter-generational dynamic: the bondage to, struggle against, reconciliation with, and the final critical, knowing, and yet respectful reverence for that parental generation that is at the root of his own existence. Early on, in the fifteenth section of *The Birth of Tragedy*, Nietzsche had spoken of how we are driven to outdo that presumptuous little nation that holds in its hands the reins of culture (1967b, 93). He makes his stance clearer in *The Gay Science* near the very end of that work when he says that though he admires the courage and wisdom of Socrates, he finds that at his death even this great man stumbled when speaking his last words, revealing how he had suffered life. Our goal must be a deeper affirmation. "Alas, my friends, we must overcome even the Greeks!" (1974*:* 272) It is at this point that Nietzsche expresses the coming Zarathustra's great teaching of the Eternal Return. Even this doctrine, however, has its pre-Socratic roots with Heraclitus. The overcoming of the Greeks is therefore done with the help of the Greeks, especially those pre-classical, pivotal figures of the Tragic Age. Thus Nietzsche's transcending of the Greek world must be read as more than simply a purification of the false

Hellenism of his day. It involves an even more intense return to the Center, and another kind of idealization, another kind of use as well. It shares with earlier Hellenism, and makes more explicit, a concern for a project of cultural self-overcoming. This is what will allow the emergence of one's deepest self, which is paradoxically both the oldest and the freshest, the most spontaneous and most "fated" moment. But for all his despair about his times, his self-realization must also involve not only the glorious ancient world, but another culture that has a more immediate claim on him. He therefore also tends to conclude his works by turning to the question of Germany, as in the *The Birth of Tragedy* and in the final essay of *On the Genealogy of Morals.*

The "radically innovative" Nietzsche attempts in his own way to be thoroughly appropriative and recapitulative in his program, in line with the best practice of the humanist tradition, though clearly he would distance himself from the Hegelian version of the same phenomenon. It is the personal and the individual, not the large-scale, world-historical process that is more important. One of Nietzsche's most heart-felt passages reads:

> *The "humaneness" of the future*—...the historical sense is still so poor and cold, and many people are attacked by it as by a frost and made still poorer and colder. To others it appears as a sign of stealthily approaching old age.... Anyone who manages to experience the history of humanity as a whole as *his own history* will feel in an enormously generalized way all the grief of an invalid who thinks of health, of an old man who thinks of the dreams of his youth, of a lover deprived of his beloved, of the martyr whose ideal is perishing, of the hero on the evening after a battle that has decided nothing but brought him wounds and the loss of his friend. But if one endured, if one *could* endure this immense sum of grief of all kinds while yet being the hero who, as the second day of battle breaks, welcomes the dawn and his fortune, being a person whose horizon encompasses thousands of years past and future, being the heir of all the nobility of all past spirit—an heir with a sense of obligation, the most aristocratic of old nobles and at the same time the first of a new nobility—the like of which no age has yet seen or dreamed of; if one could finally contain all this in one soul and crowd it into a single feeling—this would surely have to result in a happiness that humanity has not known so far: the happiness of a god full of power and love, full of tears and laughter, a happiness that, like the sun in the evening, continually bestows its inexhaustible riches, pouring them into the sea, feeling richest, as the sun does, only when even the poorest fisherman is still rowing with golden oars! This godlike feeling would then be called—humaneness. (1974, 268),

These words reveal Nietzsche's heart and his horizon. And they present his audience with a challenge. For we can not read him well without working our way toward a certain similar depth and breadth.

We can see what hermeneutical implications follow upon the perspectives we are able to bring to Nietzsche's texts when we look at those illuminating accounts that have placed Nietzsche primarily in the context of the Enlightenment. Some thinkers have presented Nietzsche as its apex or ultimate conclusion (Madigan, 1986). There is little doubt that we can make much sense of Nietzsche as the product of the Enlightenment (Rosen, 1989: 207-08). He is certainly in an intense dialogue with the modernity that shaped him. But we must remember that he was no deist, no rationalist, no anti-naturalist. He felt peculiarly "unmodern" in his sensibility. He in fact drew his inspiration directly from the ancients as well as mediately, through the more recent strands of European intellectual history. The Enlightenment itself must be contextualized in terms of antiquity (Gay, 1966-1969), and its premiere humanists (e.g., Diderot and Voltaire) in terms of earlier cultural-historical streams welling up from the Renaissance and carrying forward its deepset cultural and formational concerns: Peter Gay reminds us that enlightenment's logic pointed to the necessity of making people ready for their proper autonomy through education (Gay, 1969, 498-99).

Nietzsche knows the larger continuity in which he wants to participate: he speaks of the banner of the Enlightenment as one that bears three names, namely, Petrach, Erasmus, Voltaire (Nietzsche, 1986, 26). But because he wanted so much to *overcome* the Enlightenment's rationalism and its idealist misreading of Greek civilization, his closest affiliations can not be said to rest with the modern movement pure and simple. Our interpretations would run the risk of putting the accent in the wrong place, so to speak. For example, Stanley Rosen, who has associated Nietzsche most closely with Enlightenment thinkers, suggests that there is a lack of positive content in Nietzsche's position. Perhaps this way of reading him has brought him to his conclusion that "Nietzsche means that there is no criterion by which to identify a profound interpretation of Nietzsche" (Rosen, 1989, 206). But this view would have to be carefully qualified if we give full weight to the positive humanist ideals Nietzsche constantly suggests in passages like the those I have cited, even if we can agree that Nietzsche by no means wishes to promote a culture of servile classicist imitation. Indeed, authentic humanism aims for a *personal* and *living* appropriation, a formed and informed character that can incarnate virtues spontaneously and independently.

Thus it seems better to position Nietzsche in terms of another discernible cultural tradition that developed, concurrently with the Enlightenment, right from humanism, and from its central concern with moral values: I mean the thought of those writers usually referred to as moralists. In its French manifestations, this movement was for Nietzsche the most direct link back to the ancient world. He explictly says:

> In reading Montaigne, La Rochefoucauld, La Bruyère, Fontenelle... Vauvenargue, and Chamfort we are nearer to antiquity than in any group of six authors of other nations. Through these six the spirit of the last centuries before Christ has once more come into being, and they collectively form an important link in the great and still continuous chain of the Renaissance...To praise them in plain terms, I may say that had they been written in Greek, they would have been understood by Greeks." (1986, 362-63, as cited in Donnellan, 1982, ix)

I think that we will do better, then, to link Nietzsche directly with the humanist movement, keeping in mind this "continuous chain of the Renaissance." This field evokes that widely inclusive tradition, the broad range of which Nietzsche attempted to compress into his own soul.

But did Nietzsche consider himself a humanist? We can go well beyond the implications of passages like those just cited to some revealing evidence contained in his own self-interpretive statements. One important early item has already been noted, the programme alluded to on the back cover of the first edition of *The Gay Science.* There Nietzsche suggested his own self-understanding when he wrote:

> This book marks the conclusion of a series of writings [later identified as *Human, All Too Human-I* and *Human, All Too Human-II, The Wanderer and His Shadow, Daybreak,* and *The Gay Science*] by FRIEDRICH NIETZSCHE whose common goal it is to erect a new image and ideal of the free spirit. (1974, 30, emphasis original)

These words help us to see why Nietzsche proclaimed his idea of "humaneness" so poignantly in the glorious oratory of Section 337 of *The Gay Science* (1974, 267-69). The humanist trajectory of his early career continued on unbroken, over any supposed "great break" after the *Untimely Meditations.* Daniel Breazeale too has asserted the continuity of the themes and positions in Nietzsche's notebooks of the early period with those of later published writings, claiming that the real break is not the frequently invoked one of the distance between *Richard Wagner in Bayreuth* and *Human, All Too Human*, but between the early notebooks and the early published writings (Nietzsche, 1979, xlix). In light of our present point of view, we might also ask about how profound these changes seem when we approach Nietzsche in the context of the humanist tradition, a tradition that also deals with questions of knowledge, its value, and its uses. For example, Petrarch wrote an essay that has been entitled "On His Own Ignorance and That of Many Others," and a letter called "A Disapproval of an Unreasonable Use of the Discipline of Dialectic" (Cassirer et. al., 1948, 23-139). As an important dimension of the human life-world, problems of truth and error repeatedly appear in the epic tradition, as in the issue of true and false prophetic dreams, or as when, at the end of the *Odyssey*, Penelope tells Odysseus that he should not be upset that she has tested him, for he knows how the gods deceive us. Though the discourse in which we find such examples is certainly pre-theoretical, the sapiential use of Homer and the allegorizing hermeneutic applied to the great epic texts meant that such stories were not as far from philosophy as we might think. The same fundamental issue of appearance and reality emerges in didactic poetry, explicitly thematized as early as the account of Hesiod's encounter with the Muses, who know how to say even false things sweetly if they wish. In the important skeptical movement of early modernity, Montaigne was a key figure and perhaps the best example of humanist concern with epistemological issues. But the larger purpose of such a concern is kept foremost: how to create vibrant images of—and then real, living examples of—human authenticity, fulfillment, completeness, and so on. This is the kind of work that is so deeply rooted in the rationales of the humanistic tradition.

There is yet clearer evidence for Nietzsche's humanist self-identification. On September 22, 1886, he wrote a letter to Jacob Burckhardt—the man to whom "Basel [primarily] owes its pre-eminence in humaneness" (1954, 510). There he reveals that *he thinks they are doing the same things,* only that Burckhardt is doing them better (1969c, 255). For the older professor, Nietzsche believes, his world-shaking discoveries "will be nothing new"! Such words are hard to dismiss, given the close relationship between the two men. But we have available an even more direct confession of Nietzsche's nature as he himself understood it. It is by far the most valuable piece of evidence for his humanistic self-image. Toward the very end of his career, thrilled by the attention he is beginning to get, he confides to Georg Brandes (Turin, April 10, 1888):

> What you say about *Schopenhauer as Educator* gives me great
> This little work serves me as a touchstone; he to whom it says
> *personal* has probably nothing to do with me either. In reality it c
> the whole plan according to which I have hitherto lived; it is a ri
> *promise.* (Brandes, n.d., 79)

Now *Schopenhauer as Educator* is an extraordinarily, unmistakeably humanistic document from Nietzsche's most obviously humanistic period. It is full of rather traditional humanist accents, though these are struck at a special pitch and with an impressive originality of formulation. We hear in this essay unmistakeably intimate personal resonances that may help to account for both of these qualities. The last sentence in the citation from Nietzsche's letter to Brandes might also be translated: "Basically, therein stands the essential design by which I have lived up to this point: it is a severe *engagement." ("Im Grunde steht das Schema darin, nach dem ich bisher gelebt habe: sie ist ein strenges Versprechen.") Versprechen* indicates a kind of engagement that constitutes an act by which one commits oneself. I find it highly significant that Nietzsche, a mere nine months before the end of his career, should so enthusiastically return to this early document, "this little work," and so explicitly declare it to be a key to himself. The hermeneutical implications of these confessional words must not be ignored. We read elsewhere that this essay speaks of Nietzsche himself, and that it is perhaps even more intimate and personal than even *The Birth of Tragedy* or *Richard Wagner in Bayreuth.* In the section on the *Untimely Meditations* in *Ecce Homo,* Nietzsche stated, "The essay *Wagner in Bayreuth* is a vision of my future, while in *Schopenhauer as Educator* my innermost history, my *becoming* is inscribed. Above all, my *solemn promise [Gelöbnis]*" (1969a, 281).

Since, if we are to believe Nietzsche himself, this essay is so important for understanding his entire life, we will now dwell on it at some length. To retrieve the essentials of his innermost history and the qualities of his most solemn commitment. Once again, we have here a text whose many humanist themes are intricately interrelated, not only among themselves, but with Nietzsche's other works, and with the history of humanism as well. Thus, our reprise of *Schopenhauer as Educator* can not be a strictly systematic analysis; it will instead consist in an overview of the most relevant points, with two important "digressions" that in effect set forth other major arguments, namely, the teleological and the doctrinal. These belong here b
they direct us to precisely those central points that in a way he
define Nietzsche's horizon: his *primary goal* and his *primary t*

We will later return to the panoramic view to reformulate Nietzsche's existential arena in yet another way. But first, the essay *Schopenhauer as Educator* (Nietzsche, 1983) will give us a golden thread of coherence, and even as we discuss later works, we will find that this early essay can be understood as thoroughly integral with the themes and positions of the so-called "mature Nietzsche" of *Zarathustra* (1883-1885) and beyond.

Let us first notice that a profoundly *moral/ethical problematic* motivates *Schopenhauer as Educator.* Nietzsche worries that the leading scholars of the day "are thinking more of science than they are of mankind" (132), and he goes on in frustration:

> [O]ne finally asks oneself: where are we, scholars and unscholarly, high placed and low, to find the moral exemplars and models among our contemporaries, the visible epitome of morality for our time? What has become of any reflection on questions of morality—questions that have at all times engaged every more highly civilized society?...Thus it has come about that our schools and teachers simply abstain from an education in morality or make do with mere formalities: and virtue is a word that no longer means anything to our teachers or pupils...(132)

After claiming that Christianity's high and unattainable ideal has had much to do with the present misery, he claims that "Never have moral educators been more needed, and never has it seemed less likely that they would be found.... [W]here are the physicians for modern mankind...?" (133) This radical ethical concern is present because Nietzsche, like the humanist tradition, is focused on the issue of *humanitas,* a term which meant "the development of human virtue, in all its forms, to its fullest extent" (Grudin, 1987, 723). This concern Nietzsche expresses in a classically humanistic way. Longing for a full, real, human life, he pictures how it must be contrasted with animal life.

> Yet let us reflect: where does the animal cease, where does man begin?—man, who is nature's sole concern! As long as anyone desires life as he desires happiness he has not yet raised his eyes above the horizon of the animal, for he only desires more consciously what the animal seeks through blind impulse. But that is what we all do for the greater part of our lives: usually we fail to emerge out of animality, we ourselves are the animals whose suffering seems to be senseless. (157-58)

Now it is not just the "human" with which Nietzsche is simply concerned, but rather the "most human" or the "truly human." Again,

this is a typically humanistic way of thinking. There are ke
standards, canons by means of which one's authenticity can
mined. Hence, all writing is not "real literature"; all verse is
poetry." Homer is a poet; Ogden Nash is, well—something ... we
would be mistaken to try to apply a thinker's (say, Heidegger's) pronouncements on poetry to the works of the latter. *Qualitative distinctions are expressed ontologically.* The designation is ultimately intended to be rhetorical rather than technical. A humanist would probably admit that in a way *all* writing—even the blurbs on cereal boxes and candy wrappers—is "literature" in some technical sense, but the point of the humanist usage is ethical and evaluative. It attempts to conceive the highest forms of what is being defined and thus to distinguish the excellent and normative from the ordinary and the non-distinctive. Humanism looks to concrete "ideal models."

Nietzsche can therefore claim that we must be "lifted up" by those who are "true *men, those who are no longer animal, the philosophers, artists and saints...*" (159; emphasis original). And it is *culture* that is the way to this higher level of humanity:

> Anyone who believes in culture is thereby saying: 'I see above me something higher and more human than I am; let everyone help me to attain it, as I will help everyone who knows and suffers as I do: so that at last the man may appear who feels himself perfect and boundless in knowledge and love, perception and power, and who in his completeness is at one with nature, the judge and evaluator of things.' (162-63)

> [T]the goal of culture is to promote the production of true human beings and nothing else...(164)

The typically humanistic way of defining humanity by opposition to the animal world, occurs in ancient Greek authors, but it finds a classic formulation in Petrarch's *De Vita Solitaria*: " to take off one's beastliness and to put on humanity " (*humanitatem induere feritatemque deponere*, cited in Rico, 1986, 64). A later Renaissance humanist, Juan Luis Vives, writing on Christian education, spoke of the "arts of humanity" as those "branches of learning (*disciplinae*), by which we separate ourselves from the way of life and customs of animals and are restored to humanity..." (cited in Crane, 1967, Volume 1, 31). The other idea, that of attaining higher levels of humanity, was classically expressed by Aulus Gellius in his *Attic Nights* (Book
XIII. xvii). "*Humanitas*," this grammarian says, really means the
paideia, which in Latin implies "refinement and systematic g

ing *eruditionem institutionemque*) in the "good arts" (*bonas artes*). The contrast with animality also reappears here:

> Those who earnestly desire and seek after these are most highly humanized [*humanissimi*]. For the pursuit of that kind of knowledge, and the training given by it, have been granted to man alone of all the animals, and for that reason it is termed *humanitas*, or "humanity." (Aulus Gellius, Volume 2, 457)

This *humanissimum*, authentic humanity, is Nietzsche's ideal. The Latin superlative ending *-issimum* semantically corresponds to the *Über* in *Übermensch*, which carries, like the Greek *hyper*, the connotation of *above measure, excessively*, or *intensively*. At the basis of such a notion is a *leitmotif* that sounds forth repeatedly in Nietzsche's utterances, a "signature-theme" that links his entire life and literary corpus together, impressing them with the stamp of a *superhumanism*. That foundational and generative notion—which we must never forget is the ultimate ideal and motive and organizing principle at work in Nietzsche—is the idea of *human greatness*. This is the critically important *Grundthema* that always plays beneath the surface of all of his texts and like Leviathan often emerges. *Grösse* is the tonic in Nietzsche's tone-scale of values. It is the Copernican sun to which all that is really important to him can be related in the most economical way. *Grösse* is to Nietzsche what *Geist* is to Hegel: *the telos of his intentions and the telos within his fundamental anthropology*. It is present everywhere: in his educational ambitions to produce "real human beings"; in his mode of evaluating authors by the greatness of their personalities rather than by the consistency or comprehensiveness of their systems; in his own exaltation and painful/joyful isolation at being lifted up to a high place from which he can look down on *everything*; in his ideal of full self-realization in the lively use and harmonization of all one's talents; in the exuberance and tragic profundity of the Dionysian experience; and in countless other places. It is the center of a whole complex of themes that bind all of Nietzsche's works together and make them a part of the Western humanist tradition: nobility; good breeding; health; superabundance; power, *Macht*, Renaissance *virtù*; and ultimately, the Great Self that stands over the petty ego.

Here we can leap forward in our understandings of both Nietzsche and humanism simultaneously, for humanism can be elegantly defined as a *mystique or ethic of human greatness or nobility* (Renaudet, 1958, 32-53). Even *prima facie*, the humanists' trans-generational and trans-cultural community of great souls, sacramentalized in great books, supports such a definition, as does the "greatness of soul" that has been the inspiration and formational aim of humanist education. Henri Gouhier has expressed his admiration of Augustin Renaudet's formulation while suggesting that it could be made more specific by changing "greatness" to "sufficiency" (1987, 13-21). Gouhier believes that humanism essentially implies the confidence that humanity can achieve something by its own powers, that these powers are *natural*, and that they are developed by means of *culture*. He stresses that reflection on the relationships between nature and culture is a persistent trait of humanist thinking. Such a specification of human greatness would also manifestly apply to Nietzsche, who, even while "de-mythologizing" the notion of free will, generously invests in great achievements of powerful personalities. He often dealt with precisely those themes of nature and culture, which were both for him thoroughly involved with the theme of greatness. We see how the magnificent free power of nature was from very early on a living symbol of a thrilling trans-moral reality, when we read what he wrote to his friend Gersdorff in the April of 1866:

> Yesterday a magnificent storm was in the sky, I hurried out to a nearby hilltop, called Leusch (perhaps you can tell me what that means), found a hut up there, a man who was slaughtering two kids, and his young son. The storm broke with immense force, with wind and hail. I felt an incomparable elation (*Aufschwung*), and I knew for certain that we can rightly understand nature only when we have to run to her, away from our troubles and pressures. What to me were man and his unquiet will! What were the eternal "Thou shalt," "Thou shalt not"! How different the lightning, the wind, the hail, free powers, without ethics! How fortunate, how strong they are, pure will, without obscurings from the intellect! (1969c, 12)

The sympathy and exaltation that Nietzsche feels here indicate that culture and nature are not experienced as a simple duality. Moral imperatives and the "obscurings from the intellect," two elements *within* culture, are somehow the culprits. Culture, he says later, is rather a "new and improved *physis* [nature]," and he goes on to connect it indissolubly with his concept of greatness when he says that culture "depends upon the way in which one defines what is great" (Nietzsche, 1979, xxvii-xxviii). Gouhier's use of the word "sufficiency" itself in the definition of humanism will also strike a particularly apt note in connection with Daniel Conway's persuasive argument that "the central doctrine of Zarathustra is the sufficiency of human nature" (Conway, 1988, 264).

On the basis of either formulation, then, Nietzsche is a humanist in a radical sense. Perhaps it is his very self-conscious combination of the themes of nature, culture, and human capacities (especially that capacity to fashion an enlarged self) that marks the special superhumanism by which he attempts to extend the humanism of the past. At the end of *Beyond Good and Evil*, Nietzsche has Dionysus the philosopher say

> —"man is to my mind an agreeable, courageous, inventive animal that has no equal on earth; it finds its way in any labyrinth. I am well disposed towards him: I often reflect how I might yet advance him and make him stronger, more evil, and more profound than he is."
>
> "Stronger, more evil, and more profound?" I asked startled. "Yes," he said once more; "stronger, more evil, and more profound; also more beautiful"—and at that the tempter god smiled with his halcyon smile as though he had just paid an enchanting compliment. Here we also see: what this divinity lacks is not only a sense of shame—and there are other good reasons for conjecturing that in several respects all of the gods could learn from us humans. We humans are—more humane.— (1966, 236)

Here Nietzsche seems beguiled by a more "natural" existence whose leading feature is a greater, transmoral "weightiness," somehow incorporating the "free powers" of that storm that the young Nietzsche delighted in. But through Dionysus he also expresses his grounding in a love for this "agreeable, courageous, inventive animal that has no equal on the earth"—i.e., that is both a natural and "cultural" phenomenon. And he ironically proposes that human beings can teach the gods something about humanity, as if to say, among other things, "I know this 'enlargement' would be in our sense 'indecent' and I know that I am still somewhat attached to the old standards for what is humane—yet I am mightily tempted by this philosopher Dionysus, who, even without sharing our human condition, might actually help us to achieve in ourselves something greater."

The stress on human capacities is, for Nietzsche, consubstantial with an ethic of *mastery* and the *magisterial* that itself has no small place in the practices and ideals of the *maestros* and *magistri* of the humanist tradition (Kohl, 1988, 5). This ethic is dear to Nietzsche himself, *master-moralist* that he is, and though it can ultimately carry overtones of cruelty and selfishness that Nietzsche sometimes exploits (I believe for the sake of heuristic and rhetorical purposes rather than as naive encouragement to barbarism), we should not ignore the fact that even in his later years he sounds many a chord fully harmonious with long-standing tradition:

> It is the powerful who *understand* how to honor; this is their art, their realm of invention. The profound reverence for age and tradition—all law rests on this double reverence—the faith and prejudice in favor of ancestors and disfavor of those who are yet to come are typical of the morality of the powerful; and when the men of "modern ideas," conversely, believe almost instinctively in "progress" and "the future" and more and more lack respect for age, this in itself would sufficiently betray the ignoble origin of these "ideas." (1966, 205-06)

The images of warriors, heroes, strong and hard acts or characteristics are best understood as all part of the thematization of Nietzsche's concern with human greatness. Essentially, this quality implies *a certain substantiality of the human personality*—its depth, breadth, solidity, forcefulness, potential, unity, diversity, strength of will, "virtues," and so on. Because heroic achievement implies a certain unity and focus as well as a range of abilities that can be coordinated and brought into play according to circumstances, we find here a connection with the archetypal humanist themes of human "completeness" (wholeness, fulfillment). These are one with Nietzsche's constant concern with maturity and the vital integration of elements. Early in *Schopenhauer as Educator*, Nietzsche remembers how he wondered about the educational maxims of his day: "Develop the special strength of the student" and "Develop all the potentials of the student". He uses Cellini as an example:

> But where do we discover a harmonious whole at all, a simultaneous sounding of many voices in one nature, if not in such men as Cellini, men in whom everthing, knowledge, desire, love, hate, strives towards a central point, a root force, and where a harmonious system is constructed through the compelling domination of this living center? And so perhaps these two maxims are not opposites at all? Perhaps the one simply says that man should have a centre and the other that he should also have a periphery? That educating philosopher of whom I dreamed would, I came to think, not only discover the central force, he would also know how to prevent its acting destructively on the other forces: his educational task would, it seemed to me, be to mould the whole man into a living solar and planetary system and to understand its higher laws of motion. (1983, 131).

The same orientation to fullness and maturity appears in many ways, for example, the idea of the "great noon," which is equivalent to the "high point of humanity" (1954, 486), the moment when Zarathustra sets forth, sun-like (1954, 439). The classical background to this motif of the midday sun suggests both a moment of great danger as well as great health because it is full of daimonic presences (Roscher, 1894-1897, s.v. "Meridianus daemon," cols. 2832-2836). I note briefly here in reference to both of these examples a motif to which we will return: the overpowering force that can (in the first example) master and control other forces by means of a new, self-generating order and (in the second) bring about downfall or renewal. The most powerful classical symbol for this is another Greek god that Nietzsche often alluded to—Prometheus. That titan is, of course, the establisher of human culture who suffers as a threat to the entire Olympian order, a model of heroic defiance who suffers in order to improve humanity's lot.

Schopenhauer as Educator centers upon Nietzsche's key theme of greatness. It is oriented toward motivating readers to achieve—or at least to appreciate—some kind of completeness in personality and culture, with Schopenhauer being the leading model of greatness and the most direct route to it. The truly educative personality propels us towards wholeness by means of self-knowing self-dissatisfaction and love:

> [F]or it is love alone that can bestow on the soul, not only a clear, discriminating and self-contemptuous view of itself, but also the desire to look beyond itself and to seek with all its might for a higher self as yet still concealed from it. Thus only he who has attached his heart to some great man is by that act consecrated to culture; the sign of that consecration is that one is ashamed of oneself without any accompanying feeling of distress, that one comes to hate one's own narrowness and shrivelled nature, that one has a feeling of sympathy for the genius who again and again drags himself up out of our dryness and apathy and the same feeling in anticipation for all those who are still struggling and evolving, with the profoundest conviction that almost everywhere we encounter nature pressing towards man and again and again failing to achieve him, yet everywhere succeeding in producing the most marvellous beginnings, individual traits and forms: so that the men we live among resemble a field over which is scattered the most precious fragments of sculpture where everything calls to us: come, ...te, bring together what belongs together, we have an im- ...nging to become whole. (163)

...s of greatness in culture are universal and they are so ...an psychology that they are not limited to the political sphere, but can be found in religious, artistic, social, economic, ones as well. The humanistic tradition makes an intensive use of these dynamics with regard to cultural heroes. The principle of classicity points to concrete and empirical normative standards manifested in the Great Individuals as the models of action, as the sources most worthy of discipleship and emulation. Hence not only is a particular culture, that of ancient Greece, designated as somehow normatively "great" and endowed with all the numinosity of this greatness, but this occurs because of and by means of a whole lineage of Great Individuals who bear a similar normativity for different spheres of culture (Homer, Socrates, Euclid, Alexander). Nietzsche thoroughly understands this dynamic. He stresses in *Philosophy in the Tragic Age of the Greeks* that systems can be refuted but the great personality can not (*Philosophy in the Tragic Age of the Greeks*, Preface, 23-24).

The concrete and empirical nature of these personal guides means that from the beginning an "antinomian" tendency is ever at work in Western humanism, especially because there is no single legal code to which the heroes give witness. With this direction we might contrast the Hebraic tradition, which also helped to inform Western humanism, but often as something of a counterpoint to the Greco-Roman elements. This oriental heritage tends to put forth "heroes" of a very different type. For example, the giant-killer David is so very different from the giant-killer Hercules. The Biblical story stresses that he is the youngest boy in his family; the Greek one portrays Hercules as excessive in passion as well as physique. In his Hellenomania, Nietzsche chooses the muscular Prometheus as his inspiring emblem, not someone like the aged Abraham or the slave-born Moses. Fidelity to a covenant and its code are not as important to him as bold, passionate, and independently motivated action. This type of value is part of his enduring appeal to the adolescent in all of us insofar as we strive to "create" our identities and make our place in the world. Some type of antinomianism must be present because there is no way of completely suppressing the fact that personalities are marked by a tremendous variety; they are never directly imitable, partly because of the inevitable historical, cultural, and psychological differences. And it is often precisely through the expression of an apparently self-centered transgressive will that people come to experience themselves as distinct personal agencies, endowed with powers of initiative separate from the collectivity. In a way, then, the Great Individuals are not only "legislators," as Nietzsche often proclaims. They remain unique fulfillments of human nature that, though "normative," are unrepeatable. How can one possibly become a second Homer, except in a rather distantly analogous way? The times will have changed, along with the available technologies and the cultural repository. Altogether apart from the external forum of world-historical greatness, becoming a second "whichever person" would be quite difficult for anyone to achieve. The "second-order" norming that Nietzsche exemplifies in his use of Schopenhauer occurs in such a way that one's own individuality is not impeded but actually fostered (cf. Magnus, 1983).

Thus, operating out of the classical canon of great personalities and cultural works, Nietzsche presents his normative anthropology in a concrete, personalist, and exemplaristic way. The end of the trajectory is understandably his self-exemplarity, in *Ecce Homo*, though as he eventually realized, it was *Nietzsche* who was at issue in all the earlier works: "at bottom," he says of *Schopenhauer as Educator*, the speaker is really "Nietzsche as Educator" (1969a, 280). A strikingly distinctive trait of his texts is the fact that they teem with evocations and evaluations of particular examples of personalities and their works (which are taken to represent their spirit): Wagner, Emerson, Montaigne, Goethe, Epicurus, Socrates, and so on. This feature is highly in evidence from the *Untimely Meditations*, three of whose four titles bear the names of significant cultural figures, to *Twilight of the Idols*, in which the number of personalities discussed is especially high. It gives Nietzsche's entire corpus a humanistic tone and substance rarely, if ever, paralleled in the works of our typical professional philosophers.

Schopenhauer as Educator is Nietzsche's most intense panegyric of another personality. But in the course of his works, he does not restrict himself to the employment of particular historical figures. Rather, he dramatically, rhetorically, evangelistically sets out his "ideal type" of human authenticity by means of a persistent stream of evocative personal images: the philosopher of the future, the nobleman, the *gentilhomme*, the *grand seigneur*, the blond beast, the genius, the free spirit, the master, and of course the *Übermensch*. Over all of these looms Zarathustra. Speaking of his masterwork and its central character (explicitly designated as a "type"), Nietzsche says

> Here man has been overcome at every moment; the concept of the "overman" has here become the greatest reality—whatever was so far considered great in man lies beneath him at an infinite distance. The halcyon, the light feet, the omnipresence of malice and exuberance, and whatever else is typical of the type of Zarathustra—none of this has ever before been dreamed of as essential to greatness. Precisely in this width of space and this accessibility for what is contradictory,

> Zarathustra experiences himself as the *supreme type of all beings*, and once one hears how he defines this, one will refrain from seeking any metaphor for it.

There follows a quotation from *Zarathustra* with some telling phrases:

> "The soul that has the longest ladder and reaches down deepest—the most comprehensive soul, which can run and stray and roam farthest within itself...the most necessary soul...the soul...having being...the soul that loves itself most..." *But that is the concept of Dionysus himself.* (1969a, 305-06).

Here, then, Zarathustra, *Übermensch*, and Dionysus—that terrible Nietzschean trio—are all brought together and explicitly named "the supreme type of all beings," the overcoming of all previous human greatness. The idea of overcoming humanity then is to be interpreted in the qualitative mode of humanistic speech that we have already pointed out: "true humanity" necessarily transcends "humanity." There is the negative of the "all-too-human" and the positive of the *humanissimum*, the "intensively human."

There is not a complete disjunction between these two poles, even if the suggestion of the possibility of a grand, world-redemptive "leap in being" still remains. This is what we might gather from the thinking of Daniel Conway, who proposes that the *Übermensch* first represents an ideal eventually renounced by Zarathustra in favor of quiet self-creation (1989). Conway claims that the former ideal of human greatness, that is, greatness of the world-historical variety, is put aside for that sort of self-creation that prepares as it can for that truly great revolution that will come with the Great Individual. This happens because Zarathustra's first proclamation of the redemptive world-historical *Übermensch* is beyond his pedagogical abilities to bring about. Furthermore, Conway continues, the very idea of such a hero contradicts Nietzsche's position that humanity really does not need a "redemption from above"; he would only be fostering a new version of an old illusion by promoting a soteriology centered upon this figure. Thus, in Book III, Zarathustra gives himself rather to the practicable campaign of countering nihilism. Orienting himself towards self-creation and self-perfection, he attempts to make himself in the image of his previously proclaimed *Übermensch*. Even this fails, because he is still promoting an ideal that he has not yet personally attained (Conway, 1989, 8-9). Book IV presents a completely new strategy: he remains "quiet," and individuals come to him. He undertakes a more individual type of pedagogical effort with the "higher men," ultimately by hammering his own self into shape "as an example to them" and not by attempting to force a world-historical transformation of all culture. Conway claims, "In attaining the quiet ideal of self creation, he both has and has not become the *Übermensch*" (10-11).

To this insightful analysis, I would add that this turn in Nietzsche's 1885 conclusion to his masterwork really recalls a point at which he had stood long before, in *Schopenhauer as Educator*, which presents us with a humanistic ideal of self-creation through the transformative and transcending processes of culture. In that essay, the very same problematic of the powerful figure who transforms culture is probed with the same kind of ambivalence: the desire for the lightning bolt of the revolutionary genius is moderated by the realization that one can not simply and directly produce this as the result of one's own efforts, pedagogical or otherwise. The resistance of a sluggish and stupid general culture proves the great danger that jeopardizes all that the Great Individual might be able to accomplish. The parallels are striking. Just as Zarathustra both is and is not the *Übermensch*, as Conway says, so the authentic seeker is simultaneously one with and distant from Nietzsche's exemplaristic ego-transcending trinity:

> It is incontestable that we are all related and allied to the saint, just as we are related to the philosopher and artist; there are moments and as it were bright sparks of the fire of love in whose light we cease to understand the word 'I', there lies something beyond our being which at these moments moves across into it, and we are thus possessed of a heartfelt longing for bridges between here and there. It is true that, as we usually are, we can contribute nothing to the production of the man of redemption: that is why we hate ourselves as we usually are...Only when, in our present or in some future incarnation, we ourselves have been taken into that exalted order of philosophers, artists and saints, shall we also be given a new goal for our love and hate—in the meantime we have our task and our circle of duties, our hate and our love. For we know what culture is. Applied to the Schopenhauerean man, it demands that we prepare and promote his repeated production by getting to know what is inimical to it and removing it—in short that we unwearyingly combat that which would deprive us of the supreme fulfilment of our existence by preventing us from becoming such Schopenhauerean men ourselves. (1983, 161)

The image of the bridge, which here represents the desired mediation with the greatness that "lies beyond our being," can perhaps be glossed with the famous Zarathustran image for humanity itself. The longing for, the stretching out towards, ultimate "ideal" greatness ("supreme fulfillment") is in a way constitutive of our highest possible "real" greatness and therefore defines our being. Thus speaks Zarathustra:

> Man is a rope, tied between beast and overman—a rope over an abyss. A dangerous across, a dangerous on-the-way, a dangerous looking-back, a dangerous shuddering and stopping.
>
> What is great in man is that he is a bridge and not an end: what can be loved in man is that he is an *overture* and a *going under.* (1954, 126-27)

In *Schopenhauer as Educator,* we see that because we can not usually contribute a thing to the "man of redemption" and therefore hate ourselves, we need most of all to give ourselves to the project of culture and to attempt to remove what is inimical to the appearance of the ideal, just as Zarathustra attempts to counter nihilism locally. The early essay offers other correspondences to the ideas of Zarathustra. It even constitutes a *locus classicus* for some of the most fundamental assumptions of Nietzsche's exemplaristic way of thinking. A good example is a passage like the following:

> 'Mankind must work continually at the production of individual great men—that and nothing else is its task.' How much one would like to apply to society and its goal something that can be learned from observation of any species of the animal or plant world: that its only concern is the individual higher exemplar, the more uncommon, more powerful, more complex, more fruitful—how much one would like to do this if inculcated fancies as to the goal of society did not offer such tough resistance!...[W]hen a species has arrived at its limits and is about to go over into a higher species, the goal of its evolution lies, not in the mass of its exemplars and their well-being, let alone in those exemplars who happen to come last in point of time, but rather in those apparently scattered and chance existences which favourable conditions have here and there produced; and it ought to be just as easy to understand the demand that, because it can arrive at a conscious awareness of its goal, mankind ought to seek out and create the favourable conditions under which those great redemptive men can come into existence. (1983, 161-62)

So the "individual higher exemplar" that is the only concern of nature transcends all previous exemplars. This is significant, for it is this idea that makes of Nietzsche profoundly traditional and anti-traditional at the same time. We can not all become the great redemptive one, but we can all give ourselves to the work of culture. Such a work is traditional—the dangerous "looking back," mentioned by Zarathustra. But it has a dangerous forward impetus towards the transformative moment that outdoes all previous cultural ideals, making them seem relatively feckless. The young person

> should be taught to regard himself as a failed work of nature but at the same time as a witness to the grandiose and marvellous intentions of this artist: nature has done badly, he should say to himself; but I will honour its great intentions by serving it so that one day it may do better.
>
> By coming to this resolve he places himself within the circle of culture; for *culture* is the child of each individual's self-knowledge and dissatisfaction with himself. (1983, 162)

For Nietzsche, Greece is the perfect example of this paradoxical dissatisfaction-creating dynamic. We have already alluded to that passage in *The Birth of Tragedy* where Nietzsche mentions how

> Nearly every age and stage of culture has at some time or other sought with profound irritation to free itself from the Greeks, because in their presence everything one has achieved onself, though apparently quite original and sincerely admired, suddenly seemed to lose life and color and shriveled into a poor copy, even a caricature. (1967b, 93)

What then is the general task that Nietzsche finally recommends in *Schopenhauer as Educator*? It ultimately consists of (1) an inner consecration to culture; (2) an outer assessment of the external world; and (3) a struggle on behalf of culture, participating in the effort to produce "individual great men" or "geniuses" (161-77). This involves opposing a specific set of dangers: those coming from money-makers, the state, the pseudo-cultured, and finally the sciences and "men of learning." This last group Nietzsche portrays in detail (171-74) with the same obsession that can be found in his notes for *Wir Philologen* and throughout the polemical strains of his writings. No doubt, this criticism is his version of the negative task of removing what hinders the appearance of the Great Individual. Passages such as these evidence Nietzsche's overriding concern with *human authenticity and greatness*, for this concern is the motive behind his various portrayals of the counter-types of the ideal that we find in his representations of the "small person," the cultural philistine, the slave, the herd and so on, and in his portrayal of their traits: "weak" pessimism, nihilism, decadence, self-dissolving pity, flight from the real world. Nietzsche associates these qualities with what he perceives to be the dominant types of cultural existence, those of Christianity and Platonism. He gives a very substantial portion to delineating and discrediting "inauthentic" modes of life, and he finally comes to a specific recommendation for those who would join his company. The task

> will be to make the free spirits and those who suffer profoundly from our age acquainted with Schopenhauer, assemble them together and through them to engender a current capable of overcoming the ineptitude with which nature employs the philosopher...their goal...[is] to prepare the way for the reproduction of Schopenhauer, that is to say of the philosophical genius. (179)

But the opposition is so overwhelming that "all great human beings have to squander an incredible amount of energy in the course of their development merely to fight their way through this perversity in themselves." (179) Formation and self-creation are programmatically important, just as Conway demonstrates is the case for the Zarathustra of Book IV. In both situations, the work may be individual and solitary, yet it remains something that produces a beneficial effect upon others. This spiritual labor is culturally situated: the various types of "higher men" will be the audience.

What is different in the character of Zarathustra is the intensity of his feeling of distance above all the highest exemplars of self-creation. He simply can not remain with them, but must again move out on his own, like the sun, unique and above everything that exists; the old exemplars are all not good enough. As Nietzsche's distance from his early idols has increased, his independence, his own greatness has grown. In a similar way the Renaissance developed from a backward- and upward-looking veneration of classical antiquity to its own forward-looking self-possession (see Weisinger, 1973). Although in the penultimate section of Book IV, Zarathustra had said, "How well I like them now, these higher men!" (1954, 429), he finally states these sentiments:

> Well then, they still sleep, these higher men, while *I* am awake: *these* are not my proper companions. It is not for them that I wait here in my mountains. I want to go to my work, to my day: but they do not understand the signs of my morning; my stride is for them no summons to awaken. They still sleep in my cave, their dream still drinks of my drunken songs. The ear that listens for *me*, the *heedful* ear is lacking in their limbs. (1954, 437)

Of course, even here we perceive the same sensibility of the one who earlier had looked on all the highest human ideals and found them "human, all too human," seven years earlier (*Human, All Too Human*). In fact, this was the case even with Schopenhauer for Nietzsche in 1874. His admiration was not blind then, and we know he became less and less reluctant to spare even his own early hero from the arrows of dissatisfaction that he so often directed at himself.

> He bore many scars and open wounds, it is true; and he had acquired a disposition that may perhaps seem a little too astringent and sometimes also too pugnacious. But even the greatest of men cannot attain to his own ideal. That Schopenhauer can offer us a model is certain, all these scars and blemishes notwithstanding. One might say, indeed, that that in his nature which was imperfect and *all too human* brings us closer to him in a human sense, for it lets us see him as a fellow sufferer and not only in the remote heights of a genius. (1983, 143; emphasis added)

In this citation we can perhaps best see the validity of Conway's effort to assert Nietzsche's ultimate allegiance to the "quiet self-creation" of Book IV of *Zarathustra*, for here is an entirely "prescriptive, realistic, and concrete" greatness, as opposed to the "prophetic, romantic, and fabulous" variety we find in the world-historical culture-shakers (Conway, 1989, 5). The understanding that Conway proposes allows us to sense the traditional humanistic undercurrent deep in Nietzsche's consciousness, for self-development is a classical humanist theme from Socrates to Cicero to Petrarch to Goethe and von Humboldt. Once we have perceived this undercurrent, we are able to relate the two models of greatness more precisely.

Before returning to a consideration of *Schopenhauer as Educator* that will allow us to do that, we ought to notice that even the issue of the *necessity of a superabundance of energy* that is spoken of in *Schopenhauer as Educator* (cited above from section 7, 179) parallels what Conway presents as a later model of greatness in Nietzsche. At times Nietzsche speaks of human completeness as if on the lines of a "two-dimensional" Aristotelian moderation of virtues and vices, as in the famous Section 290 of *The Gay Science*. Conway believes that Nietzsche abandoned or altered this earlier ideal of self-integration soon after he drafted *The Gay Science*. Internal personal coherence is not enough to carry real greatness. Excess of creative energy is necessary. "The great human being...overflows, he uses himself up, he does not spare himself—and this is a calamitous, involuntary fatality, no less than a river's flooding the land" (1954, 548). Conway finds that the earlier plan gave way to a third dimension, that of Dionysian fulness that puts stress, storm, and the danger of self-destruction into the constitution of the Great One (5-6). This understanding helps us to see how Nietzsche's own special Dionysian humanism evolved from, yet eventually opposed traditional classicism. I would prefer to suggest that Nietzsche's model of greatness was actually more of a constant in his career, appearing even in his original presentation of the Dionysian. Though it is variously articulated at different times, it can be said to connote a dangerous fullness even from the arch-humanistic days of *The Birth of Tragedy*. In that essay, the Dionysian, by which we achieve access to an authentic experience of the ultimately real, is a boundary-dissolving, overwhelming joy that strains Apollonian measure and the harmony of the soul: "The individual, with all his restraint and proportion, succumbed to the self-oblivion of the Dionysian states, forgetting the precepts of Apollo. *Excess* [*Übermass*] revealed itself as truth." (1967b, 46)

It is clear that the spiritual power of Dionysus must be present for the greatness that tragic drama attempts to portray. In the 1886 preface to this book, when he had thematized this dimension of his own particular type of humanism more extensively, Nietzsche wrote concisely about this work: "What, then, would be the origin of tragedy? Perhaps *joy*, strength, overflowing health, overgreat fullness [*aus der Lust, aus der Kraft, aus überströmender Gesundheit, aus übergrosser Fülle*]?" (1967b, 21)

But the "cultural" Apollonian elements must be given their due for authentic greatness to emerge: the Dionysian energy is not available to human consciousness except to the extent that it is simultaneously "overcome again by [the] Apollonian power of transfiguration" (1967b, 143). Culture, *Bildung*, the humanistic domain, must be invoked and promoted. We have seen that this is a key theme in *Schopenhauer as Educator*. Despite Nietzsche's great polemics there about the insufficiencies of the present day, he tries, in the last pages, to give the reader some encouragement by focusing on various conditions that favor the development of greatness, using Schopenhauer again as the inspiring model.

Several elements helped Schopenhauer become who he was: "the proud, free, republican" father who had given him manliness and inflexibility, saving him from his "culturally pretentious mother"; the cosmopolitan outlook, free of parochial nationalism; the absence of political and academic constraints; immediate and early experience of life beyond the academy; the experience of genius both within himself and outside of himself in Goethe, from whom he learned all that makes a "strong and free human being" (that is, he had a *living* exemplar); a critical vision of all life from above ("he had seen the saint as judge of existence"); and freedom from the "petty necessities of life" (181-82). Self-development, then, requires a certain heroic independence and breadth of experience that can use, without completely capitulating to, one's immediate cultural environment.

Nietzsche demonstrates a readiness to leap beyond his own time by bringing the essay to a close with a lament for the disastrous conditions of philosophers in present-day Germany. He encourages keeping philosophy unencumbered both by the fetters of the state and even more by those of the academy with its system-builders. Clearly he too would like the "saintly" perspective for himself and for the philosopher. Shortly after lamenting the loss of the spirit of Friedrich August Wolf, of classical philological and academic fame, a man who appeared to Franz Passow "a genuinely patriotic, genuinely human spirit which, if it needed to, possessed the force to set a continent on fire and in ferment," Nietzsche proclaims

> It thus seems to me of the first importance that there should be created outside the universities a higher tribunal whose function would be to supervise and judge these institutions in regard to the education they are promoting; and as soon as philosophy departs from the universities, and therewith purifies itself of all unworthy considerations and prejudices, it must constitute precisely such a tribunal: devoid of official authority, without salaries or honours, it will know how to perform its duty free of the *Zeitgeist* and free from fear of it—in short, as Schopenhauer lived, as the judge of the so-called culture around him. (1983, 192-93)

So Nietzsche urges us towards this Schopenhauerian freedom, one that comes after one has attained the ability to decide what is truly great and what is certainly not, within and around oneself. Such a mode of being anticipates the solitary liberty that Zarathustra enjoys.

Now it is important to see that at the end of *Schopenhauer as Educator*, Nietzsche makes it clear that the struggle for culture is the way towards the great revolution. The philosopher, despite the apparent "quietness," is ultimately also a *disturber—even a destroyer—of culture.* The thinker is a truly powerful figure, "dynamite" in Nietzsche's favorite metaphor. On the very last page of the essay, he quotes Emerson on the danger of such a figure's effect: "*A new degree of culture would instantly revolutionize the entire system of human pursuits*" (193, emphasis original). A philosopher who enacts his quiet self-creation well is a fearsome event. Conway, perceiving the essential paradox in Nietzsche's thought, stresses those lines from the second book of *Zarathustra*:

> The greatest events are not our loudest but our stillest hours. Not around the inventors of new noise, but around the inventors of new values does the world revolve; it revolves *inaudibly.* (1954, 243)

> It is the stillest words that bring on the storm. Thoughts that come on doves' feet guide the world (1954, 258)

The Schopenhauerian person blends the Dionysian and the Apollonian in a way impossible for the Goethean and the Rousseauian ideals (1983, pp.146-55). The perfect coordinated intensification of these two dynamics is, as we know from *The Birth of Tragedy*, a major constitutive feature of tragic greatness. Thus Nietzsche describes his preferred ideal in terms of a tragic mode of existence:

> *The Schopenhauerean man voluntarily takes upon himself the suffering involved in being truthful,* and this suffering serves to destroy his own wilfulness and to prepare that complete overturning and conversion of his being, which it is the real meaning of life to lead up to. (1983, 152)

Goethe lacked the Dionysian "danger." Schopenhauer is willing to face the ultimate questions, to ask even the most dangerous questions about all of human culture and life—including that regarding its ultimate worth.

Now we can identify Nietzsche's solemn commitment, his engagement, his promise as he confessed it to Georg Brandes on April 10, 1888: *he dedicated himself to the task of culture even unto its own self-overcoming.* This is the "sanctity" that he wished to achieve. It follows upon the vision that ultimately places him in that higher tribunal from where he would sit in judgment over the living and the dead. But first it depends upon his commitment to his mission. Zarathustra at the beginning and at the end of Book IV claims that he is not concerned with his own happiness but with his work (1954, 349 and 439). In the opening pages he speaks of himself in an evangelical image. He is out to "catch fish" on the mountain with his own honey as a type of bait. This fourth book is about his ultimate temptation: *pity for the higher men.* This is the great temptation for Zarathustra because of the dialectical dedication to culture and to the transcendental moment that devalues all that had been representative of the highest ideals up to then. When Zarathustra refrains from pity for the higher men he can take possession of his own moment of greatness: "this is *my* morning, *my* day is breaking: *rise now, rise, thou great noon!*" (1954, 439).

Thus we see in the climactic book of *Zarathustra* (1885) the same dynamic delineated in *Schopenhauer as Educator* (1874). It does not work without a Great Individual and the cultural matrix which that individual must use and out of which that individual must leap. But along with the humanistic enjoyment and promotion of culture, the readiness to *renounce* it, to *surpass* it, to *look down* upon it, is also absolutely essential for one to be truest to the very principles of transcendence that originally brought about those previous moments of greatness. Therefore we have warrant to speak paradoxically: Nietzsche is a humanist; Nietzsche is an anti-humanist; Nietzsche is the latter *because* he is the former. Both moments are manifestations of greatness.

This double movement of affirmation and renunciation can be seen elsewhere. For example, Nietzsche clearly both loves and hates books. The literary world in a certain quite important way defines the horizon both of humanism and of Nietzsche's spiritual life. Humanism is oriented toward and based upon literature and the workings of language that enable literature's powers. It gives itself to philology, to etymology, to exegesis, to collections of commonplaces, to reading and re-reading, to criticism, and to writing. And Nietzsche possesses in abundance that whole archetypal humanistic fascination for texts. We find evidence of it in the story of his chance discovery of Schopenhauer while rummaging in a book store all the way to his deliberate and playful absorption in his own texts during his last intellectually sound year, when he entitled one section in *Ecce Homo* "Why I Write Such Good Books." But he pointedly realizes how one can lose vitality if one remains in the world of texts too long and does not master the "knowledge-drive." *Wissenschaft* is a tool of enlightenment, it is true, but sterile Alexandrianism, like sterile rationalism, threatens us with slavery and evisceration. Nietzsche's humanist spirit is one that travels through Alexandria to much broader horizons. He takes the path that Montaigne took when he suggested the value of experience over book-learning, that Petrarch took when he renounced his poetry for spiritual reasons, and that Seneca took when he portrayed the sage as one who knows literary culture but who values far more highly the superior worth of his own divinely-gifted soul.

But to return to our main point: both sides of the cultural project need to be moving forward, that work of minor greatness and that of major greatness. It is more than a little interesting that the very opening lines of Nietzsche's next and last "Untimely Meditation" (*Richard Wagner in Bayreuth*) give us a direct expression of these two moments and represent another formulation of the essential dimensions of great phenomena: "For an event to possess greatness two things must come together: greatness of spirit in those who accomplish it and greatness of spirit in those who experience it" (1983, 197). Without any "higher men" at all, the moment of greatness will pass unnoticed into complete oblivion, and that would be the most terrible loss. *The struggle for culture must go on, even to its self-overcoming:* "All great things bring about their own destruction through an act of self-overcoming: thus the law of life will have it..." (1969b, 61)

That tremendous moment that Nietzsche anticipates carries with it the realization that all previous ideals are mere "idols." The ambivalence in the dynamics of cultural greatness reverberates to the last hammerings of Nietzsche's career, especially in *Twilight of the Idols*. There he sounds out many traditional exemplars, and he finally closes his work with Goethe, himself, the ancients (especially the Greeks), Dionysus, and Zarathustra. Not long before this conclusion, he raises the same problematic that we have been discussing when he writes:

> Great men are necessary, the age in which they appear is accidental; that they almost always become masters over their age is only because they are stronger, because they are older, because for a longer time much was gathered for them. The relationship between a genius and his age is like that between strong and weak, or between old and young: the age is relatively always much younger, thinner, more immature, less assured, more childish (1954, 547-48).

Much has to be gathered for these great ones, who are "older" than their contemporaries: they are rooted in past greatness. Napoleon had just been mentioned as "the heir of a stronger, older, more ancient civilization than the one which was then perishing in France." Again, the third sentence of the preface to *Ecce Homo* shows that Nietzsche is not yet finished with his old theme, now referring directly to his own project: "But the disproportion between the greatness of my task and the *smallness* of my contemporaries has found expression in the fact that one has neither heard nor even seen me." (1969a, 217)

Nietzsche simply *must* write to avert the worst disaster: that he should remain unknown, unheard, misunderstood, misevaluated. Then his greatness would perish like a shipwreck in the sea, to use his early metaphor: "a brief, sharp echo, and all is over" (1983, 197). The very title of the *Untimely Meditations* refers to this dynamic of the discrepancies of popular, high, and transformative cultures.

Some readers may be quite uncomfortable with the "exemplaristic Nietzsche" which I have sharply highlighted here by focusing on that essay in which Nietzsche explicitly states "I profit from a philosopher only insofar as he can be an example" (1983, 136). Proponents of other interpretations might want to cite those strong words in *Ecce Homo*:

> The last thing I should promise would be to "improve" mankind. No new idols are erected by me; let the old ones learn what feet of clay mean. *Overthrowing idols* (my word for "ideals"—that comes closer to being part of my craft. (1969a, 217-18)

But I hope that what I have said allows for the better interpretation of these words: they refer to the paradoxically "anti-exemplaristic" nature of Nietzsche's exemplarism. And the nature of greatness as Nietzsche conceived it means that there can be no simple and direct project of imitation. With Nietzsche, exemplarism achieves an unparalleled self-consciousness about its own dynamics: *exemplary greatness is a means to the achievement of the learner's own unique authenticity.* But the dynamics were always there, and Nietzsche realized them early. The enemy is false culture, imitative culture that is used as a cosmetic. "The cultured man has degenerated to the greatest enemy of culture" (1983, 148-49). Nietzsche must stand against the stamp of conventionality that robs the individual of his or her individuality. He must stand against the frozen "ideal"—the idol. As "the anti-Christ[ian]" he attacks what he believes to be the greatest current one. Radical exemplarism fosters self-creation in the audience, the surpassing of any motive to be like another person and any "bad conscience" that one is as one is.

We can now reinterpret the world-historical *Übermensch* in a new light as *the living, real ideal carried even by the quiet self-creating cultural hero.* The coming "redemptive" figure is the one who brings about the necessary changes through the propulsion created by dissatisfaction, hope, and positive admiration. The presently great human being, endowed with our necessarily all-too-human heritage, must possess all of these characteristics in order to be truly great. The coming Great Self, carried as a present ideal, overcomes in the aspiring cultural genius any tendency to a petty egoism that would spoil the nobility and spiritual grandeur requisite for greatness. The two modes of greatness discussed by Conway can thus be linked.

Most significantly, Nietzsche uses this idea of the coming *Übermensch* who transcends all ideals as a way of surpassing the previous exemplars of the past, each of which has turned out to be disappointing in some way. Not only is there a strongly intentional gradient towards the future that guarantees the end of the self-complacency that Nietzsche found intolerable among some of the Hegelians, but there is an increased vitality that dervies from the anticipated meaning inherent in the coming Great Individual. Such a perspective reminds one of Nietzsche's own early educational enthusiasm about being involved in the formation of great individuals. And yet Nietzsche stresses that there is a distinctiveness about his ideal:

> The word "overman," as the designation of a type of supreme achievement, as opposed to "modern" men, to "good" men, to Christians and other nihilists—a word in the mouth of a Zarathustra, the annihilator of morality, becomes a very pensive word—has been understood almost everywhere with the utmost innocence in the sense of those values whose opposite Zarathustra was meant to represent—that is, as an "idealistic" type of a higher kind of man, half "saint," half "genius." (1969a, 261).

The *Übermensch* is indeed a telos, an end, a "supreme achievement," and therefore of a different order from all previous ideal figures. In *Ecce Homo* Nietzsche stresses the terrible, destructive nature of his hero, and his hero's joy in destruction, hardness, awesomeness. He makes him the ultimate "earth-shaker," and, of course identifies himself with him: "—I am, in Greek, and not only in Greek, the *Antichrist*" (1969a, 263). The Greek prefix *anti* does not merely designate opposition, but it can also mean "in place of." Nietzsche as *Übermensch* assumes the place of the redeemer, dissolving ideals by assuming the throne himself, by becoming the sun in his own solar system. Such a singular position is necessarily different from any conventional ideals that keep an individual centered upon some other reality.

The necessary relativization, devaluation, and elimination of all other ideals gives Nietzsche's ultimate ideal a radically destructive edge. As we have seen in our reading of *Schopenhauer as Educator*, it implies a humanistic anti-humanism, an indifference and renunciation that is surprisingly brought about by (and for the sake of) a genuine affirmation of humanity. The end of the second essay of *On the Genealogy of Morals*, published two years after Zarathustra's turn to quiet self-creation, portrays this dynamic in a symphonically eloquent reprise, a few fragments of which I give here:

> "What are you really doing, erecting an ideal or knocking one down?" I may perhaps be asked. But have you ever asked yourselves sufficiently how much the erection of every ideal on earth has cost?...If a temple is to be erected *a temple must be destroyed*: that is the law—let anyone who can show me a case in which it is not fulfilled! (1969b, 95)

So Nietzsche's unique ideal only follows an ancient law and eternal necessity! He continues a bit later, referring to the solemn task of self-creation:

> What gives greater offense, what separates oneself more fundamentally, than to reveal something of the severity and respect with which one treats oneself?...
>
> The attainment of this goal would require a *different* kind of spirit from that likely to appear in this present age: spirits strengthened by war and victory, for whom conquest, adventure, danger and even pain have become needs; it would require habituation to the keen air of the heights, to winter journeys, to ice and mountains in every sense; it would require even a kind of sublime wickedness, an ultimate, supremely self-confident mischievousness in knowledge that goes with great health; it would require, in brief and alas, precisely this *great health*!
>
> Is this even possible today?...But some day, in a stronger age...he must yet come to us, the *redeeming* man of great love and contempt.... This man of the future, who will redeem us not only from the hitherto reigning ideal but also from that which was bound to grow out of it, the great nausea, the will to nothingness, nihilism; this bell-stroke of noon and of the great decision that liberates the will again and restores its goal to the earth and his hope to man; this Anti-christ and antinihilist; this victor over God and nothingness—*he must come one day*. (1969b, 95-96)

Interrupting this fitful messianic reverie, Nietzsche immediately closes the essay with the claim that he is on the verge of "usurp[ing] that to which only one younger, 'heavier with future,' and stronger than I has a right—that to which only *Zarathustra* has a right, *Zarathustra the godless.*—" Here Nietzsche, the Great Individual, carries his own ideal as something that is somehow both part of and yet separate from his all-too-traditional self. In that way he attains the greatness that is possible for him in his moment: herald the new age, arouse the coming *Übermensch* by portraying him in this heroic fashion.

For the sake of an affirmation of this world, for a yea-saying of the type we cannot dissociate from the humanistic tradition, Nietzsche has launched this negative crusade against those culture builders that he portrays as nihilists. We can rightly ask whether Nietzsche wisely puts so much into jeopardy by swinging his ax energetically at the roots of the tree. But a closer look reveals that there is more pruning than uprooting, for more than a mere echo of the traditional world of humanist values comes through in the last few sentences of *Ecce Homo*, where Nietzsche's outburst against false moral ideals reaches a climax. This ideal, he rages

> is fabricated from the contradiction against the proud and well-turned-out [*wohlgeratenen*] human being who says Yes, who is sure of the future, who guarantees the future—and he is now called *evil*.—And all this was believed, as *morality*!—*Ecrasez l'infâme*!— (1969a, 335)

Not only do we hear the Voltairean voice of the assumed "higher civilization," but we see Nietzsche's ideal described in an archetypally humanistic way; that is, it is expressed in terms of a whole, balanced, self-assured personality by means of the phrase "the proud and well-turned-out human being." This very ideal is described at greater length early in *Ecce Homo,* in a passage carrying unmistakeably humanistic accents. We can even sense that Aristotle's Great-Souled Man is not far behind such a description:

> What is it, fundamentally, that allows us to recognize *who has turned out well*? That a well-turned-out person pleases our senses, that he is carved from wood that is hard, delicate, and at the same time smells good. He has a taste only for what is good for him; his pleasure, his delight cease where the measure of what is good for him is transgressed. He guesses what remedies avail against what is harmful; he exploits bad accidents to his advantage; what does not kill him makes him stronger. Instinctively, he collects from everything he sees, hears, lives through, *his* sum: he is a principle of selection, he discards much. He is always in his own company, whether he associates with books, human beings, or landscapes: he honors by *choosing*, by *admitting*, by *trusting*. He reacts slowly to all kinds of stimuli, with that slowness which long caution and deliberate pride have bred in him: he is far from meeting it halfway. He believes neither in "misfortune" nor in "guilt": he comes to terms with himself, with others; he knows how to *forget*—he is strong enough; hence everything *must* turn out for his best.
>
> Well then, I am the *opposite* of a decadent, for I have just described *myself*. (1969a, 224-25)

Once again, Nietzsche himself has told us, quite directly, something about the ideal he cherishes. It is an ideal that still significantly echoes the humanistic tradition despite a plea for that utter radicality, the "victory over God and nothingness." What postpones any easy dismissal of the Great Individual's apparently megalomaniacal self-absorption is also another humanistic motif, the idea that the *Übermensch*, even in the "quiet" mode, is still involved in some kind of redemptive work of universal relevance. It is quite clear that Nietzsche felt himself to be on such a mission on behalf of humanity, and that this destiny drew him on. The Great Self, as the central sun, still shines on the planets and gives them a course to follow. How this whole problematic of greatness, human purpose, and the intensely self-present enjoyment of life gets articulated in the humanistic tradition can be exemplified by the following passage from Petrarch's *Secret*, which gives a central place to the issue of world-weary melancholy (with which we might compare Nietzsche's struggles with nihilism):

> Augustine:...As for that complaint you have brought forward of never having lived a life of your own, what it really amounts to is not that you have lived in poverty, but more or less in subservience. I admit, as you say, that it is a thing very troublesome. However, if you look around you will find very few men who have lived a life of their own. Those whom one counts most happy, and for whom numbers of others live their lives, bear witness by the constancy of their vigils and their toils that they themselves are living for others. To quote you a striking instance, Julius Caesar, of whom some one has reported this true but arrogant saying, "The human race only lives for a small number," Julius Caesar, after he had subdued the human race to live for himself alone, did himself live for other people. (Petrarch, 1978, 94-95)

Though we can not equate the positions of Nietzsche and Petrarch's Augustine, we can still sense similarity of the intellectual and spiritual terrain. Ultimately, the project of self-affirmation deeply concerns the two thinkers, who both also at the same maintain an idea of some kind of transcendent reality for the sake of which the authentic person is ready to give his or her very life.

The Zarathustran words cited at the end of the preface to *Ecce Homo* make the point about self-affirmation and the simultaneous *return* of an ideal in a way that begins to bring to light Nietzsche's ultimate positive teaching:

> You had not yet sought yourselves; and you found me. Thus do all believers; therefore all faith amounts to so little. Now I bid you lose me and find yourselves; and only *when you have all denied me* will I return to you. (1969a, 220)

In fact the issue of finding oneself is nothing less than the *leading issue in Schopenhauer as Educator*. The first words of that work declare the difficulty that most people have in achieving their own distinct, authentic individuality (127). The teacher Nietzsche sought as a youth would put him in touch with this level of his own being, would educate him to be himself (130-36). The exemplar was needed as the pedagogical path to this self-realization. In a way, then, Nietzsche *begins* as well as *ends* beyond the exemplar. He never set out to find a hero for that hero's sake.

Zarathustra is thus fittingly subtitled *A Book for All and None*. The hero is the *ultimate educator* who wants disciples who are not disciples, but authentic individuals. Everyone is involved, as we shall see later, yet the greatness of each makes such a book and such a hero entirely dispensible. The educational persona is remarkably intact and operative, with Nietzsche even verbally linking his Zarathustra to the exemplary educational mastery he praises in *Schopenhauer as Educator*. The wordplay is highly suggestive when we recall that the German title for this essay is *Schopenhauer als ERZIEHER*:

> For *that* is what I am through and through: reeling, reeling in, raising up, raising, a raiser, cultivator, and disciplinarian, who once counseled himself, not for nothing: Become who you are!
>
> *Der nämlich bin ich von Grund und Anbeginn, ziehend, heranziehend, hinaufziehend, aufziehend, ein Zieher, Züchter, und Zuchtmeister, der sich nicht umsonst einstmals zusprach: "Werde, der du bist!"* (1954, 351)

Nietzsche's self-concept as an educator of a very high order does not ever leave him. Even in *Ecce Homo*, Nietzsche took special pride in *Schopenhauer as Educator* and *Richard Wagner in Bayreuth*, claiming

> What I was fundamentally trying to do in these essays was something altogether different from psychology: an unequaled problem of education, a new concept of self-discipline, self-defense to the point of hardness, a way to greatness and world-historical tasks as seeking its first expression. (1969a, 280)

That is to say, "What I have been doing most recently, I tried for the first time in these works." But the aspect I wish to highlight here is especially that solemn command at the end of the Zarathustran citation: "Become who you are!" The way to greatness that Nietzsche wishes to teach necessarily involves the task of self-creation and self-becoming beyond all imitation. "Become who you are"—as if to imply, "—and have no idols before yourself."

This supreme commandment occurs in his early, middle, and late periods, and it is always pregnant with a special significance. It was his epigraph to the 1867 essay on Diogenes Laertius (see 1969c, 29-32), but its special, intimate meaning can be guessed from the words he wrote to Erwin Rohde on November 3, 1867. Recalling earlier, happier times, Nietzsche thought about

> [O]ur memorial on the banks of that Leipzig river, which we christened Nirvana, and which bears the solemn words from me, which I have proved victorious: *genoi hoios essi.*
>
> If, finally, I apply these words to you, dear friend, let them contain the best my heart feels for you. Who knows when changeful fate will bring our paths together again; may it be very soon; but whenever it may happen, I shall look back with joy and pride to a time when I gained a friend *hoios essi.* (1969c, 28)

Another occurrence is found in the important Section 335 of *The Gay Science*: "We, however, *want to become those we are*—human beings who are new, unique, incomparable, who give themselves laws, who create themselves." (1974, 266) There immediately follows an echo of *Schopenhauer as Educator*'s idea of the close connection of the efforts of nature and human greatness, in the context of another educational image: "To that end we must become the best learners and discoverers of everything that is lawful and necessary in the world: we must become *physicists* in order to be able to be *creators* in this sense....." (266) Earlier, a maxim had pronounced the content of what Nietzsche's inner voice had commanded: "*What does your conscience say?*— 'You shall become the person you are.'" (219)

The great imperative flickers across the title page of *Ecce Homo*, where we find a subtitle that reads, "How One Becomes What One Is." In that work, the idea is discussed especially in Section 9 of "Why I Am So Clever" (1969a, 253-55). Most importantly, Nietzsche urges: avoid false posturing and do not subordinate yourself to unworthy secondary goals. Great things have an easiness, a fatedness about them. It is most interesting that this very section ends with a return to

Nietzsche's early philological days, to his memories of his first professional essay (the very one that bore the oracular imperative as its motto), and to his revered mentor Ritschl ("the only scholar of genius on whom I have laid eyes to this day"). In the next section, he resumes his discussion of false ideals, poses, heroes, and he ends with a pointed statement of the *Grundthema* we have identified:

> My formula for greatness in a human being is *amor fati*: that one wants nothing to be different, not forward, not backward, not in all eternity. Not merely bear what is necessary, still less conceal it—all idealism is mendaciousness in the face of what is necessary—but *love* it. (1969a, 258)

Ultimately the issue of greatness is one with the tenor of his central teaching. As he explicitly stated in *Schopenhauer as Educator*, "[B]eing great...means, in [the Great Individual's] case, being free and entirely himself" (1983, 145).

What, then, does Nietzsche's perduring attachment to his great imperative tell us? To understand the motto's significance we must first be aware that Nietzsche discovered it in the course of his classical studies, in Pindar's second Pythian Ode. Then we must realize the far-reaching significance that these words carry. In the opinion of a leading authority on classical Greek culture, *the imperative represents the essential commandment of Greek humanism* (Jaeger, 1953, 19). The center of Nietzsche's spirit and the center of Greek humanism can thus be said to coincide at this classical commonplace. This suggests that Nietzsche is at one with the classical humanist tradition in a deeply personal way. His ideas of the naturalistic bases for human greatness and of the "fatedness" of human existence serve only to underscore this close affiliation, insofar as Greece has long been associated with "naturalism" and its thematization of fate.

Once again, however, we can not go far without paradox. In the very pages of *Ecce Homo* that we have just discussed, Nietzsche forcefully sets himself against heroicism, proclaiming "I am the opposite of a heroic nature" (1969a, 255), and he counsels an apparently antihumanistic "self-forgetting" (254). Because the ethos of Greek culture might best be described as fundamentally "heroic," and because humanism has been profoundly committed to the project of human selfunderstanding, we must once again alert ourselves to the distinctively Nietzschean somersault here if we wish to understand him well. He is indeed "anti-heroic" to the extent that he despised the Romantic subservience to heroes (cf. Wagnerian *Helden* of the opera, Goethe's striving Faust; see 1969a, 255, note 6). Blaming Napoleon as the possible cause, Nietzsche railed against his century's habit of "prostration before the 'genius' and 'hero.'" He sadly noted that "even a Byron was not ashamed to say that he was a 'worm compared with such a being'" (cited in Thatcher, 1974, 149-50). As we saw in his reflections on Schopenhauer, greatness involves not submitting oneself in a certain way, but rather finding oneself. Using exemplars is necessary, but only the right type of use is acceptable, one that would be opposed to what might be called a "heroicist" use, in the way that "classic" style stands over against "classicist" or "classicizing" style. The hero is self-possessed at a deep level, somehow beyond all struggle because given greatness by fate. Thus, Nietzsche's anti-heroicist heroics parallels his anti-humanistic humanism. The self-knowledge that Nietzsche eschews is merely that absorption in one's own persona as a great individual that gives an artificiality to one's consciousness and debases one's achievements. It is clear from elsewhere that he is actually quite actively involved in a quest for self-knowledge, especially through psychological observation. The theme recurs explicitly; he has woven it into the fabric of his larger cultural programme, as we can see in this early expression of a foundational Nietzschean assumption:

> Greek antiquity provides the classical set of examples for the interpretation of our entire culture and its development. It is a means *for understanding ourselves*, a means for regulating our age—and thereby a means for overcoming it. (1979, 127)

Another notable occurrence of the theme is the opening section of the preface to *On the Genealogy of Morals*: "We are unknown to ourselves, we men of knowledge—and with good reason. We have never sought ourselves—how could it happen that we should ever *find* ourselves?" (1969b, 15)

Nietzsche's criticism of the cultural leaders of his time constitutes a relentless attempt to provoke a self-knowledge that will effect a conversion, or we might say, a revaluation of the primary values. These probings indicate that his direction in this matter follows that of Western humanism, the "primary goal" of whose inquiry was "the achievement of...psychological and cultural self-awareness" (Grudin, 1987, 731). An yet Nietzsche still knows that a self-forgetting is an important part of real self-possession.

Such a paradox shows itself in that core doctrine of self-becoming: to become who we are means that we must accept the fact that our self is as much fated as it is achieved. We already have that for which we are striving. What then to do? "Act" or "be yourself"? It turns out, however, that this "contradiction" is perfectly intelligible in light of the essential inner dynamism of Greek humanism. Moses Hadas captured its core concisely when he says that by the Greek norm, "man is not master of his fate," but "he is in the fullest sense captain of his soul, with every incentive to steer it to the highest reaches of excellence" (Hadas, 1972, 54). The leading heroes of the great epics are perfect expressions of this idea. Achilles and Odysseus are both "fated" to certain ends, but both are also agents whose potency cannot be denied. There is this tension in the humanist tradition: we must use our faculties to the fullest extent possible to become "who we are," even though we must simultaneously realize that even the greatest must fall in the end and that we depend upon what we are given. Our greatness is only "relatively absolute."

Thus there is both an eternal optimism and a pervasive melancholy in the humanist tradition—a problematic notably thematized in both Nietzsche and Greek thought through tragedy and through reflection on tragic consciousness. Melancholy is in fact a long-standing topos in Greek literature and Greek studies. William Chase Greene explicity treats this theme poses a telling question: "Why is it, we may ask, that the Greeks, on the whole a healthy, cheerful, successful people, were nevertheless constantly visited by melancholy?" (1968, 3). Nietzsche dealt with this subject as early as *The Birth of Tragedy*, which he retrospectively renamed *Hellenism and Pessimism* (1969a, 270; see also the 1886 preface to *The Birth of Tragedy*, 1967b, 17-18). Its first title had actually been *Griechische Heiterkeit* (*Greek Cheerfulness*). Nietzsche even claims that this classical pessimism, fundamentally opposed to the attitude cultivated by some later strains of Romanticism, *is distinctively characteristic of himself.* Notice also in the following citation the typical ambivalence towards traditional humanist terminology—along with the profession of faith in its substance:

> That there still *could* be an altogether different kind of pessimism, a classical type—this premonition and vision belongs to me as inseparable from me, as my *proprium* and *ipsissimum*; only the word "classical" offends my ears, it is far too trite and has become round and indistinct. I call this pessimism of the future—for it comes! I see it coming!—*Dionysian* pessimism. (1974, 330-31)

Of course the other side of the complex is also thematized in Nietzsche: the very title, *The Gay Science*, is enough to indicate that. The opening section of Book V, entitled "*The meaning of our cheerfulness*," gives more particular elucidation (279-80).

What we are happening upon here, in the midst of our discussion of self-becoming, is a crucial affective-thematic complex that runs all through Nietzsche's works and joins him closely with the long history of Western humanists' psychological probings after self-knowledge and self-understanding. This tradition expresses and often dwells upon the same bipolar emotional and psychological range that absorbed Nietzsche. We have already mentioned Petrarch and *acedia*, but we could go back towards the famous Homeric and Vergilian manifestations of melancholy or forward toward the English Renaissance best-seller by Robert Burton, *The Anatomy of Melancholy* (first edition, 1621). Long before Burton's book appeared, the Italian Renaissance hero Marsilio Ficino had revived an Aristotelian understanding of the heavy Saturnine temperament in his *De Vita Triplicis* (1482-1489). This complex merges with Nietzsche's *Grundthema* of human greatness, insofar as both the Aristotelian tradition and Ficino closely connected melancholy with genius, and with madness as well. At the peak of the Renaissance "a veritable wave of 'melancholic behavior' swept across Europe...Many great artists...were described as melancholic, among them Dürer, Raphael, and Michelangelo" (Wittowker, 1973).

In Nietzsche's writings, we find a wide range of related terms and their opposites: melancholy, pessimism, nihilism, nausea, decadence, etc. as opposed to health, life, *amor fati*, optimism, cheerfulness, laughter. We tend to hear more of Nietzsche and these other terms than of Nietzsche and melancholy, but it is clearly a major part of his explicit reflection and a noticeable feature of his psychology as well. In 1872, he penned an intricate ode "To Melancholy," which is easily related to the Dionysian complex of *The Birth of Tragedy*: the poet thirsts for "life, life, life" (Grundlehner, 1986, especially 50-62). Even in his *Einleitung*, Nietzsche added a sentence, in the context of a reference to slavery and to contemporary socialism, "*Gewisse traurige Thatsachen liegen im Wesen der Dinge*" ("Certain sad realities lie at the heart of things," [Nietzsche, 1910, 335]), an echo of the *locus classicus* of Vergilian melancholy, "*Sunt lacrimae rerum.*" Most readers of Nietzsche can not avoid seeing how he is most attentive to the issues connected with extremes of the human spiritual disposition: despair or exuberance, life-affirmation or life-denial. It is in fact the very leap from the former to the latter that is existentially at issue—*even the very motive for*—Nietzsche's turn to remembering Schopenhauer in *Schopenhauer as Educator.* Here the themes of self-possession and educators appear again:

> Certainly there may be other means of finding oneself, of coming to oneself out of the bewilderment in which one usually wanders as in a dark cloud, but I know of none better than to think on one's true educators. And so today I shall remember one of the teachers and task-masters of whom I can boast, *Arthur Schopenhauer*—and later on I shall recall others. (1983, 130)

"Coming to oneself" is opposed to wandering "as in a dark cloud."

A similar emotional problematic is at issue in Nietzsche's desire to work out a "gay science" and also in an especially striking way at the opening of *Twilight of the Idols*:

> Maintaining cheerfulness in the midst of a gloomy affair, fraught with immeasurable responsibility, is no small feat; and yet what is needed more than cheerfulness? Nothing succeeds if prankishness has no part in it. Excess of strength alone is the proof of strength.
>
> A revaluation of all values, this question mark, so black, so tremendous that it casts shadow upon the man who puts it down—such a destiny of a task compels one to run into the sun every moment to shake off a heavy, all-too-heavy seriousness. (1954, 465)

It is the weightiness of the mission, the seriousness with which Nietzsche takes human destiny, that makes gloominess a threat. Prankishness and cheer are here tied directly to excess, a hallmark of that fundamental Nietzschean category, the Dionysian. But though this connection may make the phenomenon seem quite distinctive, there is a history and a larger structure that lies behind this complex of themes. We could perhaps develop a "dispositional-thematic argument" for Nietzsche's humanistic persona: a certain kind of self-conscious focus on the emotional tonality of the spirit, as expressive of a total attitude toward life and of the existential quality of the thinker's orientations, characterized Nietzsche's awareness, and this spiritual state of being became an important explicit element in his reflection as it had in fact been in the works of many of his humanist predecessors. The humanist orientation implies a reflective self-presence that makes relevant the whole range of affectivity that is evoked by that attention. Thus there emerges a kind of reflection that rarely appears in books on metaphysics and epistemology.

If we look to the historical background of this complex, we can indeed point to one particular passage that impacted the the larger tradition and that, because of its classical provenance, probably had a direct impact on Nietzsche as well. It was also used by Montaigne in the tradition of Ficino (Screech, 1983, especially 22-36). We find it at the start of the thirtieth book of the Aristotelian *Problemata,* which asks: "Why is it that all men who are outstanding in philosophy, politics, poetry, or the arts are melancholic...?" (Aristotle, 1937, Volume 2, 155; translation slightly altered). This passage goes on to express several themes of special interest to Nietzsche: great figures who suffer; isolation; desert-existence; somatic phenomena of health and disease with special reference to sexuality and explicit mention of Dionysus and sexuality's "spiritual" or "breath-filled" dimension (cf. 1954, 561-562); suicide; madness; and epilepsy. The first example of extreme melancholy given is Herakles, who seems to have had so much black bile that he suffered somatic disturbances related to this humour, epileptic syndromes that were later named "the sacred disease" in his honor. Ajax went insane. Bellerophon became a hermit and drifter, craving solitude in the wilderness. "And many other heroes suffered in the same way as these. In later times also there have been Empedocles, Plato, Socrates, and many other well-known men. The same is true of most of those who handled poetry." This list is very interesting, for these three figures were important ones for Nietzsche. He recalls in *Schopenhauer as Educator* how the gloomy philosopher gives to the ultimate question about the value of life, the "answer of Empedocles" (1983, 146).

One of Nietzsche's reflections combines the themes of self-possession and melancholy. It is especially intriguing in connection with the Aristotelian mention of epilepsy.

> '*Flight from oneself*.—Those men given to intellectual spasms—Byron and Alfred de Musset are examples—who are impatient and gloomily inclined towards themselves and in all they do resemble rampaging horses, and who derive from their own works, indeed, only a short-lived fire and joy which almost bursts their veins and then a desolation and sourness made more wintry by the contrast it presents—how should such men endure to remain within *themselves*! They long to dissolve into something '*outside*'; if one is a Christian and is possessed by such a longing one's goal is to be dissoved into God, to 'become wholly at one with him'; if one is Shakespeare one is satisfied only with being dissolved into images of the most passionate life; if one is Byron one longs for *action*, because action draws us away from ourself even more than do thoughts, feelings or works. And so could all impulse to action

perhaps be at bottom flight from oneself?—Pascal would ask. And the proposition might indeed be demonstrated in the case of the supreme examples known to us of the impulse to action: for consider—in the light of the experience of psychiatry, as is only proper—that four of the most active men of all time were epileptics (namely Alexander, Caesar, Mohammed and Napoleon), just as Byron was also subject to this complaint. (1982, 550)

In this absorption in the themes of melancholy and euphoria that is so notable in Nietzsche and in the humanistic tradition, we see the affective manifestation of not only that tragic humanist duality that Moses Hadas has directly described, but also that classical humanist concern with the "positioning" of the human being above animals and below the gods. This theme may appear even in the obscure Pindaric passage following that famous injunction to self-becoming that Nietzsche adopted as a motto. Those lines speak of how children may call an ape "pretty," implying that mature men and women will know the far superior attractiveness of authentic humanity and render more suitable judgments. Rhadamanthos is the preferred model for a mature integrity, which is what is truly lovely:

> Be what you are, the man whose worth you have heard.
> In the eyes of a child an ape is lovely,
> Always lovely. But the best blessing came to Rhadamanthus, who
> was given the fruit
> Of mind that knows no wrong, who takes no pleasure
> Within his heart in false deceits...(Pindar, 1972, Pythian II, 94)

The thematic complex of animality, humanity, and superhumanity ("the best blessing"), and the issue of rising rather than falling on the "Chain of Being," as it were, is especially evident in some of Nietzsche's famous Zarathustran exhortations, but it appears in his intimate writings as well. An interesting passage from his correspondence explicitly connects this issue with the theme of melancholy:

I have often wondered whether happiness for human beings is the most worthy of our striving. In that case the dim-wit would really be the most beautiful representative of humanity, and our hero of the spirit, "so truly is thinking grief" at least for fools, of the species of degenerate apes or demi-gods, and the latter would truly be the worse lot. Our natural scientists prefer to derive us from apes and annul everything that is trans-animal [*überthierisch*] as unlogical. And, by Zeus, better apes than unlogical. Look at every direction of science, of art: the ape shows itself magnificently in our time, but where is God? A

> person might not even be melancholy, if Byron should not cut us a great monkey-grimace.—I should not even answer your letter in this base way, if I wanted to be not exactly an ape or could be something other. (Cited in Thatcher, 1974, 142; translation mine.)

His interest in this dilemma of being caught between lower and higher modes of life, in each of which we necessarily participate, and the choice for the "trans-animal" that Nietzsche ultimately makes, without denying the continuing presence of a deeply-rooted animality, mark him as one who is vitally involved with the humanist concern for human development and "realization." Becoming who we are ultimately demands some such understanding of the "in-betweenness" of our existence, some submission to the tensions and sorrows as well as joys involved, and some resolute choice for the "transcending" path, which leads toward human authenticity. Whatever resonances and complex thematic interrelationships we may discover here, it is easy to affirm that Nietzsche's central positive teaching of self-becoming is at one with a very powerful current in the classical humanist tradition.

We can now return to he larger view and mark out with a new formulation the broad horizons of Nietzsche's achievement. It covers a great deal to say that he thought and felt and wrote with the orientation of the Enlightenment that was heir to the Renaissance, and drawing his inspiration from the spirit of the Greeks of the Tragic Age as he could best reconstitute it. But his eyes were not on such figures and times alone. He also labored to re-invigorate German culture with a proud, ur-Romantic spirit. And yet this also fails to define the arena he chose. He is more than *philosophe*, more than Hellenist, and certainly much more than nationalist, despite all his passionate hope for Germany. In fact he had a positive desire not to be limited to these spheres: he speaks of overcoming even the Greeks and Goethe. His scorn for what he found to be German pretensions can not be missed. The clue to his real "working horizon" is given by his telos and *Grundthema* (human greatness), his core doctrine (human self-becoming), and his most vividly perceived spiritual arena (the existential problem of the value and meaning of human life). All of these help to constitute that intellectual-affective orientation that virtually defines humanism: *concern for humanity as a whole.* The ubiquity, the depth of this concern in his writings characterizes Nietzsche as quintessentially humanist.

A few citations will suggest how this *urhumanistische* mentality must be part of any adequate description of his aims. Once again, not merely the substance or the variety of expression or the repetition of the idea, but the strong affect that attaches to these passages, deserves attention. Early on, Nietzsche wrestles with the problem of what makes humanity, in "Homer's Contest" (1872), where we see how he posits the element of nature as distinctly present and vital for any adequate image of it:

> When one speaks of "humanity" the notion lies at the bottom, that humanity is that which *separates* and distinguishes us from Nature. But such a distinction does not in reality exist.... Man in his highest and noblest capacities *is* Nature and bears in himself her awful twofold character. His abilities generally considered dreadful and inhuman are perhaps indeed the fertile soil, out of which alone can grow forth all humanity in emotions, actions, and works.
>
> Thus the Greeks, the most humane of men of ancient times, have in themselves a trait of cruelty, of tiger-like pleasure in destruction... (1964c, 51)

We can here sense some of the important background to his strenuously anti-Christian formulations of the second essay of *On the Genealogy of Morals*, which keep the fundamental question of "true humanity" in the spotlight, as Nietzsche holds tight to his ultimate value of "human greatness." Notice again the humanistic concern for the "healthy," self-affirming, "well-constituted" human being:

> The more normal sickliness becomes among men...the higher should be the honor accorded the rare cases of great power of soul and body, man's *lucky hits*; the more we should protect the well-constituted from the worse kind of air, the air of the sickroom...
>
> Broadly speaking, it is not fear of man that we should desire to see diminished; for the fear compels the strong to be strong, and occasionally terrible—it *maintains* the well-constituted type of man. What is to be feared, what has a more calamitous effect than any other calamity, is that man should inspire not profound fear but profound *nausea*; also not great fear but great *pity*.
>
> But no greater or more calamitous misunderstanding is possible than for the happy, well-constituted, powerful in soul and body, to begin to doubt their *right to happiness* in this fashion...[n]o worse misunderstanding and denial of *their* task can be imagined: the higher *ought* not to degrade itself to the status of an instrument of the lower, the pathos of distance *ought* to keep their tasks eternally separate!...
>
> [Let us] guard ourselves, my friends, against the two worst contagions that may be reserved just for us—against the *great nausea at man*! against *great pity for man*! (1969b, 121;122;124-25)

Keep your eyes on "health." Revere humanity at its most vital. The point is not to be callous and indifferent to sickness because cruelty feels good, but rather to help sick humanity by maintaining a clear, self-confident image of health. It is about believing that humankind has a substantial power despite its weaknesses. Nietzsche leaves the door wide open for hubris of the worse kind with such rhetoric, especially for inattentive readers. But ultimately he acts as a cultural healer who is convinced that he needs to administer the strongest physic that he can concoct. It is a medicine that, used irresponsibly, could well result in spiritual death. But he is undertaking what he believes to be a last resort to save the human spirit from utter trivialization.

The first essay of the *Genealogy* contains similar sentiments, again with a noticeably humanistic phraseology and orientation. After complaining about the insufferability of the "ill-constituted soul," Nietzsche expresses a deep hope:

> But grant me from time to time—if there are divine goddesses in the realm beyond good and evil—grant me the sight, but one glance of something perfect, wholly achieved, happy, mighty, triumphant, something still capable of arousing fear! Of a man who justifies *man*, of a complementary and redeeming lucky hit on the part of man for the sake of which one may still *believe in man*!...
>
> Here precisely is what has become a fatality for Europe—together with the fear of man we have also lost our love of him, our reverence for him, our hopes for him, even the will to him. The sight of man now makes us weary—what is nihilism today if it is not *that*?—We are weary *of man*. (1969b, 44)

Nietzsche's consciousness of a mission to a sickly humanity grew unceasingly in his late period. He laments the stupidity of Germany at just the time he is working out his ambitious programme:

> There was never a more important moment in history—*but who knows a thing about it*? The disproportion here is altogether necessary; at a time when an undreamed-of loftiness and freedom of intellectual passion is laying hold of the *highest* problem of humanity and is calling for a decision as to human destiny, the general pettiness and obtuseness must become all the more sharply distinct from it. There is no "hostility" to me whatever—people are simply deaf to anything I say... (1969c, 315)

Another indication of the scope of his project comes from a letter of December 1888 to his sister:

> I play with the burden which would crush any other mortal...For what I have to do is *terrible*, in any sense of the word; I do not challenge individuals—I am challenging humanity as a whole with my terrible accusation... (1969c, 340)

He soon goes on to ask his sister to see "a real humanity" in this letter to her. Zarathustra, of course, meditates upon, and teaches pointedly about humanity itself. He leaves his isolation because "I love man" (1954, 123). His first words to the public are "*I teach you the overman.* Man is something that shall be overcome...Man is the meaning of the earth" (1954, 124; 125). At the climax of the key section in *Twilight of the Idols*, "How the 'True World' Finally Became a Fable," Nietzsche describes the moment of fulfillment as "Noon; moment of the briefest shadow; end of the longest error; high point of humanity; INCIPIT ZARATHUSTRA" (1954, 486). Recalling *The Birth of Tragedy* in *Ecce Homo*, Nietzsche states

> A tremendous hope speaks out of this essay...Let us look ahead a century; let us suppose that my attempt to assassinate two millennia of antinature and desecration of man were to succeed. That new part of life which would tackle the greatest of all tasks, the attempt to raise humanity higher...I promise a tragic age: the highest art in saying Yes to life, tragedy, will be reborn when humanity has weathered the consciousness of the hardest but most necessary wars *without suffering from it.* (1969a, 274)

Even as he bears his fangs, he speaks of "raising humanity higher"! All his many negative moments exist because he has such hope for a deeper and richer human existence, despite his keen awareness of the frailties of our condition. In all of these moments, we see again that tense dynamic set forth clearly in *Schopenhauer as Educator*: dissatisfaction with one's petty ego and admiration for the Great Self that we are called to become or to prepare a way for.

Nietzsche is indeed obsessed with *humanity*, the essential theme and horizon and foundation of humanism. He is always speaking *about* humanity *to* humanity. And this horizon helps to define more exactly his special mission, the *Vergrösserung* of human existence. That he had long held a similar interpretation of his chief concern he indicated in a very early note. Some words he jotted into his notebook make it quite clear how he thought of the very apex of his prospective career:

> *Plans for Life*
> *Unmodern Considerations.* For my thirties.
> *The Greeks.* For the years between forty and fifty.
> *Discourses on Humanity.* For my fifties. (1973, 5[42])

Nietzsche did not attain his fifties as a thinker, but before he stopped writing he had accomplished a good number of his "discourses on humanity." He had at last become the humanist that he had always been.

6
Nietzsche the Terrible

The humanist movement of the Italian Renaissance gave a distinctive pre-eminence to that curricular domain known as *rhetorica* (see Bouwsma, 1973, 8-9). As cultural institutions and social values shifted with changing times, not scholastic logic but grammar and rhetoric seemed to offer the most promising direction for personal and professional maturity. This emphasis on the arts of communication happened to echo the very higher educational practices of the cultures by which the humanists were most inspired. Rhetorical ambitions and cultural ideals carried and then progressively strengthened each other, producing, in a single movement, both a deeper classicism and a more sharply self-aware modernism.

Classical antiquity had established an essentially oratorical *paideia* that stretched from the the First (5th century B.C.) to the Second Sophistic (2nd century B.C.). The old program never completely disappeared, even in the scholastic era. In fact, it continued to shape much of European education for the next two millenia. Nietzsche, ever fond of rattling a few swords against Plato, that supposedly arch-conceptualist, idealist rival of Isocrates, deeply affiliated himself with this tradition. To some of his readers, the development of some of his "philosophical" positions (e.g., perspectivism) appears inconceivable apart from this association (see Nietzsche, 1989, ix-xxvii, especially xii-xvi). Knowing the complexities of language and argument elevated Nietzsche to a new level of analytical and epistemological self-knowledge. Even the importance of power in Nietzsche's work finds a counterpart in the domain of rhetoric's ultimate purpose: overcoming the listener in one fashion or another (see Ijsseling, 1976, 106).

Having worked out a series of lectures on classical rhetoric in the early 1870's, Nietzsche was quite familiar with the ancient sources. He was also pointedly aware of the "unmodern" centrality of *rhetorica* for the ancients, saying at one point that the "education of the ancient man customarily culminates in rhetoric: it is the highest spiritual activity of the well-educated political man—an odd notion for us!" He quotes Kant's understanding of rhetoric as "the art of transfiguring a serious business of the understanding as if it were a free play of the imagination..." This idea suggests to him a way by which he can characterize what is "unique" to Hellenic life. The distinctive Greek trait is "to perceive all matters of the intellect, of life's seriousness, of necessities, even of dangers, as play" (1989, 3). This statement is especially important not only because it reveals his position on the Greek spirit directly and succinctly, but also because it is a clue to some of his own leading values. The idea of play was one that Nietzsche thematized repeatedly in his works, influenced by the emphasis that a leading hero of the German *Klassik*, Friedrich Schiller, had given to the "play-drive" in the integration and fulfillment of human nature (*Letters on the Aesthetic Education of Man*). The reverberations extend to the "gaiety" of *The Gay Science*, to the Zarathustran injunctions to learn to laugh (1954, 406-08; selectively cited again at the end of the 1886 preface to *The Birth of Tragedy*), and to the "prankishness" of the preface to *Twilight of the Idols* (1954, 465).

Other vital Nietzschean themes—myth and distrust of the knowledge-drive, especially in historicism and positivism—appear in the introduction to his course on rhetoric. Nietzsche mentions that rhetoric "arises among a people who still live in mythic images and who have not yet experienced the unqualified need of historical accuracy: they would rather be persuaded than instructed" (1989, 3). The author of *The Birth of Tragedy* and *Zarathustra*, the "disciple of the philosopher Dionysus," reveals his own bias in these matters quite clearly: he chooses the rationality of *mythos* over that of *logos.* He prefers a rhetorical emphasis on style, emotion, the power of affective persuasion over that of logical consistency, historical "accuracy," positivistic certainty. These two dimensions, however, do not stand in a relationship of complete mutual exclusion. Art, and above all music, which, especially in its nineteenth-century European forms, is a domain of style, feeling, and affective absorption *par excellence*, are joined with the more intellectual lines of Nietzsche's interests in such a way that he truly believes that the most "rigorous" philosophical position must support a trans-rational dimension wherein verification has a different meaning, a more "rhetorical" one. Affective expression of the judgments made by the rationality of feeling must be given full weight.

Concerning Nietzsche's rhetorical understanding of philosophy, one can learn something important from his 1866 letter to von Gersdorff, in which he speaks of Friedrich Lange's Kantian position on the eternal elusiveness of the "thing-in-itself" and adds his own comments:

> Lange thinks, one should give the philosophers a free hand as long as they edify us in this sense [i.e., apparently, resound meaningfully for each person without universal univocality]. Art is free, also in the do-

> main of concepts. Who would refute a phrase by Beethoven, and who would find error in Raphael's *Madonna*?...if philosophy should edify I know no more edifying philosophy than our Schopenhauer. (1969c, 18)

Here we touch again upon the ethical element so important in the humanistic tradition: the edification of example in the speaker and in the speaker's imagery is thematized in the rhetorical tradition's discussion of *ethos* (e.g., see Johnson, 1984). Also, Nietzsche's long-standing musical obsession is especially relevant. The author of *The Birth of Tragedy* declared that the essay was "scientific in the highest sense," *and* that it "should have sung...and not spoken" (1967b, 20). He stated that "[p]erhaps the whole of *Zarathustra* may be reckoned as music" (1969a, 295). The "aesthetic justification" of life of which the early Nietzsche speaks so intently in *The Birth of Tragedy* is one with this way of thinking. The positive feeling of rightness, of health, of *creative* strength of *Macht,* which does not always exclude even a logical modality of speech, is chosen over any single or foundational devotion to the logic of scrupulous and univocal "correctness." We might say that *Truth* is most radically conceived as what calls forth *trust.* And trust is an existential-personal-emotional complex rather than one of disengaged, de-personalized intellectual definitions and judgments. Truth involves this holistic "feeling function," in the Jungian sense, more primordially than it does the "thinking function": thus, a thousand fine arguments fall before one well-founded conviction. Not by critical intellectual consciousness alone do we live.

Nietzsche obviously took a deeply personal delight in rhetorical experimentation and achievement, that is to say, in the whole area of *stylistics.* It is what drove him to live in that atmosphere of authors and texts that humanists find so inspiring. He seems to have made an early turn in this direction, as we can gather from a letter of 1867 that stresses how his greatest "trouble and worry" is

> my German style (not to mention Latin; once I have come to grips with the mother tongue, foreign languages will be next in turn). The scales are falling from my eyes: I lived all too long in a state of stylistic innocence. The categorical imperative, "Thou shalt and must write," has aroused me. I tried something that I had never tried except at school: to write well, and suddenly the pen froze in my hand. I could not do it, and was annoyed. And all the while Lessing's and Lichtenberg's and Schopenhauer's stylistic precepts were buzzing in my ears. It was always my solace that these three authorities unanimously agree that it is difficult to write well, that no man has a good style by nature, that one

> must work at the uphill job of acquiring one. I honestly do not want to write again so woodenly and drily, in such a logical corset, as I did, for example in my Theognis essay, at whose cradle no Graces sat (rather there was a distant thundering, as if from Königsgrätz). It would be a very sad state of affairs not to be able to write better and yet warmly to want to do so. Above all, a few gay spirits in my own style must once more be unchained; I must learn to play on them as on a keyboard, but not only pieces I have learned by heart—no—but also free fantasias, as free as possible, yet still always logical and beautiful. (1969c, 21-22)

The concluding musical metaphor is typical, along with the evocation of a different kind of "rationality." Nietzsche may think of "life as literature," as a leading Nietzsche-interpreter contends today, but let us add this: he often thinks of literature as music.

As we have just noted, Nietzsche's concern for the development of an artistic style is inseparably joined to ethical issues. An important statement from *The Gay Science* (Section 290) thematizes this typical humanist conjunction strikingly, once again exhibiting that same tradition's obsession with wholeness, with the importance of some kind of "fundamental anthropology," and with the prominent humanist leitmotif of self-fashioning:

> *One thing is needful.*—To "give style" to one's character—a great and rare art! It is practiced by those who survey all the strengths and weaknesses of their nature and then fit them into an artistic plan until every one of them appears as art and reason and even weaknesses delight the eye...It will be the strong and domineering natures that enjoy their finest gaiety in such constraint and perfection under a law of their own...Conversely it is the weak characters without power over themselves that hate the constraints of style...For one thing is needful: that a human being should attain satisfaction with himself, whether it be by means of this or that poetry and art: only then is a human being tolerable to behold (1974, 232-33).

But the stylistics of this self-fashioning, so much a concern in the Renaissance (see T. Greene, 1968, 241-64), are paralleled by those of the *literary* self-fashioning that Nehamas (1985) has highlighted so well as a profound dimension of Nietzsche's work. Somehow, Nietzsche's character is "made" by his writings, most explicitly in *Ecce Homo.* Nietzsche himself would perhaps protest that he is also "expressed" in them. He sets forth directly his concern for literary stylistics, which only intensified at the end of his career, in a striking passage in *Ecce Homo* where the connection of *ethos*, *pathos*, and style is given a new twist. Good style being the communication of an inward state, Nietzsche claims that his many different "inward states"—and therefore the whole complex of his character, along with his ability to communicate them—all mean that he has "many stylistic possibilities—the most multifarious art of style that has ever been at the disposal of one man." It is not as though he has many characters, therefore, but a character with tremendous range, the range of that broadest and deepest and most comprehensive soul he sang of in *Zarathustra* (cited also in *Ecce Homo*, 1969a, 305; see also the passage from *The Gay Science* 1974, 298). The old question of the necessary audience again arises here:

> Good style in itself—a pure folly, mere "idealism,"—...
>
> Always presupposing that there are ears—that there are those capable and worthy of the same pathos, that there is no lack of those to whom one *may* communicate oneself.—My *Zarathustra*, for example, is still looking for those—...Before me, it was not known what could be done with the German language—what could be done with language in general. The art of the *great* rhythm, the *great* style of long periods to express a tremendous up and down of sublime, of superhuman passion, was discovered only by me; with a dithyramb like the last one in the third part of *Zarathustra*, entitled "The Seven Seals," I soared a thousand miles beyond what was known as poetry hitherto. (1969a, 265)

Along with the *Grundthema* of greatness and the concluding example of the humanistic qualitative-ontological thinking that we discussed in the first argument, we see here how the theme of Germany returns and links itself with Nietzsche's stylistic obsessions. Perhaps behind this connection we may read the Schopenhauerian dictum that "The language in which a man writes is the physiognomy of his nation..." (1974, 516). If such is the case, we can see that rhetoric could well have been a way beyond the petty ego to the Great Self that, in its ultimate form, serves as a cultural "sun." The work of culture, even in its rhetorical form, is again seen to be on a gradient toward trans-national, world-historical greatness: not just the German language is at issue, but "language in general." It is worth recalling in this context that Nietzsche's first *Untimely Meditation,* was essentially an attack on David Strauss and the cultural pathology that he represented, was significantly based on his *stylistic* failings: the essay ends with a long section of the most direct rhetorical analysis—consisting of over seventy specific examples of bad style. Hollingdale notes that Nietzsche's early heroes Wagner and Schopenhauer had used a similar technique, but that it was probably the latter, following Buffon's famous equation of style and the author's self, who was probably the first German author to probe a person's rhetoric to uncover the fundamental and possibly hidden life-values that the person had chosen (Nietzsche, 1983, xii).

Nietzsche's concern with expression's inseparability from the questions of greatness of character is a significant link back to some prominent, long-standing strands of the oratorical foundations of Western humanism. The connection of style with character is in a way suggested by its double etymology, from the Latin *stilus* that makes "characters" and from the Greek *stylos* that refers to the range of specific "types" of columns in the classical orders (see Kubler, 1979). Both letters and monumental architecture demand creative, expressive effort, and both became important symbolic modes aiming at lasting "edification." The arch-orator Cicero himself suggests that speaking with a certain feeling and in a certain manner makes it happen that speech seems "to depict, as it were, the character of the speaker": *Tantum autem efficitur sensu quodam ac ratione dicendi, ut quasi mores oratoris effingat oratio* (Cicero, *De Oratore*, II. xliii.184). Even more direct is Isocrates, when he comments in the midst of his famous paean to *logos* (especially as oratorical speech rather than as philosophical reason) that this power that makes humanity distinctively human, that it helps to establish all human institutions, that it lays down laws, that it allows us to "educate the ignorant and to appraise the wise." He continues, "the power to speak well is taken as the surest index of a sound understanding" (*tou phronein eu megiston sêmeion*), and "discourse which is true and lawful and just is the outward image of a good and faithful soul" (*logos alêthês kai nomimos kai dikaios psychês agathês kai pistês eidôlon esti,* Isocrates, 1929, 326-27). Speech, as reflective of the soul, can therefore be intimately involved in the establishment of ethical integrity and human authenticity. It in fact must be so involved insofar as the public assessment of a speaker is concerned, for how will listeners allow themselves to be persuaded without some kind of positive judgment about the quality of the speaker's soul, intentions, and character? And how do they usually attain the basis for such a judgment except through the communicative action of that person? Petrarch agrees with the direction of this tradition when he writes of the isomorphism of speech and character, claiming that

> Speech is no small index of one's spirit, nor is the spirit a small moderator of one's speech. One depends upon the other...Speech can not have dignity unless its majesty were not already in the spirit...Literary

sources relate and everday experience indicates how much eloquence can fashion human life.

> *Nec enim parvus aut index animi sermo est aut sermonis moderator est animus. Alter pendet ex altero...adesse sermoni dignitas non potest, nisi animo sua maiestas affuerit... Verumtamen quantum quoque ad informationem humanae vitae possit eloquentia, et apud multos auctores lectum et quotidiana experientia monstrante compertum est.* (Petrarca, n.d., Volume 1, 45; 46 translation mine).

Seneca, another humanist authority of the first rank, had already gone further by devoting a whole letter to the linkage of style and the character, intellect, and the health of a society. He explains the corruption of literary style by citing the Greek proverb, "*talis hominibus fuit oratio qualis vita*" (Letter 114). Thus rhetoric bears upon the very issues of health and decadence in society as well as upon the state of the speaker's soul and its reliability.

For Nietzsche, style at its best is one with content. It is authenticity. It is greatness. It has to do with exemplary character that through the disciplining of the mute, brute ego far surpasses the merely subjective while remaining utterly distinct and personal. It is therefore not a leap into the abyss, not pure formalism, not aimless and unproductive "play," not total nihilism. It is inappropriate, therefore, to speak of Nietzsche's rhetorical orientation as his way of "overcoming" metaphysics; *rather it is part of his aboriginal humanistic foundations,* on which he takes a stand over and against metaphysical-theoretical abstractions. Did Isocrates "overcome" metaphysics by becoming who he was rather than a disciple of Plato? Did Petrarch, when he stood against the scholastic style? We usually do not speak this way about them. Whatever Nietzsche's reversals, whatever the implications of his epistemological critiques, he remains firmly allied to the importance of both form *and* matter, trying not to privilege one to the detriment of the other, or, better, suggesting that *form or style significantly constitutes the matter of human greatness even as the latter achieves itself through its creative, stylistic power* (cf. Nietzsche, 1974, 232-34). In the idea of this necessary conjunction he again proves his kinship to the genius of the Renaissance, which essentially aimed in its literary education for a "truer" type of cultivation than that afforded by the theological faculties of its day, a "legitimate" and "genuine" cultivation "that joins stylistic skill with an ordered knowledge of reality" (*quae litterarum peritiam cum rerum scientia conjungit,* Bruni, 1928, 6).

The unity of style and content in Nietzsche might be imagined to be the humanistic equivalent of the metaphysical position of hylomorphism, the unity of form and matter, and it is just as difficult to represent correctly when we attempt a balanced interpretation. A reader tends to veer towards either a Heideggerian Nietzsche of definite metaphysical content or a Derridean Nietzsche of a fluid indeterminacy of meaning. Charles Altieri, however, escapes this Scylla and Charybdis in a way that appears to support substantially the view that I am proposing when he says that "Nietzsche's shifting the emphases in philosophy from proposition to expression returns us to criteria of ethos and to a need for a version of traditional Humanism's concern to stage motives in relation to historical models for making and judging visions of a best self" (1985, 390). Notice that he takes us back towards the issue of exemplarism, precisely in the context of the issues of content and style (propositions and expression).

But, we ask, to what extent is *Nietzsche himself returning* to a humanist concern? Did he ever really leave it? Nehamas also comes close to a balance without going far enough. Highlighting a most revelatory passage, he mentions that a central theme of his book is Nietzsche's aestheticism, which "...results from his effort to bring style into the center of his own thought and to repeat once more what he took to be the great achievement fo the Greeks and the Romans: to make of "the grand style no longer mere art but...reality, truth, *life*" (Nehamas, 1985, 39, citing Nietzsche, 1954, 651). But it would be far better to imagine style *as radically implicated in Nietzsche's thought from the start*, or indeed as part of the matrix out of which his thought is derived. It was shaped in the context of the humanistic rhetorical education of his earliest academic years, where he first tried "to write well." This skill is one of the things that helps to constitute maturity in modern Western cultures. It proceeds as ethical formation usually does, by the imitation of models. "*Der Stil*" significantly also refers to an "exercise in translating or composition" (*Cassell's*). Just as Nietzsche attempts to achieve his own greatness through an initial discipleship to a great individual (Schopenhauer), so does he achieve the maximum of stylistic and hence *authorial* power through an initial attempt to master different styles of writing. The authorial *is* the authentic, in the last analysis. It is the creative, simultaneously self-expressing and self-creating self.

But where do we get the idea of the authorial but through concrete *exempla*? Written into humanist pedagogy is the habit of first looking up towards a model that is held out as some kind of "ideal" to be imitated. Such a "maturational dynamic" occurred in Renaissance practices as a whole. There arose then the idea of an intrinsic and autonomous verbal potency of texts, which could "produce ecstasy or order human lives" (Moss, 1989, 104) through the skillful arrangement of linguistic structures. But this intrinsic ethical and mystical power of words-in-themselves was eventually balanced by the personal reality of the writer, especially from the time of the late poetry of the premiere French Hellenist and Pindar-enthusiast, Ronsard, after 1560. "Rhetorical theories of literary production based on the imitation of model authors paradoxically led to a heightened self-consciousness in the writer" (Moss, 1989, 105). Thus character was involved on both ends, in the great model and in the aspiring writer who would thereby achieve his or her own individuality.

Schopenhauer also suggested the uniquely personal end of rhetorical training and the close interrelationship of style and character when he said, "Style is the physiognomy of the mind and such is more infallible than is that of the body. To imitate another's style is equivalent to wearing a mask" (1974, 515). Nietzsche, no stranger to masks, ultimately achieves his greatest expression of his individuality and the peak of "heightened self-consciousness" in *Ecce Homo.* The style is crucial, but the particular identity of the author even more so. Here we find the combination of subjectivity with that world-shaking greatness that apparently escapes the merely "comic" particularities of the author's own life, even while the latter are explicitly thematized. The combination as achieved here is a *ne plus ultra* in a tradition especially evocative of Renaissance humanism.

Paul Oskar Kristeller has described how, in an analogous way, the dimension of subjectivity combined with the use of key objects in the common cultural heritage to define Renaissance style and character. The humanists'

> [L]iterary production...was characterized throughout by a desire to imitate ancient authors and to emulate them in the elegance of their style, vocabulary and literary composition,...but...the humanists added...the tendency to take seriously their own personal feelings and experiences, opinions and preferences. An air of subjectivity pervades all humanist literature from Petrarch to Erasmus and Montaigne that is absent from most classical literature and also from much modern literature prior to Romanticism. It accounts for the often uninhibited gossip, flattery and polemics present in much humanist literature, and it also helps to explain the Renaissance preference for such literary genres as the invective, the dialogue, the speech, the letter and the essay. (Kristeller, 1988, 126)

It is very hard to exclude Nietzsche from this tradition, especially in the light of the genres that Kristeller points out as characteristic of the Renaissance humanists in this essay. The most popular Renaissance forms were the oration and the letter. Nietzsche was an enthusiastic and skillful letter-writer; his personal communications have at least the same importance for exploring the nature of his thinking and the features of his self-representation that Renaissance writers' letters have for discerning theirs—perhaps moreso, given Nietzsche's unusually confessional manner. Though Nietzsche never undertook the publication of his correspondence, Petrarch's practice of letter-collection, and that of his inspiring model Cicero, nevertheless constitute humanistic analogues. Nietzsche even subtitled his *The Case of Wagner* with the designation "Turinese Letter of May 1888." Much of Nietzsche's work has an undeniably "orational" quality (e.g., *The Birth of Tragedy*, *Untimely Meditations*, but also *Zarathustra* and *The Anti-Christ[ian]*), and he clearly shares the notable Renaissance preference for invective (*On the Genealogy of Morals*, subtitled "A Polemic"; *The Anti-Christ[ian]; Nietzsche Contra Wagner*; *The Case of Wagner*). Kristeller mentions other categories that have Nietzschean parallels: history and theory of history (cf. *On the Uses and Disadvantages of History for Life* and major sections of *The Gay Science* and *Beyond Good and Evil*, including those on the history of morality); treatises on philosophical and moral problems (and *Beyond Good and Evil*, subtitled "Prelude to a Philosophy of the Future"; *On the Genealogy of Morals*); biography (*Schopenhauer as Educator*; *Richard Wagner in Bayreuth*; *Ecce Homo*); and dialogue (*On the Future of Our Educational Institutions*). There were also in the Renaissance "many collections of epigrams and elegies," with which we might compare Nietzsche's many short poems that have a distinctly epigrammatic quality.

It is hard not to think of *Zarathustra* when Kristeller notes that "[t]here are quite a few long poems in epic hexameters which are historical or mythological, religious or didactic in content. Some of the didactic poems deal with philosophical or scientific topics..." (Kristeller, 1988, 125). Especially if we apply the word "historical" in a broader way to the representations of Nietzsche's own life as so closely interrelated with major issues of his time (e.g. the problems of atheism, education, scientific method, nihilism, and so on), we can affirm that *Zarathustra* has most of these elements. Nietzsche refers at different times to this epic work as a tragedy (e.g., 1974, 274; cf. 347). In this way he links it with his concerns with the latter genre in *The Birth of Tragedy*, and thus with the long-standing humanist interest in dramatic composition. Zarathustra also has satiric elements that find parallels in humanist and other Nietzschean texts (for example, compare Erasmus's *Praise of Folly*). Finally, favorite Renaissance genres included poetical theory and literary criticism, with which we might compare Nietzsche's constant aesthetical reflections, from *The Birth of Tragedy* on. Kristeller does not mention autobiography as such, but the idea of self-representation is important in epistolary literature, and the autobiographical nature of some of the texts of such figures as Petrarch, Vico, and Montaigne, serve as examples of the strongly personal flavor that can be found in Renaissance texts. As we have seen, Nietzsche's works are thoroughly imbued with this autobiographical quality.

It is of special importance that Nietzsche seems to share with the humanist tradition a distinct love of compressed expression. Though he tried many different genres and styles, he associated himself, as most of his readers do, with that complex of short sayings and reflections—the maxim, the aphorism, the apophthegm, the epigram. Even these are definitely part of his obsession with greatness and immortal "classical" exemplarity.

> The aphorism, the apothegm, in which I am the first among the Germans to be a master, are the forms of "eternity"; it is my ambition to say in ten sentences what everyone else says in a book—what everyone else does *not* say in a book. (1954, 556)

Der Spruch can be translated as "sentence, decree, judgment; verdict saying, dictum; aphorism, epigram; short gnomic poem; passage, text" (*Cassell's*). Nietzsche no doubt especially enjoys the stylistic and intellectual power that can be achieved through such forms, as he implies with the title of *"Sprüche und Pfeile"* ("Maxims and Arrows") in *Twilight of the Idols.* The ancient military imagery here parallels his more modern metaphor for the destructiveness of great philosophy: dynamite. He explicitly associates his style with that of the "*Epigramm*" in *Twilight of the Idols*, and derives it from a classical Latin source:

> My sense of style, for the epigram as a style, was awakened almost instantly when I came into contact with Sallust. I have not forgotten the surprise of my honored teacher, Corssen, when he had to give his worst Latin pupil the best grade: I had finished with one stroke. Compact, severe, with as much substance as possible, a cold sarcasm against "beautiful word" and "beautiful sentiments"—here I found myself. And even in my *Zarathustra* one will recognize a very serious ambition for a *Roman* style, for the *aere perennius* in style. (1954, 556)

Even his "epic" tragedy-parody, then, is conceived as essentially "epigrammatic." Notice also the "anti-humanistic humanism" that he attributes to his very early academic years: no "beautiful" words and sentiments are allowed. He goes on to cite as a strong influence in this connection a premiere Renaissance hero (Erasmus's favorite poet), again in terms of themes that help to constitute the "greatness-complex" in his works:

> Nor was my experience any different in my first contact with Horace. To this day, no other poet has given me the same artistic delight that a Horatian ode gave me from the first. In certain languages that which has been achieved here could not even be attempted. This mosaic of words, in which every word—as sound, as place, as concept—pours out its strength right and left and over the whole, this *minimum* in the extent and number of the signs, and the maximum thereby attained in the energy of the signs—all that is Roman and, if one will believe me, *noble* par excellence. All the rest of poetry becomes, in contrast, something too popular—a mere garrulity of feelings. (1954, 556-57)

Interestingly, Nietzsche later evokes the same Renaissance hero, suggesting a certain literary equivalence and giving his readership a direct hermeneutic clue to his own work: "That a psychologist without equal speaks from my writings, is perhaps the first insight reached by a good reader—a reader as I deserve him, who reads me the way good old philologists read their Horace." (1969a, 266)

We will become better readers of Nietzsche when we realize that the great humanists and their heroes were with him all along and that they give him his originary and perduring context of meaning. In the case of epigrammatic style, we sense that it is again not a question of mere form, but of effective, formational practice involving issues of character. We in fact feel the presence of the Renaissance, which had rediscovered and rehabilitated the epigram out of a "desire to combine rhetorical and ethical instruction" (Crane, 1986, 163).

Perhaps it is precisely the epigrammatic style that ultimately caused Nietzsche to link the French moralists so closely with the Greeks, who pioneered it. The style, of course, is not restricted to the genre (as in La Rochefoucauld's *Maximes*). Even a "rambling" essayist like Montaigne writes pieces full of sententious expressions, with pithy citations culled from classical literature. Often the sources are not even acknowledged: style and content evidently had merged with his own way of thinking and writing, and his text is thereby woven into the larger tapestry of literary compositions. We recall that, carved in to the very ceiling beams in his scriptorium, within Montaigne's view, were many brief *sententiae* from Greek and Latin authors, silently "speaking" themselves. Many similar *sententiae* hover over Nietzsche's head as well.

We thus come to the issue of the stylistic centrality of *der Spruch* for Nietzsche, one of the many royal roads that lead from him back to the Hellenic sources of Western humanism and hence toward his larger humanistic genealogy. This feature has a particularly significant resonance in this context: the uses of *der Spruch* evidently played a crucial role in the early development of the "human sciences." Jacqueline de Romilly has written a most interesting account of the dynamics involved, and it is easy to see that similar ones reverberate down through the centuries (1989, 1-15). She shows that gnomic poetry—generalizations about the human condition, hence intrinsically "humanistic" in a radical sense—really blossomed in that very period that for Nietzsche represents the "true," canonical one of ancient Greek culture: the Archaic Age of the pre-Socratics. It was especially important for Pindar and thoroughly suffused Greek drama, even down to its structure, by way of the chorus's dramatic modes of speech. The self-conscious use of the aphorism was key to the Sophists' development of reasoned argument and became "especially stimulating for knowledge of man" (6). Here we see a primal ground for the close conjunction of form and content, which we have already noted was a key ideal for the Renaissance humanists.

De Romilly mentions that Aristotle's *Rhetoric* is largely "a manual of psychology on passions and temperaments." This psychological character of the classical rhetorical tradition is highly significant for Nietzsche's work, as it is for the humanist tradition. Nietzsche's self-image certainly included the psychologist's persona, as we can tell from the last citation from *Ecce Homo* above (1969a, 266). It was in fact so important that Walter Kaufmann chose to include it as part of the subtitle in his major work on Nietzsche, whom he sees as "Philosopher, Psychologist, Anti-Christ." Since the psychological realm has so much to do with the humanist project of self-knowledge, it is easy to see why de Romilly finds that historically rhetoric was closely associated with the genesis of many different kinds of knowledge about humanity. The art of words stimulated the art of effective thinking (7). Rhetoric, de Romilly claims, "served as the complete model and source for all human sciences" (14), though, she adds, "these were not yet sciences in the sense that we might understand the word..." (15).

The sapiential, experiential qualities of this genre self-consciously combine general with specific in such a way as to give the rhetorical tradition a proto-theoretical quality often characteristic of humanism as well. Humanists do not like to leave the concrete particularities of the human lifeworld, yet they still seek rational principles by which to understand and guide thinking and living. They have an openness to more strictly scientific types of thinking, while harboring reservations about overvaluing them at the expense of other forms of rational discourse. Humanists are not necessarily eager to take Euclid out of the school curriculum, after all. We can see such an attitude at work when Nietzsche did not reject Spinoza from the start; he actually professed a great desire to undertake some scientific studies during his professional career. A "proto-scientific" quality appears directly in his own constant search for principles from the Dionysian and Apollonian drives of *The Birth of Tragedy*, to the universal and ultimate principle of self-overcoming in *Zarathustra*, to the lucubrations on the "Eternal Return," which he tried to expound as a mathematical certainty in some of his late notes.

We also see in the rhetorical foundations of humanistic thinking that *archetypally humanistic combination of idealism and realism* that is to be found in Nietzsche as well. De Romilly analyzes how Thucydides uses aphoristic thinking to present (ideal) general patterns and to give insight into real human experience. It is this same Thucydides (a model for the stylistically influential epigrammatic prose of Sallust) that Nietzsche praises in *Twilight of the Idols*: the Greek historian is a realist who stands against the *false* idealism of the Socratic-Platonic tradition. Thus Thucydides is simultaneously an ideal and a "counter-idealist," as Nietzsche elaborates in a passage bearing a particularly interesting Renaissance conjunction:

> My recreation, my preference, my *cure* from all Platonism has always been *Thucydides*. Thucydides and, perhaps, Machiavelli's *Principe* are most closely related to myself by the unconditional will not to gull oneself and to see reason in *reality*—not in "reason," still less in "morality." For the wretched embellishment of the Greeks into an ideal, which the "classically educated" youth carries into life as a prize for his classroom drill, there is no more complete cure than Thucydides. One must follow him line by line and read no less clearly between the lines: there are few thinkers who say so much between the lines. With him the culture of the Sophists, by which I mean the culture of the realists, reaches its perfect expression—this inestimable movement amid the moralistic and idealistic swindle set loose on all sides by the Socratic schools. Greek philosophy: the decadence of the Greek instinct. Thucydides: the great sum, the last revelation of that strong, severe hard factuality which was instinctive with the older Hellenes. In the

> end, it is *courage* in the face of reality that distinguishes a man like Thucydides from Plato: Plato is a coward before reality, consequently he flees into the ideal; Thucydides has control of *himself*, consequently he also maintains control of things. (1954, 558-59)

Plato had been introduced in terms of the question of style, and it is apparently expressive control that Nietzsche admires in Thucydides, "the perfect *expression*" of the culture of the realists. Once again, we find ethos and style conjoined.

The terrible conflict of real and ideal are combined for Nietzsche in a signal way in the tragic consciousness, which finds its best representation in Greek drama. Here the ultimately "real" pain of existence is directly faced by the noble, "ideal" heroic figures. It is in this genre especially that the aphorism is combined with that other radically important humanist means of arriving at leading principles for direction in life, that leading principle we have already introduced as exemplarism. Tragedy, a radically ethical type of literature that is more than text, that is oration and dialogue and soliloquy, that is music too, and action and dance—the *mousikê* that takes a leading place in Greek *paideia*—tragedy, which was for Nietzsche the most exemplary genre of the most exemplary period of the most exemplary culture—that solemn tragedy of the pre-Socratic age was not merely a "prototype of the great style" with which Nietzsche was seriously concerned. It was not merely eloquent multivocal attestation to the ultimate truth of human existence, combining extremes of joy and pain (Akiyama, 1974, 107). It was also the privileged vehicle for Nietzsche's greatest cultural and personal hopes, precisely because the Dionysian music, verbally elaborated, was mediated through certain unforgettably exemplary individuals, beings greater than whom Nietzsche hoped the hero of his own tragedy, Zarathustra, would one day be.

Greek tragedy thus represents a crucial source in Nietzsche's greater genealogy and an apparently radical ground for his humanist *Weltanschauung*. This rich theme might easily be taken as an excellent Copernican point from which to spin out a comprehensive interpretation of Nietzsche as well as of the distinctive shape of his humanism. Greek tragedy necessarily combines certain constants and ultimates in his career—the Dionysian, the idea of human greatness, the Promethean struggle against established power for some kind of greater value, the final realistic Oedipean self-knowledge and self-creation of the tragic hero. But it may be better to dwell a little longer on how important the creative use of personal paradigms was for that style of thinking employed by both Nietzsche and the humanist tradition.

Nietzsche's humanistic exemplarism could be illustrated in many ways, notably by means of his paradigmatic and heuristic figures that we have examined already (Schopenhauer, Zarathustra, *Übermensch*, the Nietzsche of *Ecce Homo*) and by means of his own practice of emulation (for example, in regard to Socrates, Montaigne, Emerson). But the passage that speaks most strikingly of this dimension of Nietzsche, that suggests that it is a matter of both "poetic power"—and therefore rhetorical in some sense—and real character, a passage that is also suffused with archetypal humanist phraseology and sentiment welling up from deep in Nietzsche's soul, is the following (with italic-highlights added to the most important typical humanist themes):

> *The poet as signpost to the future.*—That poetic power available to men of today which is not used up in the depiction of life ought to be dedicated, not so much to the representation of the contemporary world or to the reanimation and imaginative reconstruction of the past, but to signposting the future...What he will do...is *emulate the artists of earlier times who imaginatively developed the existing images of the gods and imaginatively develop a fair image of man*; he will scent out those cases in which, in the *midst of our modern world* and reality and without any artificial withdrawal from or warding off of this world, *the great and beautiful soul is still possible, still able to embody itself in the harmonious and well-proportioned and thus acquire visibility, duration and the status of a model, and in so doing through the excitation of envy and emulation help to create the future.* The poems of such poets will be distinguished by the fact that they appear to be secluded and secured against the fire and breath of the *passions*: the incorrigible error, the shattering of the entire human instrument, mocking laughter and gnashing of teeth, and *everything tragic and comic in the old customary sense will be experienced as a tedious archaisizing coarsening of the human image* when confronted with his new art. *Strength, goodness, mildness, purity and an involuntary inborn moderation in the characters and their actions*: a level ground which it is repose and joy to the feet to walk upon: countenances and events mirroring a luminous sky: *knowledge and art blended to a new unity: the spirit dwelling together with its sister, the soul*, without presumptuousness or jealousy and evoking from what divides them not impatience and contention *but a graceful seriousness*:—all this would make up the general and all-embracing golden ground upon which alone the tender *distinctions* between the different *embodied ideals would then constitute the actual painting—that of the ever increasing elevation of man.*—Many a path to this poetry of the future

> starts out from *Goethe*: but it requires good path-finders and above all a much greater power than present-day poets—that is to say the *innocuous depicters of the semi-animal and of immaturity and abnormality confused with force and naturalness*—possess. (1986, 235-36)

Behind the "imaginatively-developed" image of the human person we can see the long file of paradigmatic figures in the humanist tradition as they have been variously portrayed, described, suggested: Byron's Manfred; the moralists' *honnête homme*; Machiavelli's Prince; Castiglione's Courtier; Sidney's and Petrarch's and Virgil's *poeta*; Plutarch's noble Greeks and Romans; Seneca's *sapiens*; Cicero's and Isocrates's orator; Aristotle's "great-souled man," the *megalopsychos*; Plato's myth-making philosopher and also his "empirical ideal," Socrates; Sophocles's Antigone and Oedipus; and Homer's Achilles, Penelope, and Odysseus. These figures are the universal, transsubjective, yet personal models that, humanists have proposed, can help us to achieve something like our own particular, authentic "humanity," at least in terms of the raising, in a uniquely effective way, our self-consciousness of what all human beings already are or to some extent share.

The humanist tradition becomes especially self-conscious about its exemplaristic mode with Giambattista Vico's theory of "imaginative universals." Vico claims that these first appear in poetic characters in fables. In heroic times, they are often used to express qualities of character: valor, persistence, courage, cleverness, and so on (Verene, 1976, 22-23). This practice probably goes far back beyond recorded history, but it is knowingly employed by Homer in his use of *paradeigmata* that suggest best courses of action to follow, as in Phoenix's advice to Achilles in *Iliad* IX. Also the early allegorization of the Homeric poems made the heroes representative of moral forces. When commenting on the intrinsically ethical dimension of rhetoric, Isocrates claims that if one wishes to speak or write well,

> [I]t is not conceivable that he will support causes which are unjust or petty or devoted to private quarrels, and not rather those which are *great and honourable, devoted to the welfare of man and our common good*; for if he fails to find causes of this character, he will accomplish nothing to the purpose. In the second place, he will *select from all the actions of men which bear upon his subject those examples which are the most illustrious and the most edifying; and, habituating himself to contemplate and appraise such examples, he will feel their influence not only in the preparation of a given discourse but in all the actions of his life.* It follows, then, that the *power to speak well and think right* will reward

> the man who approaches the art of discourse with love of wisdom and love of honour. (Isocrates, 1929, 337, 339, emphasis added)

Exemplars, used in the context of learning to communicate well, shape and refine one's character as well as one's oratorical performance. R. B. Rutherford has indicated how broad and intense was the "ancient, and especially Roman, passion for exemplary figures," who tended to be rather simplistically portrayed "in terms of very clearly defined virtues and vices" (1989, 56). Even beyond the realm of poetry, rhetoric, and history, the philosophers developed this practice, especially that "the example of a revered moral preceptor should be kept continuously in one's mind" (58). In a way exemplarism is a practice that encapsulates something essential in the Hellenic sources of humanistic tradition. Werner Jaeger in a highly significant and highly untimely passage says:

> We can now define the specific character of Hellenism...By discovering man, the Greeks did not discover the subjective self, but realized the universal laws of human nature. The intellectual principle of the Greeks is not individualism but 'humanism,' to use the word in its original and classical sense...It meant the process of educating man into his true form, the real and genuine human nature. That is the true Greek *paideia*, adopted by the Roman stateman as a model. It starts from the ideal, not from the individual. Above man as a member of the horde, and man as a supposedly independent personality, stands man as an ideal; and that ideal was the pattern towards which Greek educators as well as Greek poets, artists, and philosophers always looked. But what is the ideal man? It is the universally valid model of humanity which all individuals are bound to imitate. We have pointed out that the essence of education is to make each individual in the image of the community; the Greeks started by shaping human character on that communal model, became more and more conscious of the meaning of that process, and finally, entering more deeply into the problem of education, grasped its basic principles...(Jaeger, 1965, Volume 1, xxiii-xxiv).

Jaeger goes on to say that the ideal was not an empty, abstract pattern, but one rooted in the cultural-historical specifics of time and place. Perhaps this excerpt tells us why the classical world and the epigrammatic style appealed to Nietzsche so much: a certain hardness, compression, abstraction, universality of importance, and grandeur seem to attach to concise, significant expression and to exemplary characters severely drawn and powerfully presented, as they are in Greek tragedy. The spiritual-pedagogical impact of these figures should not be underestimated. Nietzsche actually praises this type of idealization explicitly, thereby revealing his own sympathy with the abstractive aesthetics of classicism:

> What is essential in such frenzy [the physiological presupposition of all art] is the feeling of increased strength and fullness. Out of this feeling one lends to things, one *forces* them to accept from us, one violates them—this process is called *idealizing*. Let us get rid of a prejudice here: idealizing does not consist, as is commonly held, in subtracting or discounting the petty and inconsequential. What is decisive is rather a tremendous drive to bring out the main features so that the others disappear in the process (1954, 518).

In light of such sentiments, it is not surprising that Nietzsche abhorred any "sickly" Romantic wallowing in the immediately subjective. Such indulgence could never provide a good example for anyone. Suffer, Nietzsche seems to counsel, but suffer strongly, with a sense of radicality, ultimacy, eternity. Pass from the petty ego to the Great Self. This suffering is what finally constitutes greatness: it is a matter of the creation of oneself as a work of art, as a "complete" and "finished" human being. The human person is therefore the ultimate "product" of the ultimate creative act (Nietzsche, 1967b, 37; cf. Jaeger, 1965, xxii). A radical humanism indeed!

Ida Overbeck once spoke most insightfully of the cost of Nietzsche's self-fashioning, revealing how profound was his involvement in these dynamics of exemplarism:

> He was a distinct character by nature and he trained himself in that direction...How could Nietzsche's work ever seem other than that of a heroically tragic person! In theory absolute exemplariness was his burning ambition; at any rate he is a very developed individual (Gilman, 1987a, 145).

His greatness, as a tragic kind of greatness, had to be equally self-destructive and self-creative, combining effective achievement and complete downfall in the manner of the tragic hero. *Übergehen* means *untergehen* for Zarathustra. The "most spiritual human beings" suffer "the most painful tragedies," honoring life, however, because "it pits its greatest opposition against them" (1954, 524). The image of dynamite too suggests something of the conjunction of powerful inner potency and final self-destruction that characterizes the great individual.

> The danger that lies in great men and ages is extraordinary; exhaustion of every kind, sterility, follow in their wake. The great human being is a finale; the great age—the Renaissance, for example—is a finale. The genius, in work and deed, is necessarily a squanderer: that he squanders himself, that is his greatness. The instinct of self-preservation is suspended, as it were; the overpowering pressure of outflowing forces forbids him any such care or caution...He flows out, he overflows, he uses himself up, he does not spare himself—and this is a calamitous, involuntary fatality, no less than a river's flooding the land. Yet, because much is owed to such explosives, much has also been given them in return: for example, a kind of higher morality (1954, 548).

This paradox parallels and participates in that of the anti-humanistic humanism we have already explored in Nietzsche's thought from his earliest period, his struggle for culture even to its own self-overcoming. The greatest creation involves the greatest destruction.

Nietzsche used a special term to highlight this idea and he exuberantly applied it both to himself and to his ultimate ideal in *Ecce Homo*, in that section where it begins its rumbling towards the final explosive conclusion, perhaps the most forceful of all epigrammatic utterances.

> [M]y truth is *terrible* [*furchtbar*]...It is my fate that I have to be the first decent human being...(1969a, 326).

> I am by far the most terrible human being [*der furchtbarste Mensche*] that has existed...I obey my Dionysian nature...(1969a, 327).

> "What is great is so alien to your souls that the overman would be *terrifying* [*furchtbar*] to you in his goodness." [Quoted from *Zarathustra* II] It is here and nowhere else that one must make a start to comprehend what Zarathustra wants: this type of man that he conceives, conceives reality *as it is*, being strong enough to do so; this type is not estranged or removed from reality but is reality itself and exemplifies all that is terrible [*Furchtbares*] and questionable in it—*only in that way can a man attain greatness* (1969a, 331).

The concept of *Das Furchtbar* is reminiscent of nothing so much as an ultimate aesthetic-ethical-technical category of High Renaissance Classicism that has deep roots in the ancient Greek rhetorical tradition—*terribilità*. This term designates not only the forcefulness and expressiveness of the object created but also the tremendous versatility and heroic style or personality of the artist (Summers, 1981, 234-241). Michelangelo was a leading example of the Renaissance *terribilità*, in character, range of skill, and artistic effects. The word translates the Greek *deinotes*, which was an important rhetorical idea in the Hellenic tradition. For Hermogenes it was in fact the most important of rhetorical values, indicating the very summit of oratorical excellence that can use language and thought both variously and appropriately. It in fact achieves the status of a "quintessential rhetoric" itself in his definition. As he considers the seventh and last type of style, he says

> In my opinion Force (*Deinotes*) in a speech is nothing other than the proper use of all the kinds of style previously discussed and of their opposites and of whatever other elements are used to create the body of a speech. (Hermogenes, 1987, 101)

It represents what Nietzsche sought stylistically and ethically—powerful expression, which to be truly effective must be understood as emanating from a great personality and ability, a person of great *virtù*, in the Renaissance sense or *aretê* in the Greek one. Hermogenes's description of particular forms of *deinotes* even seems to apply to some of Nietzsche's preferred oratorical aesthetic quite well, including the epigrammatic style:

> Thus thoughts that are typical of this sort of Force are paradoxical, profound, compelling, or, in general, any cleverly contrived thoughts...
>
> But the figures and the word order and all the other elements that are characteristic of Force are not those that are typical of those types that produce Grandeur, but those that are appropriate to Solemnity and Florescence and Brilliance and Abundance. The figure that involves concentrating many thoughts concisely into one sentence is especially suitable. (104, 105)

Of course Nietzsche allies his rhetorical forcefulness and his epigrammatic power to a large cultural program, his "task" and "mission," which goes far beyond the scope of the paradigmatic Demosthenes or any classical orator. Nevertheless the orientation toward *effect* and even toward that so highly praised Dionysian state could have been closely analogous to what Nietzsche had in mind. Dionysius of Halicarnassus, often cited in Nietzsche's lectures on rhetoric, clearly relates *deinotes* both to Demosthenes and to the Dionysian realm as he reveals the inward effects of his reading of the great orator:

> But when I take up a work of Demosthenes, I am as one inspired, I am swept this way and that, one emotion follows another, incredulity, anxiety, fear, contempt, hatred, pity, sympathy, rage, envy, a succession of all the passions that can sway the human heart. I think that at such times I am in exactly the same state as the initiates at the mystery of the Mother of the Corybantes, or the like...(Cited from *De Demosthene*, in Summers, 1981, 238)

Other overtones from antiquity and the Renaissance also make themselves felt in this connection, ones that link the humanist tradition to the idea of the "terrible one" (*deinos*) and to Nietzsche's *Übermensch*. I cite the following reminiscence at length not only for the immediately relevant content, but for the whole web of associations that seem lost on so many today and for the revealing testimony of an early witness to Nietzsche's humanistic character. Ludwig von Scheffler recalls:

> For my approaching graduation took me back to Freiburg...to be inaugurated as a humanist in the great hall of the university amid Basel's very impressive Renaissance aura. When I held my doctoral lecture, the picture of Aeneas Sylvius Piccolomini was on the wall behind my head! And in the "corona" before me sat Jakob Burckhardt, the greatest and most genuine humanist the modern age has ever known!...Had I really, on this solemn occasion, not missed him, Nietzsche?

A little later he also recounts another string of striking associations:

> But I was to hear of him again and in a strange way that reminded me of his Plato lectures...In Florence! I was then writing my *Michelangelo*...[I saw Michelangelo's] allegorical figure of "night," with its dismal, death-weary face bowed over the hollow mask of death. Yes, a "mask" no longer struck me as a chance symbol of the serious impression! Not the rigid grandeur, as ancient fantasy formed the allegory of the "illusory dream," no, still full of painful life, full of reality, like everything that stems from Michelangelo's very personal conception!... No wonder that I too was seized by the living, painful memory of Basel!
>
> Then, to cast out the depressing idea, I reached into my pocket and pulled out a newspaper. Literary news from Germany! And the first name that my eye fell on was...Nietzsche. As one greets a dear relative again after a long separation, I rejoiced at this discovery. Then I devoured what the article said about Nietzsche. A new turn in his philosophy! The doctrine of the "superman," of the happiness of the su-

> pra-morality which feels itself to be "beyond good and evil" and recognizes the value of existence only in its own freedom and strength!... I had to smile to myself. So that was how the "wise man in the cave" had worked his way up to the light of day, abandoning the "pessimist" Plato and going over to the camp of those who joyously affirm, the "many" whom just this Plato had attacked so bitterly. Of course, all said in Nietzschean terms and transfigured to a high, indeed the highest, ethical level. Yet I had read the basic idea of this in *Gorgias* and in the *Republic.* The magnificent apostrophes of Casticles [Callicles], of Thrasymachus! That "justice [is] merely what the strong man finds advantageous!" That "those who pass laws and recognize them are the great herd and the weak"! That the "freedom and right of the more noble" begin only "beyond them"!! And as the Greek "superman" necessarily seemed to be merely the prototype of the Nietzschean one, a different image arose before my soul: the memory of how Burckhardt had once spoken to us (presumably also to Nietzsche) of the *dei[n]os,* the Hellenic "all-man"! This most resplendent characterization which found its counterpart only in the description of the "demonic man," the "terrible one," of the Renaissance! Was Nietzsche too thinking of this when, guided by Plato the writer, not Plato the philosopher, he found his way to a new world-view? For though he later despised Plato, he always remained a Hellene in his whole formation and temperament. Even his Zarathustra cloak, strange as it fits in places, fall in Greek folds. I at least have felt that what is most delightful in Nietzsche's wealth of imagery and in his language is always the reflection of great Hellenic impressions (Gilman, 1987a, 102, 103-04).

Yes, Nietzsche, the associate of Burckhardt, wanted to be terrible too, we are easily persuaded to say, adding that he wanted to be terrible in a way that was partly analogous to the classical archetypes of greatness and partly without parallel. For only with the latter quality would he have felt that he had become "who he was," and only with the former would he have felt that he had become anything at all.

Perhaps that word *deinotes* shows us the best path to the inner structure of Nietzsche's peculiarly aggressive kind of humanistic greatness, for in the Homeric epics, *deinos* applies to what inspires awe and terror and fear in the manner of Achilles as well as to the verbal skill that Odysseus uses and came to symbolize, as Hermogenes stresses (102-03). These two Homeric archetypes of heroic greatness between them seem to provide primal sources for the two sides to Nietzsche's own versions thereof, as Daniel Conway has described them (1989): the fanciful, powerful, fabulous one (most appropriate symbolized by militaristic imagery) and the more cultured, quiet, yet equally revolutionary one of self-creation. On the one hand, there is the world-historical nemesis of Troy, who cuts down Hektor its last hope, and whose anger almost destroys the Greeks as well; on the other, the patiently suffering rhetorician, who devises a clever ruse that unfolds by night, which yet works the actual downfall of the city. Nietzsche was an Odyssean wanderer, yearning for new seas, a solitary survivor who perhaps had despaired of ever finding his true home; and he was also a withdrawn but passionate Achillean warrior ready to overturn civilization, some will say, out of his own type of *ressentiment.* But beneath all this terribleness lies the amazing phenomenon of mere humanity, exaggerated greatly enough to catch our attention: Sophocles's famous ode from the Antigone says that there is nothing more *deinos* than the human being.

Whatever the case about these archetypes, it seems that if one listens carefully enough, one can hear the Homeric heartbeat of the Hellenic and humanistic traditions working away until the end. Nietzsche shows his kinship with Homer most unmistakeably in his desire for a realism and a naturalism that is simultaneously artistic and ideal. For Nietzsche, culture is a transfigured nature. Even in the face of the dangers of that dessicated Alexandrianism that loses the vitality of Alexander, the cultural process should carry nature toward its own aim: maximum power, which is not ever the same as mere brute force. The vital natural drives are meant to impel cultural creativity. "My task: the dehumanizing of nature and then the naturalizing of humanity, after the latter has acquired the pure concept 'nature'" (cited in Rosen, 1989, 219).

No wonder Nietzsche should come to stress the theme of the human body in a way that recalls to us its pervasive importance for the great humanist cultures of Greece and Renaissance Italy. And we are no less reminded here of the assertion of *Schopenhauer as Educator* that the great individual is the ultimate intention of *nature,* and of *Zarathustra* that "Man [as the *Übermensch*] is the meaning of the earth." The Homeric world carries a not-so-dissimilar aura of the remarkable interfusion of the natural, supernatural, and human levels, despite or perhaps at the very root of the tragic greatness of the heroes (who can appear both "god-like" and "dog-like"). Like Homer, Nietzsche seems to find human authenticity in the fullness of the creative exercise of the distinctively human powers of speech and deed. And like Homer he achieves his own greatness in the celebration and in the castigation of examples of greatness and smalless, and especially in the singing of his own epic hero Zarathustra.

There is little doubt, then, that Nietzsche was quite intensely invested in rhetorical practices. These pervade his works, and they help to constitute as well as communicate his positions in notably humanistic manner. Even without a lengthy elaboration of the many connections with issues of human psychology, the nature of philosophy, perspectivism, national character, "true humanity," art, self-creation, edification, body, and so on, we can sense Nietzsche's profound absorption in and assimilation of this complex rhetorical tradition and its stylistic-ethical concerns. No matter what his despair about "ultimate truth," he never gave up his enthusiasm for the arts of communication and he did find there, in fact, much empirical, culturally concrete aesthetic-ethical "truth" in the sense of "that on which someone can ultimately rely, that which calls forth our deepest conviction." In this alliance, Nietzsche is profoundly wedded to the heart of the Western humanities. As a leading humanist of our own day has said:

> [A]t the center of the humanities lies always the study of human expression in all its manifestations and of human culture, which grows in and around human expression as this expression grows in and around culture. (Ong, 1971, 305)

7
Reprise and Ascent

The rhetorical argument closes the circle of our demonstrations, returning us to the larger linguistic domain of humanist philology from which we, and Nietzsche, set out. Over the course of the inquiry, we have surveyed ample evidence that in origins and foundations, in form, in general and specific content, in scope, in intentionality, and in manner, Nietzsche is so thoroughly implicated in the traditions of Western humanism that an understanding of his humanist character seems essential to any faithful interpretation of his work. Highly suspect is any reading that would detach him from that larger sphere of cultural-historical meaning to which he inalienably belongs. A reader without a sense of that background will have to be hermeneutically crippled. Likewise, this study points us insistently toward the conclusion that any general reading of Nietzsche must not disregard the positive content and the coherent intelligibility of his works and life-project. Having put to rest the gross interpretive distortions that make Nietzsche a Nazi or an anti-Semite does not mean that there are no equally grievous misreadings that we yet need to overcome. Nor does it mean that Nietzsche is cleared of all charges of incendiary rhetoric or grossly distortive bias.

I hope that at minimum I have made more systematically explicit a framework for understanding that not only challenges many current misleading treatments but also facilitates an especially rich, balanced reading of Nietzsche. If there are some who would like to pinpoint Nietzsche's particular place in the history of humanism using a more focused intellectual-historical approach than I have employed, then I hope that these reflections prove to be helpful prolegomena for them. To conclude my own project here, I will first mention several corroborations for the approach that I have proposed, and then I will probe the larger complex of issues that are at stake. We will arrive at a point well beyond beyond the special hermeneutical issues of this study, but we will not leave them behind completely. Humanism, of course, always directs us back to the exigencies of our own particular life-world. Such a turn is important to make here because the issues are vital in themselves and never to be forgotten. But they are also that which helps to motivate and to condition our reading of Nietzsche in the first place. They ground our estimation of his larger contemporary significance, and they can affect the way we interpret his own intentions. Of what use might his works be? And how might we begin to go about evaluating him as a kind of exemplar? What, in short, are we to "make" of him? Certainly he himself would not engage an author without pressing on to the larger evaluation. In fact, his evaluation and interpretation would take shape *pari passu,* or he might even give the lion's share to evaluation. Achieving a better understanding of an author is a fine thing, he might say, but it is certainly not in itself sufficient for a "full" reading, nor can such a reading really be achieved unless the questions of value and relevance are explicitly probed, however preliminarily, for the sake of the understanding itself.

First, then, are there any corroborations for what I have proposed? Certainly some contemporary currents in Nietzsche-interpretation support my approach. For example, there are thinkers like Daniel Conway and Bernd Magnus, who are de-emphasizing the importance of the supposedly "leading" categories of Nietzsche's philosophy—Will to Power, the *Übermensch,* and Eternal Recurrence—to allow the existential, experiential, and humanistic qualities of Nietzsche's thought to emerge more clearly. Others have attempted to illuminate more clearly the positive and pedagogical sides of Nietzsche's thought. Such readings are *prima facie* supportive of my position (Hillesheim, 1969b, 1985; Cooper, 1983; Golomb, 1985; Loew, 1984; Murphy, 1984; Rosenow, 1986; Aloni, 1989). My second argument was fashioned mostly out of relatively recent materials, which, taken together, also indicate a promising, sympathetic trend in Nietzsche-interpretation. They effectively clarify Nietzsche's many close ties to many primary sources of humanism.

A second major corroboration of this understanding of Nietzsche flows from the realization that many of the well-known Nietzschean personae are ones that are thoroughly coherent with those of the humanist tradition. It is a commonplace to suggest that Nietzsche has "many sides" or "belongs to many histories." Now is the time to gather this plurality into what seems to me a most appropriate "arch-persona"—that of the humanist. Under such a category we can place Nietzsche as philosopher, educator, classicist, scholar, rhetorician, sophist, linguistic analyst, stylist, *littérateur* and aesthete, psychologist, moralist, polemicist, panegyricist, belletrist, cultural critic and reformer, lyric and epic poet, musician, autobiographer. No single one of these terms carries quite the complex adequacy that "*humanist*" does as a descriptive term for Nietzsche. Even as a "critic of science" and as a "critic of religion," Nietzsche wears masks that are identifiably a major part of the humanistic tradition. His very readiness to wear that variety of masks supports the humanist designation, for all the various personae I have mentioned are very often part, but never the whole of a bona fide humanist. For example, being a philologist does not *eo ipso* make one a humanist. One could be a mere technician professing that specialty, as Nietzsche well knew. Being a humanist, however, almost always implies having, to a significant degree, some kind of philological consciousness. The humanist emphasis is consistently placed on a wholeness that specialization stands in danger of missing because of its own purified pieties. It does not matter, of course, that the humanist does not in fact achieve all the postulated ideal wholeness. A thing is defined by its end, says Aristotle. The imagined goal makes all the difference in character of one's consciousness. Vision is transformative.

Even those who would claim that Nietzsche is in fact *anti*-humanistic might unwittingly help to confirm the position presented here, for an "anti-humanism" characterizes humanism also: the great humanists always stood against over-specialization and over-exaltation of the very practices of their own tradition. Montaigne discovered, and readily confessed, that reading the *Tusculan Disputations* was not really a help in preparing him to die, and he questioned the wisdom of his own age's paying such a high price to learn the classical languages. Erasmus rebuked the Ciceronian purists. Vico was deeply antipathetic to pedantry of all sorts. In the paradigmatic humanist movement, that of the Renaissance, careful critical attention to the ancients eventually led to the supersession of the old masters or at least to their fair emulation in the "vulgar languages" by the moderns who had attentively absorbed the best that they had to offer. These new masters naturally developed a distaste for "false culture" and for any cheap use of rare material, even as they attained a deepening sensitivity to "true culture." The humanists made a habit of exercising their faculties of artistic and intellectual judgment. Quality was all. Phoniness and easy imitation were nothing more than schoolboy preparations for the real thing. What other kind of education could one possibly want to undertake other than one that used Great Books, Great Ideas, Great Individuals, Great Moments, Great Music? Mediocre works were to be judged and rooted out; not even tomes of venerable antiquity were immune from criticism. And how could the worthy writings be appreciated except by labor and life-investment and a quasi-heroic reaching up to a new height? Thus we find it to be the case with Nietzsche. He campaigned against the facile false-culture of his day; he made a constant effort to write "good books" and unmask the overly "pretty" versions of humanism that he found in his milieu.

As for anti-humanism in that other current sense of a vision based upon a radical denial of the individual subject, the humanist tradition again provides a relevant if not totally harmonious background, for, as we have seen, it contains much that is "non-subjective" or "anti-subjective"—even while it probes the domain of human interiority. The description of Greek humanism by Werner Jaeger that I cited above suffices to indicate the tradition's concern with the *trans*-subjective "objectivity" and "universality" of the "true self." Thus subjectivity is relativized, and to a certain extent Romantic impulses are thereby held in check. But humanism is not so foolish as to efface the whole personal self entirely, for that would simply take us out of the life-world of human experience. Just so, Nietzsche re-instates the self, and his writing exalts it, even though he distances himself from the self of immediate subjectivity and supposedly "deconstructs" a certain version of "the self" for his polemical purposes (see Miller, 1981). For him, no transcendental, independent, and freely willing self is "given" to a person, but there remains the universal exigency to become who we are, some kind of culturally and historically constituted "fatedness," and empirical examples of "self-created" human works of art like Goethe.

Yet another type of corroboration can be found when we read summary accounts of humanism that describe it in terms that seem to apply extraordinarily well to Nietzsche himself. Two examples will suggest adequately what I mean. Here is a passage from Robert Grudin:

> *Humanitas* called for a fine balance of action and contemplation, a balance born not of compromise but of complementarity. The goal of such fulfilled and balanced virtue was political in the broadest sense of the word. The purview of Renaissance humanism included not only the education of the young but also the guidance of adults (including rulers) via philosophical poetry and strategic rhetoric. It included not only realistic social criticism but also utopian hypotheses, not only painstaking reassessments of history but also bold reshapings of the future. In short, humanism called for the comprehensive reform of culture, the transfiguration of what humanists termed the passive and ignorant society of the "dark" ages into a new order that would reflect and encourage the grandest human potentialities. Humanism had an

> evangelical dimension. It sought to project *humanitas* from the individual into the state at large. (Grudin, 1987, 723)

Nietzsche too aimed for an active and comprehensive reform of culture; wanted to transcend "dark ages" by a superior educational and cultural leadership; approached politics through the individual rather than through institutional governmental structures; grandly conceived a utopian future while sharpening a realistic critique of present and past; adopted an evangelistic tone and attitude; and invested himself in a pedagogical mission employing philosophical poetry and strategic rhetoric. Another authority on Renaissance culture gives us the occasion to notice in the humanist heritage a strong resemblance to Nietzsche's long obsession with will, power, and the irrational. Linking this concern directly with the educational impetus at the heart of humanism, Charles Trinkaus writes the following:

> The central conclusion of this book is that the Italian Renaissance, conceived essentially along Burckhardtian lines, was accompanied by a powerful assertion of a philosophy of will by leading representatives of Italian humanism and among philosophical circles influenced by them. Humanist moralism, rather than stressing rationalistic restraint and inhibition of human action, emphasised the dominance of irrational or arational elements in man's psychic make-up. In so doing this movement was consistent with its rhetorical nature and with its conception of its educational role as one of psychagogy....The assertion of an energetic, individualist drive for fulfilment as a major motif of Renaissance culture by Burckhardt thus found its theoretical statement and justification among the humanists. (Trinkaus, 1970, Volume 1, xx)

Such obvious affinities between Nietzsche and the Renaissance humanist movement continue in the other historical direction as well. Nietzsche has a *de facto* connection with movements that explicitly or implicitly evoke some idea of "humanism," for example, F. C. S. Schiller's pragmatism and Germany's *fin-de-siècle* Renaissancism. Of course, one still must judge whether these connections are organic or forced, since the Third Reich has made clear how group-bias can distort the meanings of a person's works. But it seems that Nietzsche's work provided a significant impetus for both of these movements (Stack, 1982; Ükermann, 1985). From the perspective of philosophical circles, Nietzsche clearly sustains a profound interest in what might be termed "philosophical anthropology," which is itself synonymous with a version of humanism (Schacht, 1988, 71-72). Richard Schacht has suggested that ultimately Nietzsche makes this philosophical anthropology the fundamental philosophical activity, more basic than epistemology or metaphysics.

A final corroboration that I will mention here is something of a pragmatic-intellectual one. It is the fact that with this approach one evidently solves the "coherence problem" in Nietzsche's works and certain interpretive advantages result (see Solomon and Higgins, 1988, 7-8). For example there would be less puzzling than there is now over how *Zarathustra* fits into the Nietzschean corpus (Higgins, 1987, ix-xv). Humanists are much given to the appreciation—and sometimes to the composition—of grand, epic poetical works even as they take delight in essays and epigrams, disputations and declamations. In fact, in the tradition, it is to be expected that one aspiring to be a truly great writer might give some thought to the composition of such an extended poetical work of distilled and solemnly proclaimed wisdom.

Given such an array of corroborations, then, the argument presented in this study is fairly secure, although clearly, much more can be said about Nietzsche's distinctive relationship to the humanist tradition, and about that tradition itself. My task in these pages has been conditioned by the attention I have wanted to give to a second focus that in the long run may be even more fruitful than the first one. I would like to turn now toward some of the larger issues relevant to this side of the work.

I have been trying to promote a deeper knowledge of the particular qualities and constitution of the humanist heritage. I hope that my many concrete references and definitions culled from a broad range of thinkers have provided the beginnings of a more articulate understanding of this polysemous, vastly significant term *humanism.* By way of concise summary, I would simply draw attention here, among its interrelated strands of concern, to those that are *pedagogical, philological, rhetorical, aesthetic, ethical, heroic, and sapiential.* Certainly I would propose—and this presentation has I hope borne out—that one must best understand humanism as a *complex* of such concerns rather than as a simple reality. I would be cautious about making too deep a distinction between a literary Italian *umanesimo* and other more ethos-oriented humanisms as Vito Giustiani does, even though I admit the historical variances involved (see Giustiani, 1985, 171; 188). Since classical literature carried concrete images of human virtues and provided a wide range of forms of self-realization, the Italian humanist program never stood far from the profound ethical and anthropological implications cultivated by later figures who were also frequently in touch with the classical tradition in one way or another. The two early meanings of *humanus* ("learned" or "benevolent," see Giustiani, 168) can not be easily separated in a culture in which literary study entails exposure to and self-conscious assimilation of ethical ideals that transcend mere scholarship. There may also be an even deeper *de facto* connection between education and the broadening of human sympathies that led the ancient Italians to use the same word for these different meanings. We need not posit that any *automatic* moral improvement attends literary instruction, nor need we imagine that the grand claims made about humanist education were actually realized (see Grafton and Jardine, 1986), but we can nevertheless entertain the plausibility of the proposition that there has been some perceived, or even some likely correlation between a tradition of particular literary-educational practices and broadened sensibilities.

It is not my purpose systematically to evaluate the whole tradition's graces and shortcomings, many of which Nietzsche exemplifies, but I will point to some of the features that underscore the significance of the present undertaking. Humanism seems to me an important cultural heritage because it is a valuable, life-promoting tradition of formational practices by which we can heighten our self-consciousness to such a degree that we become articulately aware of our individual and collective virtues and vices, or, as Nietzsche might prefer to say, strengths and weaknesses. As we attain such critical self-knowledge, we can become progressively more capable of working towards the achievement of our own authenticity. I find humanism to be an especially important tradition for our times, as we attempt to arrive at a cosmopolitan consciousness and a respectful pluralism while resisting a capitulative relativism and an irresponsible skepticism that fears to make value-judgments on anything other than idiosyncratic or crassly pragmatic grounds. Humanism is pragmatic and skeptical itself, but in a way that is balanced by a positive and realistic idealism: it tends to seek highest common factors rather than lowest common denominators. Humanism also gives us a mechanism for fostering our sense of the whole and the humanly meaningful in a world that has struck so many as fragmented, specialized, individualistic, technological, coldly professional, utilitarian. It directly promotes and even helps to constitute a human community on the basis of shared cultural and historical phenomena, especially those of the literate past. Many elements of this heritage can stand as truly universal rather than narrowly nationalistic or tribalistic possessions. Without that shared cultural-historical archive we can not so easily or fully become who we are, much less a unified world-wide community, because in its absence we would have lost the *via regia* to self-knowledge and to cultural-historical self-appropriation. Indeed, without historical and cultural memories, how could we say that there was any "self" to appropriate? On the personal level, who would you be if you recognized neither relatives, nor your native language, nor any places or objects in your environs? Selfhood is an ongoing achievement. It requires learning how to remember, and the continual enactment of that remembering.

We ultramoderns seem to prefer an all-embracing hermeneutic of suspicion. We achieve our own moralistic discourse through the dismantlement and the demythologization of almost any ideal. Partly for that reason, no doubt, the humanist tradition stands suspect in the eyes of many as dangerously ethnocentric. Even if we rightly recognize ethnocentrism as a widespread human trait, we might want to ask "What is this tradition that dares to tell us what 'true humanity' is?" Certainly I would not want to dismiss the dangers of this universal human bias towards self-glorification or overly dull our own vigilance against its destructive aspects (a vigilance which of course owes a great deal to the critical insights attained via the humanistic tradition). And I would certainly want to avoid such phrases as "true humanity," but I would do so primarily because of consequences that follow more from *universal* human self-concern, arrogance, and avarice than from their intended meanings. A humanist, of course, would be especially likely to have become sensitive to the complex uses of language and thus would tend to take *true* in a *humanistic* rather than in a technically philosophical (ontological) sense. The humanist would therefore tend to interpret *true humanity* as a symbolic expression meaning "what we have honestly found to be most trustworthy, admirable, and valuable in human character in the long run and most expressive of its greatest potential and most glorious power—that something that we at our best hope to draw out of ourselves and out of all others who are open to it." There is something about this intended meaning that should be preserved: we know, in a rather commonsensical and pragmatic way, that there is some kind of "greater fulfillment" of oneself if one learns about language, history, literature, and philosophy than that which would be possible if one neglects such learning, and if one acts by the values of figures like Lincoln and Gandhi rather than by those of figures like Idi Amin and Nicolai Ceausescu. Humanism helps to keep images of heroes and villains before our eyes so that we may choose our paths wisely, realizing that we have the potential to resemble either.

In practice, the humanist tradition progresses along a gradient through but decidedly beyond myopic tribalisms, nationalisms, and ethnocentrisms. It in fact supports the idea of a "common humanity" that vitally nourishes universal sympathy. *"Sunt lacrimae rerum et mentem mortalia tangunt."* So said that singer of Dido and Aeneas who today might be too easily tossed aside as just one more spokesperson for oppressive imperial might. An even more suspicious character, one of the most admired humanist heroes, has written even more explicit words about universal sympathy:

> Those who say, however, that we have to have consideration for citizens and not for foreigners rip to shreds the shared fellowship of humankind; when that has been removed, kindness, generosity, goodness and justice are removed. The ones who take these things away must be condemned as rebels against the immortal gods. For they are overturning the fellowship established by the gods among human beings: its strongest bond is thinking that it is more against nature to diminish another person for the sake of one's advantage than to endure all inconvenience of property or body...or even of the spirit itself—provided that these inconveniences are not involved in questions of justice. For this one virtue is mistress of all of them. It is the queen of virtues.
>
> Qui autem civium rationem dicunt habendam, externorum negant, ii dirimunt communem humani generis societatem; qua sublata beneficentia, liberalitas, bonitas, iustitia funditus tollitur; quae qui tollunt, etiam adversus deos immortales impii iudicandi sunt. Ab iis enim constitutam inter homines societatem evertunt, cuius societatis artissimum vinculum est magis arbitrari esse contra naturam hominem homini detrahere sui commodi causa quam omnia incommoda subire vel externa vel corporis...vel etiam ipsius animi, quae vacent iustitia; haec enim una virtus omnium est domina et regina virtutum. (Cicero, *De Officiis*, III.vi.28, translation mine)

The most dangerous idea afloat today is not the one that tries to wash out cultural differences for the sake of harmonious universalism—something that humanists who love cultures as much as they love "Culture" would not really want to do. Rather I believe a far more sinister idea is the one that seems to deny that there are more deep-likenesses than there are deep-differences between any two human beings on the face of the earth. Such a line of thinking suggests that there is no common ground allowing us to make valid value-judgments that are initiated beyond the borders of our own particular minds. A humanist consciousness helps us to realize that there is a notable breadth of consensus on values that people everywhere seem to support, admittedly in a variety of particular ways, as ultimately important. C. S. Lewis has said that "[t]here never has been, and never will be, a radically new judgement of value in the history of the world" (Lewis, 1978, 56).

Of course there is an irony in remembering these words here, for Lewis castigates Nietzsche in the very essay from which this citation is taken. I would agree with Lewis that Nietzsche did seem to deny the Tao its due, while I would claim that he remained sensitive to the authority of "natural" processes even in human psychology and creativity, and he gave to this authority a religious name, Dionysus. Nietzsche himself never abandoned his mission to achieve what he thought was the ultimate good of "humanity." Nor did he ever stop looking for the universal determinants in human and natural processes. Thus we can say that he persistently maintained a universalist sensibity. Apart from all argument about the ontological status of the transcendentals, it remains quite meaningful to ask: Are there people anywhere who do not seek the life-preserving, the useful, the just, the intelligible, the true, the real, the beautiful, the good, the vital, the fitting, the lasting, the holy? Culture is what gives shape to such transcendentals; it is that actual ongoing expression, promotion, and deepening discovery of these motives.

We might well ask "What really are the best ways out of a bad ethnocentrism, ways that do not obliterate a positive regard for the particular achievements of one's own and others' cultures?" Is not a tradition of attentive, historically informed, self-knowing, critical, linguistically and rhetorically sensitive, reflective wisdom one of them? It seems to me that humanism can provide an excellent meeting-ground for peoples of many particular traditions as well as a set of techniques for attaining an enlightened, corporate, pluralistic, cosmopolitan consciousness. In fact it does: Nietzsche, a "barbarian" who stretched his consciousness well beyond (and even against) the Reich toward world-wide scope, is a prime example of how it works. We need to realize more clearly how even classical Western European humanism is intrinsically anti-ethnocentric as well as anti-temporocentric, for we are not the ancient Greeks, and we never were, except by common participation in the complex web of humanity. We have mentioned how the Greeks themselves profited extensively from their older civilizations of Asia and Africa. Homer's profound humanism allows for sympathy for the "enemies" Hector and Andromache as well as for criticism even of the best of the Achaeans. Euripides' dramatic art in his *Medea* lets us know something about how hard it must be for a foreign woman living in an alien culture. Plato's *Republic* is the text that first raises a radical feminist question in its most direct form. The Stoics first worked out an articulate cosmopolitanism and challenged the nearly universally-accepted practice of slavery. And if we judge by his initial statement of purpose, Herodotus was as keen to write about "the barbarians" (that is, those who did not speak his language) as he was to write about the Greeks, for he saw that the great works of any cultures should not be forgotten.

The "our" in "our story" grows ever greater as humanism works towards its ends. Without being able to include every voice from every walk of life, the canon has been remarkably open from that moment at which peasant Hesiod took his place beside the wandering minstrel Homer as cultural pedagogues. The fact that it has also been progressively aggregative helps us to see how humanist praxis has become ever more challenging for us to maintain. A simple ethnocentrism would not abide such complexity. If we want authentic multiculturalism and multitemporalism in a way that makes the most of our complex and still expanding cultural resources, we must ask ourselves whether we should abandon the practices and the contents that have constituted the humanistic tradition. It is far more likely that our consciousness is weaker now than it might be, not because of an overuse of that mythically oppressive "canon of Western civilization," but because of the overwhelming obscurity of our heritage. How many typical undergraduates today read a fair amount of Petrarch, Montaigne, and Goethe—not to mention categories like Polish poetry, or old favorites like Valerius Maximus, Plutarch, and the *Gesta Romanorum*? And yes, other continents, other voices await us. We need to expand upon the contents and practices of Western humanism, not to deracinate them. Our failure to learn the long-standing European background does not speak well for our prospects for integrating world-wide cultural materials into our educational practices. Without canonical practices, new talents with much to say will be swallowed up in general bureaucratized, often politicized distraction, and education will indeed become, as Richard Lanham has put it, "a random walk through a great K-Mart of the human spirit" (Lanham, 139).

Now I do not want to imply that humanism is salvation, as I would not want to suggest that Nietzsche is the best of models for us. There remains the whole issue of moral, let alone religious, conversion. Nietzsche most pointedly raises the question of morality, the question about how we can best evaluate moral systems, but his suspicions did not always assist his vision. And in fact, Nietzsche in fact missed a great deal, for example, the world-affirming character of Christianity and the faultiness of some of his own Enlightenment-inspired presuppositions. Even with all his capacity for high spirits, he was certainly a man who struggled to the end, who deeply sensed his own insufficiencies, and who failed to achieve *amor fati* to the extent that he deeply wished that things were otherwise than he believed them to be. We can find in Nietzsche a living expression of that famous Kierkegaardian moment in which the one who was the life of the party is yet full of a melancholic and self-destructive dissatisfaction.

Likewise a bare, "self-reliant" humanism clearly has its weaknesses, which can only become more evident the more acutely one examines the human condition. Since it has to be carried by the "all-too-human," humanism is easily affected by moral impotence and infected by spiritual diseases that undo and reverse the good that it intends. But if its reasonable and positive capacities for self-criticism perdure, humanism will provide us with a tool which we can use to operate against the causes of personal and social decline. Despite popular misconceptions, humanism at its best is not at all opposed to, but is rather fully coherent with ecological, cosmological, and theological interests. The Greeks certainly realized that knowing one's self meant knowing and respectfully keeping one's own limits over against the powers that be. Their best wisdom is anti-hybristic. Humanism clearly places us in that middle ground of the "*metaxy*." Even that "anti-Platonic" Nietzsche takes it fully into account: we are a bridge that stretches from bestiality, through the all-too-human, to the superlatively human. Zarathustra has his coming *Übermensch,* Nietzsche has his Zarathustra (or his philosopher or philologist of the future), and perhaps the reader might be persuaded to adopt an ideal found in a certain Dionysian song sung by one particular Hellenist-humanist-educator. Or the reader might discover a greater model of greatness.

I hope it has been clear that I do not deny the value of other approaches to Nietzsche. However, I have been attempting to deal with an issue that others have not sufficiently considered: *How do we best go about reading Nietzsche most faithfully and comprehensively?* It has not been merely a question of finding a single facet from which one can work one's way to others. Rather it has had to do with understanding the general gestalt of all facets as they appear, dynamically and integrally related over the course of the thinker's development. I believe in the hermeneutic value of working on the basis of some sense of the whole, through particulars, to a differentiated, deeper, more concrete sense of the whole. Without general conceptions, we are lost. Granting that there are gaps, complexities, rough edges, contradictions, inner tensions, reversals over time, relatively independent and autonomously developing streams of interest, intangibles, and so on, might we find one gestalt in particular that has a greater appropriateness or hermeneutical value than others? Even if we eventually decide this question negatively, our position will be irresponsibly lacking to the extent that we have not really engaged the question as searchingly as we are able to. Admittedly, my attempt here is but a beginning. It is comprehensive insofar as it treats a wide range of Nietzsche's works, and it is systematic insofar as it relates many strands and levels of meaning to one another, but it obviously remains far from exhaustive. For example, I have not dealt at any great length with important issues like Nietzsche's critique of Christianity, or his reception of Darwinian ideas. And yet I have tried to propose a general context in which the meanings of such elements as these can be understood and integrated with other major dimensions of Nietzsche's life and works. Perspective on Christian morality has historically been an aspect of the humanist tradition (which, to mention just one element, developed critical philology to the point at which the authoritative texts of the tradition were subjected to a new kind of scrutiny); and Nietzsche's interest in Darwinian ideas may reflect in his own particular career the long-standing humanist concern with nature, the natural causes of things, the materialist schools of Epicurus and Democritus, the human body and passions, etc.

Of course, all is connected with all, and the humanist tradition covers an amazing array of positions and themes. But I hope to have shown that the concept of humanism, though highly complex, is not so hopelessly broad as to be meaningless. And it is certain that not every general framework accommodates equally well an equally great range of elements. Even in the case of several favorable options, we must still confront, say, the questions of biographical particularities that may help us to decide to give priority to one over the others. Thus "Nietzsche as humanist" will have demonstrable advantages over "Nietzsche as critic of science" or "Nietzsche as materialist" or "Nietzsche as anti-Christian." To those who might claim that I have been overly selective in my evidence, I will appeal to the abundance and depth of supporting material mentioned here, coming from many different times and sources. In addition, I have given enough of his own reflections on his work to be able to claim that Nietzsche himself has in effect set his seal of approval on the essential proposal of this study. It is no great matter that he might demur because of the connotations of the word *humanist.* He had similar feelings about how the word *classical* had lost its strength in his day.

Apart from all such judgments on the value of my understanding of the best basis for reading Nietzsche, the approach I have developed maintains a certain pedagogical value. By far the most significant result for Nietzsche-interpretation seems to be the identification of Nietzsche's *Grundthema* as human greatness. It is an important finding not only because of the intelligibility it gives, but because it challenges the hyperaestheticist, panskeptical, nihilistic Nietzsche of postmodernism. There are uses and there are misuses of authors. We ultimately misuse Nietzsche, I believe, if we suppress the realization that in his idea of greatness he indeed had a practical criterion, historically embodied in many exemplars, for human life at its fullest and most authentic. Nietzsche, who wants us to have our own and not necessarily his thoughts, still does not want to be misrepresented. And he certainly demands that we engage him responsibly: he was always ready to counsel "good philology." Would Nietzsche himself not be quite wary of, or rather, would he not be intensely acerbic towards, postmodern devaluation and deflation of human aspirations? I think there is little doubt that he would. Far from deconstructing the self, he above all wanted to prepare the way for the "Great Individual," and he made a tremendous effort to rouse his readers to great expectations. He himself indicates that destroying temples is the means to building new ones. Destruction takes place for reconstruction. His "turn to the (great) subject" even transcends the Cartesian and Kantian strategies that loom so large in disciplinary philosophy, for Nietzsche's turn takes place within the whole range of human "life," within all its interrelated complexes of natural and cultural-historical dynamics and memories.

The theme of greatness in Nietzsche is important for another reason, one that is cultural, pragmatic, and existential. For Nietzsche's "greatness" is the thematic expression of the idea of human authenticity, and only on the grounds of the quest for this authenticity can a humanism adequate to our time be rehabilitated. Many of us are at a stage at which we can no longer afford a naive, fundamentalistic attribution of normativity to a particular cultural or philosophical or moral system. Our affiliations must be carefully, consciously, critically, responsibly, and sensitively made. It will help us to attain a superior affective and intellectual appropriation of our own subjectivity, on the basis of which we might better judge the models of authenticity that are available and that have in part already in our pre-critical years helped to shape the orientations of that very subjectivity. Both the psychological and the pedagogical sides of this endeavor are well represented in Nietzsche's work. However incomplete he was and knew himself to be, Nietzsche is thus to this extent an exemplary figure for us to engage and evaluate. With deepening self-awareness, he constantly encounters, critiques, revalues important representations of human authenticity, thus fulfilling one of the best possible uses of the humanist canon. A humanism for our day will continue such a practice of self-consciously retrieving and evaluating such models of human authenticity, in the context of all the leading individual and corporate questions of the present, and with the age-old universalist humanist concerns for humanity at large. Western Enlightenment has especially reveled in the progressive development of a consciousness that is both critical and culturally and historically informed. An appropriate contemporary humanism will not undo the advances of this movement that is historically derivative of humanism, but it will also promote, to a greater extent than the Enlightenment did, a responsible affiliation to traditions on the basis of which a fuller "maturity" and a larger human community can be achieved. The concreteness and cultural-historical particularities of humanistic practices can be used as a wedge against any tendency to a new naive myth of "Absolute Reason." We cannot do without such elements today, if we are to live as well as we might. For this kind of inattention to our life-world leads inevitably to inauthenticity, and inauthenticity leads inevitably to decline.

Between the general needs for a rehabilitated humanism that promotes human authenticity and the particular exigencies of Nietzsche-criticism for a more thorough understanding of his works, there also emerge some practical academic issues to which this study may directly and indirectly contribute. For the academy is still—or still has the best chance of being—the institution most focally, self-consciously, systematically, and comprehensively concerned with a wide range of personal and public, formational and cultural values. These are in practice promoted through critical engagements with thinkers like Nietzsche. His particular project to broaden the soul of humanity can most dramatically call our attention to the ways in which we have failed to make our universities as profoundly educative as they might be. Nietzsche used classical studies as a means of engaging, critiquing, and transcending some important cultural-historical influences shaping the subjectivities of his day. His exemplary work encourages us to continue our own skirmishes against the forces of positivism, over-specialization, fragmentation, and over-professionalization in all of our humanistic educational practices. His life-long effort to select, to appropriate, to integrate, and to extend what he was able to discern as most valuable and necessary for himself and his own time can inspire us to sharpen our own formational planning.

The next generation, always one of our worthiest concerns, desperately needs both to sense a depth of purpose and meaning in the educational enterprise—which ultimately must involve the sense of the students' own significance—and to begin to develop a certain mastery of basic elements that will eventually allow for a heightened consciousness, an increased freedom and creativity, and a profounder capacity for critique and affirmation. These two dimensions—educational particularities and a sense of their larger significance—are more closely interrelated than we usually suspect. Though we might all naturally desire to make a quick leap to some ultimately free, *übermenschliche* stage of consciousness, Nietzsche himself remains sensitive to the necessity of a careful, committed, anti-narcissistic perseverance in the less exhilarating aspects of human development:

> What is essential "in heaven and on earth" seems to be, to say it once more, that there should be *obedience* over a long period of time and in a *single* direction: given that, something always develops, and has developed, for whose sake it is worth while to live on earth; for example, virtue, art, music, dance, reason, spirituality—something transfiguring, subtle, mad, and divine.
>
> "You shall obey—someone and for a long time: else you will perish and lose the last respect for yourself"—this appears to me to be the moral imperative of nature which, to be sure, is neither "categorical" as the old Kant would have it (hence the "else") nor addressed to the individual (what do individuals matter to her?), but to peoples, races, ages, classes—but above all to the whole human animal, to *man.* (1966, 101, 102)

If we neglect the more restricted stage of the load-bearing camel, will we ever arrive at those of the lion or the child proclaimed by Zarathustra (1954, 137-39)? Our author suggests not.

Despite Nietzsche's apparent elitism, he would nevertheless stress that all people should strive to appreciate all the excellence that they can, to the fullest extent of their powers. *Without the greatness of the "many," there can be no great events whatsoever* (cf. 1983, 197). Here is an example of how the larger tradition can carry a meaning that to some extent corrects what can easily be exaggerated into distortion in Nietzsche's thought. And if the "exaggerations" are judged to be in fact a part of his thinking, the larger context can still suggest how there might be a problematic, or at least a spiritually intriguing whisper of a "yes and no" involved, a simultaneous respect and distance. Thus, to be sure, Nietzsche was no democrat; nevertheless, his thought is so allied to a tradition that carries democratic as well as anti-democratic elements that even his own symbolism, when probed, can lead us toward an appreciation for the many. Does Dionysus not have a "democratic" soul, inviting women and slaves as well as kings and philosophers to join in the rural, nocturnal, communal mysteries? And on the other hand, is a love of excellence or a keen sensitivity to rank not a profoundly *popular* trait? Is it not "the people" who demand and support what they consider to be "the best," who constantly create their own canons—of singers, athletes, writers, actors, leaders, and entertainers? Though he would press for a ranking of genres and for a more demanding set of criteria than "the many" might use, Nietzsche nevertheless knew from the days of *The Birth of Tragedy* that without the chorus of common satyrs, there are no tragic visions, and without the tragic visions, there are no heroes.

Again, as he is no democrat, Nietzsche is certainly no Christian. But once more we need to look closely. No doubt his understanding would have been far different had he not lived in a semi-enlightened scholarly world bent on "demythologization" and in a culture eager for thorough secularization. One wonders what he might have done with the works of his contemporary Gerard Manley Hopkins ("the world is charged with the grandeur of God"), or those of his near-contemporary Teilhard de Chardin ("holy matter"). His reading would certainly have brought him around to the statement of Saint Irenaeus—that Greek in Old Gaul—that "[t]he glory of God is the human person fully alive." It would then have been harder for him to fail to recognize the deeper affirmation of life that Christians can claim an Incarnational vision provides. But despite his major oversight, what does the "blasphemous" spirit do *in The Anti-Christ(ian)*? He names Jesus a *free spirit.* The ultimate exemplar, the one whose spirit is poured out on all his true followers, is thus given one of Nietzsche's highest designations of praise! At the core of Christianity, then, *even in Nietzsche's view,* we find a representative bearer of spiritual freedom.

Those who may feel that I have offered here some kind of domesticated, conventionalized, "defanged" Nietzsche might reconsider first, subtleties such as these and secondly, the dynamic transformational power to be found in the humanist tradition. And then there is always a great question to be asked even about Nietzsche's ranting, scornful, vituperative polemics—indeed about all of his works. That is the question raised by an arresting comment found in his late scribblings:

> Assuming one thinks of a philosopher as a great educator, powerful enough to draw up to his lonely height a long chain of generations, then one must also grant him the uncanny privileges of the great educator. An educator never says what he himself thinks, but always only what he thinks of a thing in relation to the requirements of those he educates. He must not be detected in this dissimulation... (1968, 512-13)

The hermeneutical implications of these words are far-reaching. They tell us that even Nietzsche's grand campaigns may not exactly represent his own positions pure and simple. He perhaps prefers playing the philosopher who is ultimately, he suggests, a good educator. It is the effect on his students that he is after; it is their needs that he attends to. In the end, Nietzsche wanted to be an educator on a great mission, opening a new age. Like Heraclitus, he would have us listen not to *his* voice, but to the tune he tries to carry—to that Dionysian music that the pre-Socratic Greek would perhaps call the *Logos*. And ultimately he would not have us become mere philologists of his writings, but he would want us renewed, transformed, fully alive, playing child-like on the shores of eternity, in the only existence that he thinks we can know now.

The classical studies that Nietzsche loved so intensely were once conceived as foundational for education in its deepest sense. They had the character of a field of disciplined and "preliminary" yet necessary learning, opening upon many other areas. Standing at the other end of the academic ladder, especially for a "post-theological" age, was another disciplinary endeavor that from early on captured Nietzsche's educational imagination—philosophy. He in fact early on sought to be transferred from his philological chair to a philosophical one, professing as one of his qualifications for it an interest in "educational questions and inquiries" (Nietzsche, 1969c, 77). As we conclude our reflections here, it is important to mention that Nietzsche can also contribute to a more refined self-consciousness in this discipline, offering timely warnings against distractions from philosophy's most vital purposes. From *Schopenhauer as Educator* to *Twilight of the Idols*, Nietzsche points us toward the older meanings of philosophy as an experiential, existential, sapiential enterprise integral with one's whole life. Far from being primarily a "way of writing" it is radically a "way of living" that may include, but should never be reduced to, a closed set of technical questions. It is, in fact, ultimately confessional, a "decisive witness to *who [the philosopher] is*" (1966, 13-14). Those who would claim that philosophy is primarily analysis of the use of language should make an analysis of the language used to express the understanding of philosophy in important humanist texts like the one that says

> [The philosopher is]...he who strives to know the meaning, nature, and genesis of all divine and human realities, and to pursue and live out an entire plan for living well.
>
> *[I]s, qui studeat omnium rerum divinarum atque humanarum vim naturam causasque nosse et omnem bene vivendi rationem tenere et persequi* (Cicero, *De Oratore*, I. xlix. 212).

Another witness writes:

> This is what philosophy offers more than anything else: the sound judgment that is common to all, a refined sensibility appropriate to our existence as human beings, and companionship.
>
> *Hoc primum philosophia promittit, sensum communem, humanitatem et congregationem* (Seneca, *Epistulae*, 5).

With such a philosophic spirit knowing itself and informing our humanistic and academic practices, perhaps Nietzsche's work will help to lead not only philosophy but the university itself to become what it is—a generative, formational institution integral to contemporary culture, working to reverse cycles of decline in the individual and in society, a place where leading values are highlighted, communicated, and critically appreciated, where human authenticity is deepened and arrogance overcome. Nietzsche is far from being the perfect guide. More than a few times he seems to stumble badly on some very large rocks, or he stands frozen in solitary Promethean agony. He cannot take us the entire way. But in that divine comedy, how far would Dante pilgrim have gotten without his pagan Vergil?

Nietzsche's Works

1910. "Einleitung in das Studium der Klassischen Philologie." In *Nietzsches Werke*, Band XVII, Dritte Abteilung, Band I. Leipzig: Alfred Kroner.

1954. *The Portable Nietzsche.* Translated by Walter Kaufmann. New York: Viking.

1962. *Philosophy in the Tragic Age of the Greeks.* Translated and Introduced by Marianne Cowan. Washington, D.C.: Regnery Gateway.

1963a. "Nietzsche on Classics and Classicists." Selected, translated, and introduced by William Arrowsmith. *Arion* 2, no. 1, 5-18.

1963b. "Nietzsche on Classics and Classicists." Selected, translated, and introduced by William Arrowsmith. *Arion* 2, no. 2, 5-27.

1963c. "Nietzsche on Classics and Classicists." Selected, translated, and introduced by William Arrowsmith. *Arion* 2, no. 4, 5-31.

1964a. *The Complete Works of Friedrich Nietzsche.* Edited by Dr. Oscar Levy. New York: Russell and Russell, (rpt. of Edinburgh and London: Foulis 1910).

1964b. *On the Future of Our Educational Institutions.* Translated by J. M. Kennedy. In 1964a, Vol. 3, 1-142.

1964c. "Homer's Contest." Translated by M. A. Muegge. In 1964a, Vol 2, 49-62.

1964d. "Homer and Classical Philology." Translated by J. M. Kennedy. In 1964a, Vol. 3, pp.145-170.

1966. *Beyond Good and Evil: Prelude to a Philosophy of the Future.* Translated by Walter Kaufmann. New York: Vintage.

1967a. *Nietzsche: Werke. Kritische Gesamtausgabe.* Herausgegeben von G. Colli und M. Montinari. Berlin: De Gruyter.

1967b. *The Birth of Tragedy Out of the Spirit of Music.* Translated by Walter Kaufmann. New York: Vintage.

1967c. *The Case of Wagner: Turinese Letter of May 1888.* Translated by Walter Kaufmann. New York: Vintage.

1967d. *Friedrich Nietzsche: Sämtliche Werke. Kritische Studienausgabe.* Herausgegeben von G. Colli und M. Montinari. Berlin: De Gruyter Dünndruck-Ausgabe.

1968. *Will to Power.* Translated by Walter Kaufmann and R. J. Hollingdale. New York: Vintage.

1969a. *Ecce Homo: How One Becomes What One Is.* Translated by Walter Kaufmann. New York: Vintage.

1969b. *On the Genealogy of Morals: A Polemic.* Translated by Walter Kaufmann and R. J. Hollingdale. New York: Vintage.

1969c. *Selected Letters of Friedrich Nietzsche.* Translated by Christopher Middleton. Chicago: University of Chicago.

1973. "Nietzsche: Notes for *We Philologists.*" Translated by William Arrowsmith. *Arion* N.S. 1/2 : 279-380.

1974. *The Gay Science "la gaya scienza".* Translated by Walter Kaufmann. New York: Vintage.

1975-1984. *Nietzsche: Briefwechsel. Kritische Gesamtausgabe.* Herausgegeben von G. Colli und M. Montinari. Berlin: De Gruyter.

1979. *Philosophy and Truth: Selections from Nietzsche's Notebooks of the Early 1870's.* Translated, edited, introduced, and annotated by Daniel Breazeale. Foreword by Walter Kaufmann. New Jersey: Humanities; Sussex: Harvester.

1982. *Daybreak: Thoughts on the Prejudices of Morality.* Translated by R. J. Hollingdale. Cambridge: Cambridge.

1983. *Untimely Meditations.* Translated by R. J. Hollingdale. Cambridge: Cambridge.

1986. *Human, All Too Human: A Book for Free Spirits.* Translated by R. J. Hollingdale. Cambridge: Cambridge.

1989. *Friedrich Nietzsche on Rhetoric and Language.* Edited, translated, and with a critical introduction by Sander L. Gilman; Carole Blair; David J. Parent. New York: Oxford University.

1990. *Unmodern Observations: Unzeitgemässe Betrachtungen.* Edited by William Arrowsmith. New Haven: Yale University Press.

General Bibliography

Akiyama, Hideo. 1974. "Nietzsches Idee des 'Grossen Stils'." *Nietzsche-Studien* 3, 105-14.

Alderman, Harold. 1977. *Nietzsche's Gift*. Athens: Ohio.

Allison, David B., ed. 1985. *The New Nietzsche: Contemporary Styles of Interpretation*. Dell, Cambridge, Mass. and London, England: MIT, 1985.

Aloni, Nimrod. 1989. "The Three Pedagogical Dimensions of Nietzsche's Philosophy." *Educational Theory* 39, no. 4, 301-06.

Altieri, Charles. 1985. "Ecce Homo: Narcissism, Power, Pathos, and the Status of Autobiographical Representations." In O'Hara, 1985a. Bloomington: Indiana.

Andler, Charles. 1958. *Nietzsche, sa vie et sa pensée, Volume I: Les précurseurs de Nietzsche; La jeunesse de Nietzsche*. 2nd ed. Paris: Librairie Gallimard.

Ansell-Pearson, Keith J. 1987. "Nietzsche's Overcoming of Kant and Metaphysics: From Tragedy to Nihilism." *Nietzsche-Studien* 16, 310-39.

Aristotle, *Problemata*. 1937. 2 Vols. Translated by W. W. Hett. Loeb Classical Library. Cambridge: Harvard; London: William Heinemann.

Aulus Gellius. 1927-1928. *The Attic Nights of Aulus Gellius*. 3 Vols. Translated by John C. Rolfe. Loeb Classical Library. London: William Heinemann; New York: G. P. Putnam's Sons.

Ausführliches Lexicon der Griechischen und Römischen Mythologie. 1894-1897. Edited by W. H. Roscher. Zweiter Band, Zweite Abteilung, Leipzig: B. G. Teubner, s.v. "Meridianus daemon." cols. 2832-2836.

Baeumer, Max L. 1976. "Nietzsche and the Tradition of the Dionysian." Trans. Timothy F. Sellner. In O'Flaherty et al., 1976, 165-89.

Baron, Hans. 1971. "Petrarch: His Inner Struggles and the Humanistic Discovery of Man's Nature." In *Florilegium Historiale*, 18-51. Edited by J. G. Rowe and W. H. Stockdale Toronto: University of Toronto.

Behler, Ernst. 1978a. "Nietzsche und die Frühromantische Schule." *Nietzsche-Studien* 7, 59-87.

———. 1978b. "Nietzsche's Challenge to Romantic Humanism." *Canadian Review of Comparative Literature* 5, 30-52.

Bell, Desmond. 1984. "Nietzsche and the *Geisteswissenschaften*." *Journal of European Studies* 14, 187-210.

Bergmann, Peter. 1987. *Nietzsche, "the Last Antipolitical German." Bloomington: Indiana.*

Berman, David. 1988. "Nietzsche's Three Phases of Atheism." *History of Philosophy Quarterly* 5, no. 3, 273-86.

Blasche, Siegfried. 1986. "Hegelianismen im Umfeld in Nietzsches *Geburt der Tragödie*." *Nietzsche-Studien* 15, 59-71.

Boeschenstein, Hermann. 1982. "Nietzsche und das Problem der Humanität." *MLN* 97, 636-55.

Bolter, Jay. 1980. "Friedrich August Wolf and the Scientific Study of Antiquity." *Greek, Roman, and Byzantine Studies* 21, no. 1, 83-99.

Boulby, Mark. 1976. "Nietzsche and the *Finis Latinorum*." In O'Flaherty et al., 1976, 214-33.

Bouwsma, William J. 1973. *The Culture of Renaissance Humanism*, AHA Pamphlets 401 Washington, D.C.: American Historical Association.

Boyle, Nicholas. 1986. "Nietzsche and the 'Middle Mode of Discourse'." *In Realism in European Literature: Essays in Honour of J. P. Stern*, 123-57. Edited by Nicholas Boyle and Martin Swales. Cambridge: Cambridge.

Brandes, Georg. No date. *Friedrich Nietzsche*. Translated by A. G. Chater. London: Heinemann.

Breazeale, J. Daniel. 1975a. "The Hegel-Nietzsche Problem." *Nietzsche-Studien* 4, 146-64.

———. 1975b. "The Word, the World, and Nietzsche." *Philosophical Forum* 6, nos. 2-3, 301-20.

———. 1979. *Philosophy and Truth: Selections from Nietzsche's Notebooks of the Early 1870's*. New Jersey: Humanities Press.

Bruni Aretino, Leonardo. 1928. "De studiis et litteris liber." In *Humanistisch-Philosophische Schriften*, 5-19. Herausgegeben und erlaütert von Dr. Hans Baron Leipzig; Berlin: B. G. Teubner.

Burckhardt, Jacob. 1979. *Reflections on History*. Translated by M. D. Hotinger. Indianapolis: Liberty Classics.

Cassirer, Ernst; Kristeller, Paul Oskar; Randall, John Herman, Jr., eds. 1948. *The Renaissance Philosophy of Man*. Chicago: University of Chicago.

Cicero, *De Oratore*. 1942. 2 Vols. Translated by E. W. Sutton and H. Rackham. Loeb Classical Library. Cambridge: Harvard; London: Heinemann.

Conroy, Mark. 1981. "The Artist-Philosopher in Nietzsche's *Jenseits von Gut und Böse*." *MLN* 96, 615-28.

Conway, Daniel. 1988. "Solving the Problem of Socrates: Nietzsche's *Zarathustra* as Political Irony." Political Theory 16, no. 2, 257-80.

———. 1989. "Overcoming the *Übermensch*: Nietzsche's Revaluation of Values." *Journal of the British Society for Phenomenology* 22, no. 3, 1-14.

Cooper, D. E. 1983. *Authenticity and Learning: Nietzsche's Educational Philosophy*. London: Routledge and Kegan Paul.

Copleston, Frederick. 1968. "Foreground and Background in Nietzsche." *Review of Metaphysics* 21, no. 3, 506-23.

Crane, Mary Thomas. 1986. "*Intret Cato*: Authority and the Epigram in Sixteenth-Century England." In *Renaissance Genres: Essays on Theory, History, and Interpretation*, 158-86. Edited by Barbara Kiefer Lewalski. Cambridge: Harvard.

Crane, R. 1967. S. "Shifting Definitions and Evaluations of the Humanities from the Renaissance to the Present." In *The Idea of the Humanities and Other Essays*, 16-170. Chicago: University of Chicago.

Dannhauser, Werner J. 1974. *Nietzsche's View of Socrates.* Ithaca: Cornell.

Danto, Arthur C. 1980. *Nietzsche as Philosopher.* New York: Macmillan, Morningside, 1980

de Romilly, Jacqueline. 1989. "From Aphorisms to Theoretical Analyses: The Birth of Human Sciences in the Fifth Century B. C." *Diogenes* 144, 1-15.

Del Caro, Adrian. 1985. "Towards a Genealogy of an Image: Nietzsche's Achievement According to Nietzsche." *University of Toronto Quarterly* 54, no. 3, 234-50.

Donnellan, Brendan. 1982. *Nietzsche and the French Moralists.* Bonn: Bouvier Verlag Herbert Grundmann.

———. 1986. "Nietzsche and Montaigne." *Colloquia Germanica* 19, no. 1, 1-20.

Eliot, T. S. 1916. Review of *The Philosophy of Nietzsche* by A. Wolf, *International Journal of Ethics* 26, 426-27.

Faber, Marion. 1986. "The Metamorphosis of the French Aphorism: La Rochefoucauld and Nietzsche." *Comparative Literature Studies* 23, no. 3, 205-17.

Flecheux, Andre. 1985. "Nietzsche, la science, et l'université." In *Nouvelles Lectures de Nietzsche,* 119-129. Edited by Dominique Janicaud. Lausanne: L'Age d'Homme.

Françon, Marcel. 1936. "Petrarch, Disciple of Heraclitus." *Speculum* 11, 265-71.

Gasché, Rodolphe. 1985. "Autobiography as *Gestalt*: Nietzsche's *Ecce Homo.*" In O'Hara, 1985a. Bloomington: Indiana UP.

Gay, Peter. 1966. *The Enlightenment: An Interpretation.* Vol. I: *The Rise of Modern Paganism* New York: W. W. Norton.

———. 1969. *The Enlightenment: An Interpretation.* Vol. II: *The Science of Freedom* New York: W. W. Norton.

Geertz, Clifford. 1973. "Thick Description: Toward an Interpretive Theory of Culture." In *The Interpretation of Cultures,* 3-30. New York: Basic Books.

Gerber, Rudolf. 1968. "Nietzsche: Reason as Power for Humanism." *Philosophy Today* 12, 75-93.

Gillespie, Michael Allen and Strong, Tracy B. 1988. *Nietzsche's New Seas: Explorations in Philosophy, Aesthetics, and Politics.* Chicago and London: University of Chicago.

Gilman, Sander. 1987a. *Begegnungen mit Nietzsche.* Bonn: Bouvier Verlag Herbert Grundmann.

———, ed. 1987. *Conversations with Nietzsche: A Life in the Words of His Contemporaries.* Translated by David J. Parent. New York; Oxford: Oxford.

Giustiani, Vito R. 1985. "*Homo, Humanus,* and the Meanings of Humanism." *Journal of the History of Ideas* 46, no. 2, 167-95.

Golomb, Jacob J. 1985. "Nietzsche's Early Educational Thought." *Journal of the Philosophy of Education* 19 no. 1, 99-109.

Gouhier, Henri. 1987. *L'Anti-humanisme au XVIIe Siècle.* Paris: Librairie Philosophique J. Vrin.

Grafton, Anthony and Jardine, Lisa. 1986. *From Humanism to the Humanities: Education and the Liberal Arts in Fifteenth and Sixteenth Century Europe.* Cambridge, Mass.: Harvard.

Greene, Thomas. 1968. "The Flexibility of the Self in Renaissance Literature." In *The Discipline of Criticism: Essays in Literary Theory, Interpretation, and History,* 241-264. Edited by Peter Demetz; Thomas Greene; Lowry Nelson, Jr. New Haven: Yale.

Greene, William Chase. 1968. *Moira: Fate, Good, and Evil in Greek Thought.* Gloucester, Massachusetts: Peter Smith, 1968.

Gregory, John. 1983. "Order, Grace, and *Terribilità.*" In *The Classical Temper in Western Europe,* 10-23. Edited by J. P. Hardy and A. D. McCreadie. Melbourne: Oxford.

Gronigen, van, B. 1953. A. *In the Grip of the Past: Essay on an Aspect of Greek Thought.* Leiden: E. J. Brill.

Grudin, Robert. 1987. "Humanism." *Encyclopedia Britannica,* 15th edition.

Grundlehner, Philip. 1986. *The Poetry of Friedrich Nietzsche.* New York: Oxford.

Gusdorf, Georges Paul and Tiles, Mary Elizabeth. 1987. "Philosophical Anthropology." *Encyclopedia Britannica,* 15th edition.

Hadas, Moses. 1972. *Humanism: The Greek Ideal and Its Survival.* Gloucester, Massachusetts: Peter Smith.

Hayman, Ronald. 1982. *Nietzsche: A Critical Life.* Harmondsworth: Penguin, 1982.

Heftrich, Eckhard. 1989. "Die Geburt der Tragödie: Eine Präfiguration von Nietzsches Philosophie?" *Nietzsche-Studien* 18, 103-26.

Heller, Peter. 1976. "Nietzsche in His Relation to Voltaire and Rousseau." In O'Flaherty et al., 1976, 109-33.

Hermogenes of Tarsus. 1987. *Hermogenes's On Types of Style.* Translated by Cecil W. Wooten. Chapel Hill: University of North Carolina.

Higgins, Kathleen Marie. 1987. *Nietzsche's Zarathustra.* Philadelphia: Temple.

Hillesheim, James W. 1969a. "Action and Solitude: A Nietzschean View." *Educational Theory* no. 4 (1969), 357-62; 371.

———. 1969b. "The Scholar as Educator? A Nietzschean View." *Journal of Educational Thought* 3, 20-28.

———. 1973. "Nietzsche Agonistes." *Educational Theory* 23, 343-53.

———. 1986. "Suffering and Self-Cultivation: The Case of Nietzsche." *Educational Theory* 36, no. 2, 171-78.

Houlgate, Stephen. 1986. *Hegel, Nietzsche, and the Criticism of Metaphysics.* Cambridge: Cambridge.

Howey, Richard Lowell. 1973. *Heidegger and Jaspers on Nietzsche: A Critical Examination of Heidegger's and Jaspers' Interpretations of Nietzsche.* The Hague: Martinus Nijhoff.

Hummel, Hermann. 1946. "Emerson and Nietzsche." *The New England Quarterly* 1946), 63-84.

Ijsewijn, Jozef. 1973. "Humanistic Autobiography. " In *Studia Humanitatis: Ernesto Grassi zum 70. Geburtstag*, 209-19. Herausgegeben von Eginhard Hora und Eckhard Kessler. Muenchen: Wilhelm Fink.

Ijsseling, Samuel. 1976. *Rhetoric and Philosophy in Conflict: A Historical Survey*. Trans. Paul Dunphy The Hague: Martinus Nijhoff.

Isocrates. 1929. *Works*. 3 Vols. Translated by George Norlin and Larue van Hook. Loeb Classical Library. Cambridge: Harvard; London: William Heinemann.

Jaeger, Werner. 1953. "The Greeks and the Education of Man" New York: Annandale-on-Hudson: Bard College Papers.

———. 1965. *Paideia: The Ideals of Greek Culture*. Translated by Gilbert Highet. Volume 1: Archaic Greece; The Mind of Athens. New York: Oxford.

Janz, Curt Paul. 1974. "Friedrich Nietzsches Akademisches Lehrtätigkeit in Basel, 1869-1879." *Nietzsche-Studien* 3, 192-203.

Jaspers, Karl. 1980. "Zu Nietzsches Bedeutung in der Geschichte der Philosophie." In Salaquarda, 1980a, 50-62.

———. 1985. *Nietzsche: An Introduction to the Understanding of His Philosophical Activity*. Translated by Charles F. Wallraff and Frederick J. Schmitz. Lanham: University Press of America.

Johnson, Nan. 1984. "Ethos and the Aims of Rhetoric." In *Essays on Classical Rhetoric and Modern Discourse*, 98-114. Edited by Robert J. Connors; Lisa S. Ede; Andrea A. Lunsford. Carbondale: Southern Illinois.

Kaufmann, Walter. 1974. *Nietzsche: Philosopher, Psychologist, Anti-Christ*. 4th ed. Princeton: Princeton.

Kohl, Benjamin G. 1988. "Humanism and Education," 5-22, in Rabil 1988, Volume 3. Philadelphia: University of Pennsylvania.

Krailsheimer, A. J., ed. 1978. *The Continental Renaissance, 1500-1600*. New Jersey: Humanities Press.

Kristeller, Paul Oskar and Randall, John Herman, Jr. 1948. "General Introduction." In Cassirer et al., 1948, 120.

———. 1961. *Renaissance Thought: The Classic, Scholastic, and Humanist Strains*. New York: Harper and Row.

———. 1972. "Petrarch." In the *Encyclopedia of Philosophy*. New York: Macmillan and the Free Press.

———. 1988. "Humanism." In *The Cambridge History of Renaissance Philosophy*, 113-37. Cambridge: Cambridge.

Kubler, George. 1979. "Toward a Reductive Theory of Visual Style." In *The Concept of Style*, 119-128. Edited by Berel Lang. Philadelphia: University of Pennsylvania.

Lanham, Richard A. 1993. *The Electronic Word: Democracy, Technology, and the Arts*. Chicago: University of Chicago.

Lampert, Lawrence. 1986. *Nietzsche's Teaching: An Interpretation of Thus Spoke Zarathustra.* New Haven and London: Yale.

Leibrich, Louis. 1983. "Nietzschéisme et humanisme Nietzschéen: Une lecture de Nietzsche à la lumière de Goethe." *Nietzsche-Studien* 12, 287-334.

Leventhal, Robert S. 1986. "The Emergence of Philological Discourse in the German States, 1770-1810." *Isis* 77, 243-60.

Levi, Albert William. 1969. *Humanism and Politics: Studies in the Relationship of Power and Value in the Western Tradition.* Bloomington and London: Indiana.

Levi, Albert William. 1983. "The Humanities: Their Essence, Nature, Future." *Journal of Aesthetic Education* 17, no. 2, 5-17.

Lewis, C. S. 1978. *The Abolition of Man: How Education Develops Man's Sense of Morality.* New York: Macmillan.

Lloyd-Jones, Hugh. 1976. "Nietzsche and the Study of the Ancient World." In In O'Flaherty et al., 1976, 115.

Löw, Reinhardt. 1984. *Nietzsche—Sophist und Erzieher: Philosophische Untersuchungen zum Systematischen Ort von Friedrich Nietzsches Denken.* Weinheim: Acta Humaniora.

Love, Nancy S. 1986. *Marx, Nietzsche, and Modernity.* New York: Columbia.

Madigan, Patrick. 1986. *The Modern Project to Rigor: Descartes to Nietzsche.* Lanham, Maryland: University Press of America.

Magnus, Bernd. 1978. *Nietzsche's Existential Imperative.* Bloomington: Indiana.

———. 1983a. "Nietzsche Today: A View From America." *International Studies in Philosophy* 15, no. 2, 95-103.

———. 1983b. "Perfectibility and Attitude in Nietzsche's *Übermensche.*" *Review of Metaphysics* 36, 633-59.

———. 1986. "Nietzsche's Philosophy in 1888: The Will to Power and the *Übermensch.*" *Journal of the History of Philosophy* 24, no. 1, 79-98

Mann, Nicholas. 1984. *Petrarch.* Oxford: Oxford.

Marcel, Raymond. 1951. "'Saint' Socrate, Patron de l'Humanisme." *Revue Internationale de Philosophie* 5, no. 2, 135-43.

Martin, Alfred von *Nietzsche und Burckhardt: Zwei Geistige Welten im Dialog.* 1947. 4th ed. München: ErasmusVerlag.

McGinn, Robert E. 1975. "Culture as Prophylactic: the Birth of Tragedy as Culture-Criticism." *Nietzsche-Studien* 4, 75-138.

Megill, Allan. 1985. *Prophets of Extremity: Nietzsche, Heidegger, Foucault, Derrida.* Berkeley: University of California.

Moran, Michael. 1972. "Ralph Waldo Emerson." In *The Encyclopedia of Philosophy.* New York: Macmillan and the Free Press.

Miller, J. Hillis. 1981. "The Disarticulation of the Self in Nietzsche." *Monist* 64, 247-61.

Molitorisz, Joseph, Jr. 1983. *Toward a New Humanism: A Study of Diderot's and Nietzsche's Methodologies.* Ph.D. Dissertation, University of Washington.

Molner, David. 1993. "The Influence of Montaigne on Nietzsche: A Raison d'Etre in the Sun," in *Nietzsche-Studien* 22, 80-93.

Moroney, Patrick. 1986. *Nietzsche's Dionysian Aristocratic Culture: The Influence of Ancient Greco-Roman Thought on Nietzsche's Philosophy.* Maynooth, Ireland: Kairos Publications.

Moss, Ann. 1989. "Rhetoric and the Evolution of Ideas and Styles in the Renaissance." *Renaissance Studies* 3, no. 2, 99-105.

Murphy, Timothy F. 1984. *Nietzsche as Educator.* Lanham, Maryland: University Press of America.

Nehamas, Alexander. 1985. *Nietzsche: Life as Literature.* Cambridge: Harvard.

Neumann, Harry. 1976. "Superman or Last Man? Nietzsche's Interpretation of Athens and Jerusalem." *Nietzsche-Studien* 5, 1-28.

O'Flaherty, James C., Sellner, Timothy F. Helm, Robert M., eds. 1976. *Studies in Nietzsche and the Classical Tradition.* Chapel Hill: University of North Carolina.

O'Hara, Daniel T., ed. 1985a. *Why Nietzsche Now?* Bloomington: Indiana.

———. 1985b. "The Prophet of Our Laughter: Or Nietzsche as—Educator?" In O'Hara, 1985a, 119.

Ong, Walter J. 1962. "Educationists and the Tradition of Learning." In *The Barbarian Within and Other Fugitive Essays,* 149-63. N.Y.: Macmillan.

———. 1971. "Crisis and Understanding in the Humanities." In *Rhetoric, Romance, and Technology: Studies in the Interaction of Expression and Culture,* 304-36. Ithaca: Cornell.

———. 1983. *Ramus, Method, and the Decay of Dialogue.* Cambridge, Massachusetts.

Petrarca, Francesco. No date. *Le Familiari.* Edited by Vittorio Rossi. Vol. 1. Firenze: G. C. Sansone.

———. 1948. "On His Own Ignorance and That of Many Others." In Cassirer et al., 1948, 47-133.

———. 1978. *Petrarch's Secret.* Translated by William H. Draper. Westport, Connecticut: Hyperion.

Pindar. 1972. *The Odes of Pindar.* Translated by Geoffrey S. Conway. London: J. M. Dent and Sons.

Politicky, Matthias. 1981. *Der Frühe Nietzsche und die Deutsche Klassik: Studien zur Problemen Literarische Wertung.* Straubing, München: Donauverlag.

Pomper, Philip. 1985. *The Structure of Mind in History: Five Major Figures in Psychohistory.* New York: Columbia.

Pöschl, Viktor. 1979. "Nietzsche und die klassische Philologie" In *Philologie und Hermeneutik im 19. Jahrhundert: Zur Geschichte und Methodologie des Geisteswissenschaften,* 141-155. Edited by Helmut Flashar; Karlfried Grunder; Axel Horstmann. Goettingen: Vandenhoeck und Ruprecht.

Rabil, Albert, Jr., editor. 1988. *Renaissance Humanism: Foundations, Forms, and Legacy.* Volumes 1-3. Philadelphia: University of Pennsylvania.

Renaudet, Augustin. 1958. "Autour d'une Definition de l'Humanisme." In *Humanisme et Renaissance,* 32-53. *Travaux d'Humanisme et Renaissance* XXX. Geneve: Librairie E. Droz.

Rico, Francisco. 1986. "Philology and Philosophy in Petrarch." In *Intellectuals and Writers in Fourteenth-Century Europe,* 45-66. Edited by Piero Boitano and Anna Torti. Tuebingen: Gunter Narr; Cambridge: D. S. Brewer.

Roscher. W. H. 1894, editor. *Ausführliches Lexicon der Griechischen und Römischen Mythologie.* Leipzig: B. G. Teubner.

Rosen, Stanley. 1989. *The Ancients and the Moderns: Rethinking Modernity.* New Haven: Yale.

Rosenow, Eliyahu. 1986. "Nietzsche's Concept of Education." In *Nietzsche as Affirmative Thinker,* 119-31. Edited by Y. Yovel. Dordrecht, Boston, Landcaster: Martinus Nijhoff.

Rutherford, R. B. 1989. *The Meditations of Marcus Aurelius: A Study.* Oxford: Clarendon.

Salaquarda, Jörg, ed. 1980a. *Nietzsche.* In *Wege der Forschung,* Band 521. Darmstadt: Wissenschaftliche Buchgesellschaft.

———. 1980b. "Einleitung." In Salaquarda, 1980a, 1-20.

Schacht, Richard. 1983. *Nietzsche.* London: Routledge and Kegan Paul.

———. 1988. "Nietzsche's *Gay Science,* or How to Naturalize Cheerfully." In Solomon and Higgins, 1988, 68-86.

Schmidt, Hermann Josef. 1969. *Nietzsche und Sokrates: Philosophische Untersuchungen zu Nietzsches Sokratesbild.* Meisenheim am Glan: Anton Hain.

Schmidt, Rüdiger. 1984. "Auf der Suche nach dem Humanum: Elemente der Frühen Kulturkritik Friedrich Nietzsches." *Nietzsche-Studien* 13, 129-154.

Schopenhauer, Arthur. 1974. *Parerga and Paralipomena: Short Philosophical Essays.* Translated by E. F. J. Payne. Oxford: Clarendon.

Schottlaender, Rudolf. 1940. "Two Dionysians: Emerson and Nietzsche." *South Atlantic Quarterly* 39, 330-43.

Schrift, Alan D. 1987. "Between Perspectivism and Philology: Genealogy as Hermeneutic." *Nietzsche-Studien* 16, 91-111.

Screech, M. 1983. A. *Montaigne and Melancholy: The Wisdom of the Essays.* London: Duckworth.

Shaw, Daniel C. 1986. "Nietzsche as Sophist: A Polemic." *International Philosophical Quarterly* 26, no. 4, 331-39.

Silk, M. 1981. S. and J. P. Stern. *Nietzsche on Tragedy.* Cambridge: Cambridge.

Solomon, Robert C. 1980. *Nietzsche: A Collection of Critical Essays.* Notre Dame, Indiana: Notre Dame, 1980.

Solomon, Robert C. and Higgins, Kathleen M., eds. 1988. *Reading Nietzsche.* New York: Oxford.

Spiegelberg, Herbert, ed. in collaboration with Bayard Quincy Morgan. 1964. *The Socratic Enigma: A Collection of Testimonies Through Twenty-Four Centuries.* Indianapolis: Bobbs Merrill.

Stack, George J. 1982. "Nietzsche's Influence on Pragmatic Humanism." *Journal of the History of Philosophy* 20, no. 4, 369-406.

Stack, George J. 1983. *Lange and Nietzsche.* Berlin: Walter de Gruyter.

———. 1989. "Emerson's Influence on Nietzsche's Concept of the Will to Power." *The Modern Schoolman* 66, 175-95.

———. 1992. *Nietzsche and Emerson: An Elective Affinity.* Athens: Ohio University Press.

Stern, J. P. 1978. "Nietzsche and the Idea of Metaphor." In *Nietzsche: Imagery and Thought: A Collection of Critical Essays,* 64-82. Edited by Malcolm Pasley. Berkeley: University of California.

———. 1979. *A Study of Nietzsche.* Cambridge: Cambridge.

Stone, Donald D. 1988. "Arnold, Nietzsche, and the 'Revaluation of Values'." *Nineteenth-Century Literature* 43, no. 3, 289-318.

Strong, Tracy B. 1975. *Friedrich Nietzsche and the Politics of Transfiguration.* Los Angeles, Berkeley, London: University of California.

Summers, David. 1981. *Michelangelo and the Language of Art.* Princeton: Princeton.

Thatcher, David S. 1974. "Nietzsche and Byron." *Nietzsche-Studien* 3, 149-50.

Trinkaus, Charles. 1963. "Humanism." *Encyclopedia of World Art.* N.Y.: McGraw-Hill.

———. 1970. *In Our Image and Likeness: Humanity and Divinity in Italian Humanist Thought.* London: Constable.

———. 1979. *The Poet as Philosopher: Petrarch and the Formation of Renaissance Consciousness.* New Haven: Yale.

Ükermann, Gerd. 1985. *Renaissancismus und Fin de Siècle: Die Italienische Renaissance in der Deutschen Dramatik der letzten Jahrhundertwenden.* Berlin: Walter de Gruyter.

Verene, Donald Phillip. 1976. "Vico's Philosophy of Imagination," in *Vico and Contemporary Thought,* 20-43. Edited by Giorgio Tagliacozzo; Michael Mooney; Donald Phillip Verene. Atlantic Highlands, New Jersey: Humanities Press.

Versenyi, Laszlo. 1963. *Socratic Humanism.* Foreword by Robert S. Brumbaugh. New Haven: Yale.

Weinberg, Kurt. 1976. "The Impact of Ancient Greece and French Classicism on Nietzsche's Concept of Tragedy." In O'Flaherty et al., 1976, 165-89.

Weisinger, Herbert. 1973. "Renaissance Literature and Historiography." *Dictionary of the History of Ideas: Studies of Selected Pivotal Ideas.* New York: Scribners.

Weitz, Morris. 1977. *The Opening Mind.* Chicago: University of Chicago.

Westphal, Kenneth R. 1984. "Nietzsche's Sting and the Possibility of Good Philology." *International Studies in Philosophy* 16, no. 2, 71-90.

White, Richard. 1988. "Art and the Individual in Nietzsche's *Birth of Tragedy.*" *British Journal of Aesthetics* 28, no. 1, 59-67.

Whitman, James. 1986. "Nietzsche in the Magisterial Tradition of German Philology." *The Journal of the History of Ideas* 47, no. 3, 453-68.

Wittowker, Rudolph. 1973. "Genius: Individualism in Art and Artists." *Dictionary of the History of Ideas.* New York: Scribner's.

Wurzer, William S. 1975. *Nietzsche und Spinoza.* Meisenheim am Glan: Anton Hain.

Zuckert, Catherine. 1976. "Nature, History, and the Self: Friedrich Nietzsche's Untimely Considerations." *Nietzsche-Studien* 5, 55-82.

Index

Works

Subjects

Names